GARRISON KEILLOR

We Are Still Married

faber and faber

LONDON · BOSTON

First published in the USA in 1989
by Viking Penguin Inc., New York
and simultaneously in Canada
by Penguin Books Canada Ltd Ontario
First published in Great Britain in 1989
by Faber and Faber Limited
3 Queen Square London WC1N 3AU
Revised paperback edition first published in 1990
This paperback edition first published in 1993

Printed in England by Clays Ltd, St Ives plc

"Maybe You Can, Too", "The Current Crisis in Remorse", "Who We Were and
What We Meant by It", "We Are Still Married", "End of the Trail", "The
People vs. Jim", "What Did We Do Wrong?" "End of an Era", "Hollywood in
the Fifties", "Your Book Saved My Life, Mister", "Three New Twins Join Club
in Spring", and "Meeting Famous People" first appeared as signed contributions
in *The New Yorker*. "After a Fall" was originally published in *The New Yorker*.

In addition, seventeen essays, observations, and reflections appeared as "Notes
and Comment" and "Talk of the Town" pieces in *The New Yorker*.

Other selections in this book first appeared, some under different titles or in
slightly different form, in *The Atlantic*, *The Gettysburg Review*, *Harper's*, *Life*,
Minnesota Monthly, *The New York Times*, *Newsweek*, *Sports Illustrated*, and *TWA
Ambassador*.

Grateful acknowledgment is made for permission to reprint the following works:
"How to Write a Letter" (originally entitled "How to Write a Personal Letter").
Reprinted by permission of International Paper. Excerpts from "Gentle on My
Mind", by John Hartford. Copyright © 1967, 1968 by Ensign Music
Corporation. Excerpts from *The Washington Post* article, July 3, 1988. © *The
Washington Post*, 1988. Excerpt from "An Irish Airman foresees his Death", from
The Poems: A New Edition, by W. B. Yeats, edited by Richard J. Finneran.
Copyright 1919 by Macmillan Publishing Company, renewed 1947 by Bertha
Georgie Yeats. Reprinted with permission of Macmillan Publishing Company
and A. P. Watt Ltd. on behalf of Michael B. Yeats and Macmillan London Ltd.

A CIP record for this book is available
from the British Library
ISBN 0-571-17009-9

2 4 6 8 10 9 7 5 3

Garrison Keillor is the bestselling author of *Lake Wobegon Days*, *Happy to be Here*, *Leaving Home*, *We Are Still Married* and *Radio Romance*. He was born in Minnesota in 1942 and graduated from the University of Minnesota in 1966. He has four children. From 1974 to 1987 he was host of the popular live radio show *A Prairie Home Companion*. He lives in St Paul, Minnesota.

by the same author

LAKE WOBEGON DAYS
HAPPY TO BE HERE
LEAVING HOME
RADIO ROMANCE

To the memory
of my classmate
Corinne Guntzel
(1942–1986)

My parents think I'm crazy,
My kids think I'm bourgeois—
My true love thinks I'm wonderful,
The handsomest she ever saw,
And who am I to disagree
With one so sensible as she?

CONTENTS

2

THE LAKE

3

LETTERS

4

HOUSE POEMS

5

STORIES

INTRODUCTION

There's a lot to be said for lack of communication and so many problems we can't talk about simply go away after a while, such as the problem of mortality, for example, but a writer's duty is to keep trying, to wake up every afternoon and saddle up the mare and bear the sacred *plume de literature* over the next ridge, and here, to show I've been on the job and not just sunning myself in Denmark, is a book, collecting in one neat pile some stories, poems, and letters mostly written at the time of Ronald Reagan, the President who never told bad news to the American people.

I've written for *The New Yorker* since I was in high school, though they weren't aware of it at the time, and many of these stories first appeared there; most of the letters in Section 3 appeared there, unsigned, in "The Talk of the Town." When I first met up with the magazine, I was thirteen, sitting in the periodicals room at the Minneapolis Public Library, surrounded by ruined old men collapsed in the big oak chairs, who I took to be retired teachers. I read Talk as the voice of inexhaustible youth, charged with curiosity and skepticism, dashing around the big city at a slow crawl, and tried to imitate its casual worldly tone, which, for a boy growing up in the potato fields of Brooklyn Park township, was a hard row to hoe, but I tried. The magazine was studded with distinguished men of initials, including E.B., A.J., S.J., E.J., J.F., and J.D., so I signed myself G. E. Keillor for a while, hoping lightning would strike. The summer after college I hitched a ride to New York and got a room in a boardinghouse on West 20th next door to a convent and walked up to *The New Yorker* on West 43rd to apply for a job as a Talk reporter. I was twenty-three, had a faceful of beard and long hair, and was dazed with ambition. There were plenty of exclusive clubs on 43rd and 44th, including the Harvard, Princeton, New York Yacht, and Century, but only one worth trying for, in my eyes, and I took the elevator up and tried. A woman named Patricia Mosher talked with me for an hour. She was friendly and encouraging, and sent me home to write more, which I've been doing ever since. Three years later, I got a letter from Roger Angell at *The New Yorker* buying a story of mine and sat down on the front steps of my house and enjoyed his three or four lovely paragraphs two or three dozen times. I felt grateful that my life would not be completely wasted. Over the years, Roger turned out to be a tireless editor, and a great coach, telling me how much the magazine *needed* me, hoping I'd become one of his starters, a cleanup humorist, and only gradually did he come to accept me for who I am, a tall serious man with a knack for the long pause, slow to write and easily distracted, whose association with the magazine has been modest, if undistinguished. In 1971 I became the first writer in its history to have his name misspelled on a byline (Kiellor), and a few years later I wrote the story "Don: The True Story of a Younger Person," which contains a quintuple interior quote, a quote of a quote of a quote of a quote of a quote, the deepest interior quote ever published there, I guess. You could look it up. In 1974, having written a piece about the Grand Ole Opry, I became one of the few writers in *New Yorker* annals to try to live the life I had written about, when I started "A Prairie Home Companion." Mark Singer did not open a bank after writing *Funny Money*, nor did Calvin Trillin buy a rib joint with the proceeds of *Alice, Let's Eat*. Yes, I am aware of Roger Angell's pinch-hit appearance (7/12/49) at the Polo Grounds, a long poke off the bat handle that scooted into the left-field corner under the Macy's clock and caromed off the groundskeeper's roller for a skinny triple, driving in one run, and that's why I said I was one of the "few"—Pauline Kael, who directed Joanne Woodward and John Wayne in *Canaan*, is another, but you look at that picture, you can't help but feel the sparks flying between the stars and you see how precise and single-minded and *knowing* the camera is, and you wonder, "Why couldn't she just let those two loose?" And Roger's hit, in any other ballpark, would've been a double, except in Fenway, where it would've been foul.

It was a long reach for a writer, to do a radio show all those years, like a dairy farmer sailing the Atlantic, but that sort of thing happens all the time. The open sea casts a powerful lure and dairy farmers are particularly susceptible. The monotony of twice-daily lactation and the steady throbbing of the milking machines make them feel like the engine-room crew of a ferryboat that's going nowhere, and they dream of taking the helm and getting salt spray in their faces. Wiping the immense udders, they imagine a billowing spinnaker—a manure-crusted tail switches across their face and they see the mainsheet taut as the *Francesca* rounds Bermuda—and next thing they're at the Clay County library to check out *How to Build a Boat from a Sixty-Foot Pole Barn*. One year and eighteen months later their pole barn is gone, the *Francesca* is finished and loaded on a flatbed truck and all the comedians of Chatterton, South Dakota, who have watched Ray build the boat, stand around and hoot and howl as he chugs out of the driveway. He's glad to pull out of the dusty little town and past the soybean fields and see the water tower disappear in the rearview mirror, but six months later, after weeks of thirty- and forty-foot swells and close calls with icebergs and flying sharks and the morning when the tanker loomed out of the fog and the misery of wet socks and damp underwear and rope burns on his hands that never heal and the sullenness among his crew since the whiskey ran out, Ray thinks back on Chatterton as a jewel of civility and he is glad to return and see his cows and get back on the tractor and hold *seeds* in his hand, and so was I glad to rejoin *The New Yorker*—

its faded yellow walls and scraps of furniture, its burrows stuffed with books and manuscripts, the glass bookcases and the long table piled with newspapers, the archives full of black scrapbooks and the little library crammed with reference books where Eve and Dusty and Hal and all the checkers slave away—and to be back among *paper*.

My cash crop is humor, a bastard genre of literature that includes Mark Twain and the gentlemen of the old firm of Benchley, Thurber, Perelman & White and also includes *How to Talk Suth'n, Buddy's Big Book of Booger Jokes* and *Funny Fotos of Cats in Hats,* a mixed field.

Humor is a knife and what it cuts off doesn't grow back right away, just look at journalists. They are gentle and thoughtful people given to good work in a dark world, but they have been withered by thousands of journalist jokes, portraying members of the Fourth Estate as peabrains. Humor has dropped a rock on them, just as it has withered Iowans, Clevelanders, Jerseyites, Dan Quayle, proctologists, and people named Elmer, and yet no victims dare complain lest they be accused of having no sense of humor, the worst charge that can be leveled against an American citizen. Even someone who was convicted of selling the nation's last three nuclear secrets to the Russians—if, before sentencing, the judge were to lean across the bench and say, "You know, you have a very poor sense of humor," the defense would leap to its feet and object. Humor, a good sense of it, is to Americans what manhood is to Spaniards and we will go to great lengths to prove it. Experiments with laboratory rats have shown that, if one psychologist in the room laughs at something a rat does, all of the other psychologists in the room will laugh equally. Nobody wants to be left holding the joke. The funniest line in English is "Get it?" When you say that, *everyone* chortles.

For a long time, most Americans have considered humor to be much funnier than it really is. Sometimes I wish I could quit writing humor and just write irritation for a while. I grow old and irritable. I once was a tall dark heartbreaker who, when I slouched into a room, women jumped up and asked if they could get me something, and now they only smile and say, "My mother is a big fan of yours. You sure are a day-brightener for her. You sure make her chuckle." I grow old. Boys and girls in their thirties who compose essays on the majestic sorrows of aging—*give me a break*. I'm forty-seven. Wait until you're forty-seven and then tell me about it. I'll be sixty then.

I grew up in a gentler, slower time. When Ike was President, Christmases were years apart, and now it's about five months from one to the next, and in a decade it'll be the end of the century, the year 2000, a fiction. I grow old and irritable and forgetful and often forget what irritated me in the first place, though the misery is still there. It's enough to make a person psychopathic if you had the energy for it but irritation is all I can manage. It irritates me when news people explain things that everyone knows, such as who Rocky Marciano was or Edward R. Murrow or John Foster Dulles, names that don't pop up often, but when they do, the teenage anchorman says, "Dulles, the bass player of the Crickets, gave up his seat on the plane to Richie Valens," as if you didn't know this. Of course you do. Last November, on the anniversary of the assassination, the tube was jammed with bozos explaining about the Kennedy years, implying that it was long ago, but twenty-five years isn't that long. You learn this as you grow up.

Like everybody, I mark time by who's in the White House, starting with Truman, who presided over my childhood, a man in a bow tie who resembled my uncle Bill Anderson who hiked around Minnesota as a young man and swam across rivers stripped naked, his clothes wrapped in a bundle and fastened on his head with his belt looped under his chin. He shot pool, a daring thing in a Christian family, and knew all the counties of Minnesota by heart. About Truman, however, dark things were intimated in our house. He used the Lord's name in vain and was weak on Communism. In the playground at Benson School, we played war during recess and killed North Koreans by the zillions. Our teacher Floyd Lewis brought a

television set to sixth grade so we could watch Eisenhower's inau-
guration. He looked like Uncle Merrill who traveled the Midwest
aboard the North Coast Limited and Hiawatha and other crack trains,
extending the domain of Northrup, King seed corn. Ike's benign rule
saw me through high school and I started at the University of Minnesota the fall Kennedy was elected. Being eighteen, free, and rea-
sonably intelligent, I decided I was a Democrat, of course, and admired
him feverishly and was—except for an afternoon during the Cuban
blockade when I was afraid the world was about to end—as patriotic
as a person could possibly be, right up to November 22, 1963, that
deep cold cave, the day of our national murder, when Lyndon Johnson
was ushered in. He was the first President I voted for and the first
who threatened my life. My son was born at the beginning of Nixon,
1969, who resigned in 1974, missing my thirty-second birthday by
a day, ending the epic Watergate story, since when newspaper reading
hasn't been one fourth as much fun. Ford didn't register on me.
Carter only showed that I didn't know beans about politics: I thought
he was a decent hardworking God-fearing President and never understood how Republicans could get elected simply by saying his name
out loud. Everybody understood this joke except me, so I took an
eight-year vacation under Reagan and didn't have a political thought,
except to admire the old masseur as he applied his craft. Then came
Gentleman George Bush, the man who gave Dan Quayle to the nation,
and there we are now.

Of all those Presidents, Reagan was the best storyteller. He saw
America as a fabulous land, a small town of sixty million Christian
families who work hard, play ball, and handle their own problems.
He truly believed in his story and was disinterested in other, gloomier
visions. He was a Midwesterner who had long since left home to
escape the Law of the Provinces (*Don't think you're somebody. If
you were, you wouldn't be here, you'd be on the Coast*) but who
remained true to the Midwest's distrust of intellect, its virtuousness
and sweet sense of isolation, its nostalgia, and he retained a cozy

philosophy common to successful men his age in small towns all
along the Mississippi. He himself was a huge success, the most out-
rageously successful authentic high-flying Irish politician of his day,
with a honey voice and a twinkle and a wave and a duck of the head,
the most boyish seventy-five-year-old man in America, hard to lay
a glove on, as light as a kite. Nothing he said ever came back to haunt
him. His mastery of the air baffled and dazed his enemies, who
couldn't take seriously a man who refused to face up to the facts of
the American decline. They were serious men, who trusted schol-
arship and experience and competence, but he revealed their crucial
flaw: they had no story, and a man who has no story is a man with
no truth to offer. They thought him shallow, which was irrelevant,
like accusing Will Rogers of not writing a novel: so what? His talent
was to be a hearty, graceful public man, a royal President. A genial
uncle, the first one you'd want at your wedding to make a toast and
charm the in-laws, the last one you would choose to trouble with the
information that you are pregnant and feel lousy. He himself went
out of his way to avoid upsetting people. He told no bad news. He
never uttered a sentence that didn't have at least a ninety-percent
chance of public approval.

When Reagan retired from the field, he left his opponents covered
with dust, discouraged. Few had the heart to argue that he was a
dishonest and disastrous President because the ones he was most
dishonest to (Christian fundamentalists) and most disastrous for (people under thirty) supported him in droves, and when the people speak
so clearly, the minority ought to shut up and listen. In 1984 when I
went in the booth and voted for Mondale-Ferraro, the lever felt cold
and dry, as if untouched by human hands. I went home and before
supper was over Mondale had lost forty-nine states, carrying only
Minnesota. If you could win only one state out of the Union, I suppose
Minnesota would be your first choice, but it made for a short evening.
Tom Arndt and I zipped over to Democratic headquarters at a hockey
rink in St. Paul to cheer for our man and found a small crowd thinly

milling around, people looking for people who weren't there, like a fortieth annual reunion of something. Wan liberal faces from civil-rights and antiwar days, snooty feminists, old union guys, hairy leftists: My Old Gang. We had been so right for so long about so many things that the American people refused to vote for us out of pure resentment. The sheer mass of Reagan's victory loomed above us like Mount McKinley.

In Lake Wobegon, we grew up with bad news. Since I was a little kid I heard it wafting up through the heat duct from the kitchen below. Our relatives came to visit on Saturday evenings and after we kids were packed off to bed, the grownups sat up late until ten-thirty or eleven and talked about sickness, unhappiness, divorce, violence, and all the sorrows they felt obliged to shelter children from, and I lay on the bedroom floor and listened in, soaking up information. Two high-school boys and a girl, killed when the car slammed into a tree at ninety miles an hour, at 2:00 A.M. the night before grad-uation, only the driver survived, the one who was drunk. A cousin was sick, whose husband had run away and whose son had drowned at age eighteen, doctors didn't give her long. The son's girlfriend had never recovered from the shock. That sweet black-haired girl had tried to kill herself twice. The drunk driver was the husband's nephew. The voices were soft and low. "I donno. He's like a different person entirely. He doesn't look good at all but he won't hear about seeing a doctor. I think it's his heart. His mother died of heart trouble and she was heavy like him. I think he drinks too." A chair creaked *shnkknk* and someone shuffled over *stiplstoplstiplstople* and poured a cup of coffee, *blibliblibliblibliblib*. An edgy silence. Throat clear-ing. "She tried to kill herself by dropping an electric fan in the bathtub. Then she tried to row out on the lake but the waves were too high. I don't know. She never got over him, that's for sure. You want more banana bread? It's fresh, I just baked it. Here."

They are still down there in the kitchen, my beloved aunts and dear uncles, drinking coffee, murmuring, discussing the sorrows of the world, protecting me from bad news, and I'm still in the bedroom, listening at the grate.

Farewell, Mr. President.

Long live American humor.

We are getting old, a terrible mistake, and that's no joke.

What's really funny is that we are still married.

1

PIECES

END OF THE TRAIL

THE LAST CIGARETTE SMOKERS in America were located in a box canyon south of Donner Pass in the High Sierra by two federal tobacco agents in a helicopter who spotted the little smoke puffs just before noon. One of them, Ames, the district chief, called in the ground team by air-to-ground radio. Six men in camouflage outfits, members of a crack anti-smoking joggers unit, moved quickly across the rugged terrain, surrounded the bunch in their hideout, subdued them with tear gas, and made them lie face down on the gravel in the hot August sun. There were three females and two males, all in their mid-forties. They had been on the run since the adoption of the Twenty-eighth Amendment.

Ames, a trim, muscular man in neatly pressed khakis who carried a riding crop, paced back and forth along the row of prisoners, their shoe soles motionless. "What are you people using for brains? Can't you read?" he snapped, flicking the crop at their ankles. He bent down and snatched up an empty Marlboro pack and thrust it in the face of a pale, sweaty man whose breath came in short, terrified gasps. "Look at this! This warning has been there for decades! Want me to read it to you? Want me to give you the statistics? What does it take to make you understand? Look at me! Speak up! I can't hear you!"

In fact, the smokers had been very subdued since long, long before the acrid tear-gas fumes drifted into their hideout, a narrow cave near the canyon mouth. They knew the end was near. Days before, they had lost radio contact with the only other band of smokers they knew of: five writers holed up in an Oakland apartment. It had been three weeks since the Donner group's last supply drop from the air, forty pounds of barbecued ribs, ten Picnic Tubs of Jimbo deep-fried chicken, and six cartons of smokes, all mentholated. Agents who searched the cave found exactly two cigarettes. There was not a single shred of tobacco found in any of the thousands of discarded butts. The two cigarettes were hidden in the lining of a sleeping bag, and the general disorder in the cave—clothing and personal effects strewn from hell to breakfast—indicated that some smokers had searched frantically for a smoke that very morning. Blackened remnants of what appeared to be cabbage leaves lay in the smoldering campfire.

"Move 'em out of here!" Ames said. "They disgust me."

*   *   *

Among the personal effects were four empty packs, carefully slit open, the blank insides covered with handwriting. An agent picked them up and put them in a plastic bag, for evidence. They read:

Dear Lindsay & Matt—
This is to let y. know I'm OK & w. friends tho how this w. reach you I dont know. 5 of us are in the mts (dont know where). I never thot it wld come to this. All those yrs as ashtrays vanishd fr parties & old pals made sarc remarks & FAA crackd down & smoke sect. became closet, I thot if I just was discreet & smokd in prv & took mints I'd get by but then yr dad quit & I had to go undergrnd. Bsmnt, gar., wet twls, A/C, etc. Felt guilty but contd, couldnt stop. Or didnt. Too late for that now. Gotta go on midnt watch. More soon.

Love,
Mother.

My Dear Children—
Down to 1 cart. PlMls. Not my fav. Down to 1 cg/day. After
supper. Hate to say it but it tastes fant. So rich, so mild. I
know you never approvd. Sorry. In 50s it was diffrnt, we all
smokd like movie stars. So gracefl, tak'g cg from pk, the mtch,
the lite, one smooth move. Food, sex, then smoke. Lng drags.
Lrnd Fr. exh. Then sudd. it was 82 and signs apprd (Thanx
for Not S). In my home! Kids naggng like fishwives & yr dad
sudd. went out for track. I felt *ambushed*. Bob Dylan smokd,
Carson, Beatles. I mean WE'RE NOT CRIMINALS. Sorry. Too late
now. More soon.

Love,
Mother.

Dear Kids—
This may be last letter, theyre closing in. Planes o'head every
day now. Dogs in dist. Men w. ldspkrs. Flares. Oakland chapt
got busted last pm. Was w. them on radio when feds came.
Reminded me of when yr dad turnd me in. After supper. Knew
he was a nut but didnt know he was a creep. Cops surr. hse,
I snk away thru bushes. No time to say g-b to y. Sorry. Wld
you believe I quit twice yrs ago, once fr 8 mo. I'm not a
terrible wom. y'know. Sorry. Know this is hard on y. Me too.
We're down to 2 pks & everybody's tense. Got to go chk
perimtr. Goodbye.

Love,
Mother.

Dear L & M—
This is it. They saw us. I have one left and am smokng it
now. Gd it tastes gd. My last cg. Then its all over. I'm OK.
I'm ready. Its a better thng I do now than I hv ever done. I
love you both. . . .

*   *   *

The five smokers were handcuffed and transported to a federal detention camp in Oregon, where they were held in pup tents for months. They were charged with conspiracy to obtain, and willful possession of, tobacco, and were convicted in minutes, and were sentenced to write twenty-thousand words apiece on the topic "Personal Integrity" by a judge who had quit cigarettes when the price went to thirty-five cents and he could not justify the expense.

The author of the letters was soon reunited with her children, and one night, while crossing a busy intersection near their home in Chicago, she saved them from sure death by pulling them back from the path of a speeding car. Her husband, who had just been telling her she could stand to lose some weight, was killed instantly, however.

THREE NEW TWINS JOIN
CLUB IN SPRING

My TEAM WON the World Series. You thought we couldn't but we knew we would and we did, and what did your team do? Not much. Now we're heading down to spring training looking even better than before, and your team that looked pitiful then looks even less hot now. Your hometown paper doesn't say so, but your lead-off guy had a bad ear infection in January and now he gets dizzy at the first sign of stress and falls down in a heap. Sad. Your cleanup guy spent the winter cleaning his plate. He had to buy new clothes in a size they don't sell at regular stores. Your great relief guy, his life has been changed by the Rama Lama Ding Dong, and he is now serenely throwing the ball from a place deep within himself, near his gallbladder. What a shame. Your rookie outfielder set a world record for throwing a frozen chicken, at a promotional appearance for Grandma Fanny's Farm Foods. Something snapped in his armpit and now he can't even throw a pair of dice. Tough beans. Your big left-hander tried hypnosis to stop smoking and while in a trancelike state discovered he hated his mother for tying his tiny right hand behind his back and making him eat and draw and tinkle with his left. So he's right-handed now, a little awkward but gradually learning to point with it and wave goodbye. That's what your whole team'll be doing by early May.

Meanwhile, my team, the world-champion Minnesota Twins, are top dogs who look like a lead-pipe cinch to take all the marbles in a slow walk. My guys had a good winter doing youth work. Last October they pooled their Series pay to purchase a farm, Twin Acres, north of Willmar, where they could stay in shape doing chores in the off-season, and they loved it so much they stayed through Thanksgiving and Christmas (celebrating them the good old-fashioned Midwestern way), and raised a new barn, bought a powerful new seed drill to plant winter wheat with, built up the flock of purebred Leghorns, chopped wood, carried water, etc., along with their guests—delinquent boys and girls from St. Louis and Detroit who needed to get out of those sick destructive environments and learn personal values such as honesty and personal cleanliness. Meanwhile, back in Minneapolis, the Twins front office wasn't asleep on its laurels but through shrewd deals made mostly before 8:15 A.M. added to what they had while giving up nothing in return. They did so great, it seems unfair.

OTHER TEAMS GNASH TEETH OR SULK

It's considered impossible to obtain *three top premium players* without paying a red cent, but the Twins:

¶Traded away some useless air rights and obtained Chuck Johnson (23, 187 lbs., 6'1", bats left, throws left), a native of Little Falls, Minnesota. Maybe that's why the scouts who work the Finger Lakes League ignored his phenomenal season with the Seneca Falls Susans. They figured, "Minnesota? Forget it!" But how can you forget thirty-eight doubles, twenty-two triples, and twenty-nine round-trippers—and in spacious Elizabeth Cady Stanton Stadium! That's a lot of power for a lifelong liberal like Chuck. And what's more, he *never struck out*. Not once. Plays all positions cheerfully.

¶Sent a couple in their mid-forties to the San Diego Padres in exchange for Duane (Madman) Mueller (29, 280 lbs., 6'2", right/right, a.k.a. Mule, Hired Hand, The Barber). Duane is a big secret because after he was suspended by the Texas League for throwing too hard he played Nicaraguan winter ball for three years and then spent two more doing humanitarian stuff, so scouts forgot how, back when he was with the Amarillo Compadres, nobody wanted to be behind the plate, Duane threw so hard. His own team kept yelling, "Not so *hard*, man!" If that sounds dumb, then you never saw him throw: he threw *hard*. A devoted Lutheran, he never ever hit a batter, but in one game a pitch of his nicked the bill of an opponent's batting helmet and spun it so hard it burned off the man's eyebrows. No serious injury, but big Duane took himself out of organized ball until he could learn an off-speed pitch. He's from Brainerd, Minnesota, where he lives across the street from his folks. His mom played kittenball in the fifties and had a good arm but not like her son's. She thinks he got it from delivering papers and whipping cake mix. "I'd sure hate to have to bat against him," she says.

¶Gave up a dingy two-bedroom house in St. Paul (it needs more than just a paint job and a new roof, and it's near a rendering plant) to acquire and activate Bob Berg (24, 112 lbs., 5'3", right/left), the fastest man on the basepaths today (we *think*), but he sat out last year and the year before last and the year before *that* because he didn't have shoes. Reason: he's so fast he runs the shoes right off his feet. Now athletic foot specialists have studied his film clips (sad to see: three lightning strides, a look of dismay on Bob's face, and down he goes with his loose laces like a lasso round his ankles) and come up with a new pair of pigskin shoes with barbed cleats that stick in the turf and slow him down. Born and raised in Eveleth, Minnesota, he is probably the nicest fast man in baseball. Nicknamed The Hulk ("berg" means "mountain" in Norwegian). He used those three years on the bench to earn a B.A. in history, by the way.

THAT'S NOT ALL

¶Joining the team later will be Wally Gunderson (17, 191 lbs., 6'4", left/right), who dons a Twins uniform June 8, the day after he graduates from West High in Minneapolis. The Twins have saved him a number, 18, and assigned him a locker and paid him a bonus, twelve hundred dollars, which was all he would accept. He's thrilled just to be on the team. A big lanky loose-jointed kid with long wavy blond hair and a goofy grin, he throws a screwball that comes in and up, a slider that suddenly jumps, a curve that drops off the table, and a stinkball that hangs in the air so long some batters swing twice. You don't expect so much junk from an Eagle Scout, but Wally's got one more: a fastball that decelerates rapidly halfway to the plate—a braking pitch. Some he learned from his dad and the rest he invented for a Science Fair project. "Pitching is physics, that's all," he says, looking down at his size-13 shoes, uneasy at all the acclaim.

Detroit and St. Louis offered the lad millions in cash, land, jewelry, servants, tax abatements, but he wasn't listening. "I want to play my ball where my roots are," he says quietly.

Twinsville wasn't one bit surprised. Personal character and loyalty and dedication are what got us where we are right now, and that's on top. We're No. 1. We knew it first and now you know it, too. You thought we were quiet and modest in the Midwest but that's because you're dumb, as dumb as a stump, dumber than dirt.

You're so dumb you don't know that we're on top and you're below. Our team wins and your team loses; we need your team to amuse us. Minnesota soybeans, corn, and barley; we're the best, so beat it, Charley, or we'll shell ya like a pea pod, dunk ya like a doughnut—sure be nice when the game's over, won't it—take ya to the cleaners for a brand-new hairdo. We can beat ya anytime we care to. Shave and a haircut, two bits.

YOUR BOOK SAVED
MY LIFE, MISTER

ALL OF MY BOOKS, including *Wagons Westward!!! Hiiiii-YAW* and *Ck-ck Giddup Beauty! C'mon Big Girl, Awaaaaayy!* and *Pa! Look Out! It's—Aiiiiieee!*, have been difficult for my readers, I guess, judging from their reactions when they see me shopping at Val-Mar or sitting in the Quad County Library & Media Center. After a rough morning at the keyboard, I sort of like to slip into my black leather vest, big white hat, and red kerchief, same as in the book-jacket photos, and saunter up and down the aisle by the fruit and other perishable items and let my fans have the thrill of running into me, and if nobody does I park myself at a table dead smack in front of the Western-adventure shelf in Quad County's fiction department, lean back, plant my big boots on the table, and prepare to endure the terrible price of celebrity, but it's not uncommon for a reader to come by, glance down, and say, "Aren't you Dusty Pages, the author of *Ck-ck Giddup Beauty! C'mon Big Girl, Awaaaaayy!*" and when I look down and blush and say, "Well, yes, ma'am, I reckon I am him," she says, "I thought so. You look just like him." Then an awful silence while she studies the shelf and selects Ray A. James, Jr., or Chuck Young or another of my rivals. It's a painful moment for an author, the reader two feet away and moments passing during which she does not say, "Your books have meant so much to me," or "I can't tell you how much I admire your work." She just reaches past the author like he was a sack of potatoes and chooses a book by

11

somebody else. Same thing happens with men. They say, "You're an author, aren'tcha? I read a book of yours once, what was the name of it?"

I try to be helpful. "Could it have been *Wagons Westward!!! Hiiiii-YAW!*"

"No, it had someone's name in the title."

"Well, I wrote a book entitled *Pa! Look Out! It's—Aiiiiieee!*"

"No, I think it had the name of a horse."

"Could it have been *Ck-ck Giddup Beauty! C'mon Big Girl, Awaaaaayy!*"

"That's the one. Did you write that?"

"Yes, sir, I did."

"Huh. I thought so."

And right there you brace yourself for him to say, "Y'know, I never was one for books and then my brother gave me yours for Christmas and I said, 'Naw, I don't read books, Craig, you know that,' and he said, 'But this is different, Jim Earl, read this, this isn't the girls' literature they stuffed down our throats in high school, this is the real potatoes,' so I read it and by George I couldn't put the sucker down, I ran out and did the chores and tore out and back in the pickup to check on those dogies and I read for two days and two nights without a minute of shuteye. Your book changed my life, mister. I'm glad I got a chance to tell you that. You cleared up a bunch of stuff that has bothered me for years—you took something that had been inside me and you put it into words so I could feel, I donno, not so weird, feel sorta like *understood*, y'might say. That was me you put in that book of yours, mister. That was my life you wrote about there, and I want to say thanks. Just remember, anytime you're ever in Big Junction, Wyoming, you got a friend there name o' Jim Earl Wilcox"—but instead he says, "You wouldn't know where the little boys' room is, wouldja?," as if I were a library employee and not a book author. So it's clear to me that when people read my books they like me a little less at the end than at the beginning. My fourth book, *Company A, Chaaaaaaarge!*, is evidently the worst. Nobody bought it at all.

I know what it's like to be disappointed by a hero. You think I don't know? Believe me, I know. I met my idol, Smokey W. Kaiser, when I was twelve. I'd read every one of his books twice—the Curly Bob and Lefty Slim series, the Lazy A Gang series, the Powder River Hank series—and I had waited outside the YMCA in Des Moines for three hours while he regaled the Rotary with humorous anecdotes, and when he emerged at the side door, a fat man in tight green pants tucked into silver-studded boots, he looked down and growled, "I don't sign pieces of paper, kid. I sign books. No paper. You want my autograph, you can buy a book. That's a rule of mine. Don't waste my time and I won't waste yours."

Smokey's problem was that he was a jerk, but mine is that I get halfway through a story and everything goes to pieces. In *Wagons Westward!!! Hiiiii-YAW!* the pioneers reach Council Bluffs, having endured two hundred solid pages of Indian attacks, smallpox, cattle stampedes, thirst, terror, bitter backbiting, scattered atheism, and adulterous inclinations, and then they sit on the bluffs and have a meeting to decide whether they really want to forge onward to Oregon or whether maybe they should head east toward Oak Park or Evanston instead. Buck Bradley, the tall, taciturn, sandy-haired, God-fearing man who led them through the rough stuff, stands up and says, "Well, it's up to the rest of you. Makes no nevermind to yours truly, I could go either way and be happy—west, south, you name it. I don't *need* to go west or anything. You choose. I'll go along with whatever."

I don't know. I wrote that scene the way I heard it in my head but now I see it in print, it looks dumb. I can certainly see why it would throw a reader, same as in *Giddup Beauty! C'mon Big Girl, Awaaaaayy!*, when Buck rides two thousand miles across blazing deserts searching for Julie Ann and finally, after killing twenty men and wearing out three mounts and surviving two avalanches, a prairie fire, a blizzard, and a passel of varmints, he finds her held captive by the bloodthirsty Arapaho. "So, how are you doing?" he asks her. "Oh, all right, I guess," she says, gazing up at him, wiping the sweat from her brow. "You want to come in for a cup of coffee?" "Naw, I just wanted to make sure you were okay. You *look* okay." "Yeah, I lost some weight, about twenty pounds." "Oh, really. How?" "Eating toads and grasshoppers." "Uh-huh. Well, now that I look at you, you *do* look lighter." "Sure you won't have coffee?" "Naw, I gotta ride. Be seein' ya, now." "Okay, bye!" To me it seemed more realistic that way, but maybe to the guy reader it sounded sort of unfocused or something. I don't know. Guys have always been a tough audience for me. The other day a guy grabbed my arm in the Quad County and said, "Hey, Dusty! Dusty Pages! That right? Am I right or am I right?"

"Both," I said.

"Mister," he said, "your book saved my life. My brother gave it to me and said, 'Buck, read this sometime when you're sober,' and I put it in my pocket and didn't think about it until, October, I was elk hunting up in the Big Coulee country, other side of the Little Crazy River, and suddenly *wham* it felt like somebody swung a bat and hit me in the left nipple. I fell over and lay there and, doggone it, I felt around and didn't find blood—I go 'Huh???????' Well, it was your book in my jacket pocket saved my life—bullet tore through the first half of it, stopping at page 143. So, by Jim, I thought, 'This is too crazy, I got to *read* this,' and I started to read and I couldn't believe it. That was me in the book—my life, my thoughts, it was weird. Names, dates, places—it was my life down to the last detail, except for the beer. I don't drink Coors. The rest you got right. Here." And he slipped an envelope into my hand. "This is for you," he said.

It was a subpoena to appear in U.S. District Court the 27th of November to defend myself in a civil suit for wrongful misuse of the life of another for literary gain. I appeared and I tried to defend, but I lost. My attorney, a very, very nice man named Howard Furst, was simply outgunned by three tall ferret-faced bushwhackers in black pinstripes who flew in from Houston and tore him limb from limb in two and a half hours in that cold windy courtroom. They and their client, Buck Bradley, toted away three saddlebags full of my bank account, leaving me with nothing except this latest book. It's the first in a new series, the Lonesome Bud series, called *The Case of the Black Mesa*, and it begins with a snake biting Bud in the wrist as he hangs from a cliff while Navajo shoot flaming arrows at him from below and a torrent of sharp gravel showers down on his old bald head. From there to the end, it never lets up, except maybe in Chapter 4, where he and the boys shop for bunk beds. I don't know what I had in mind there at all.

WHO WE WERE AND WHAT
WE MEANT BY IT

THE BREAKUP OF THE MOMENTIST MOVEMENT in 1962 in St. Paul was a deliberate decision on the part of all four of us. We were sitting in Swedlund's Drugstore one afternoon when Patty said, "It's great being together and all but—you know, it's never going to be this good again, so I think it's time we said goodbye."

So we left town, or so I thought until last Christmas, when I saw Ed's book, *Once There Was a Time*, a "memoir" of that St. Paul scene—a book riddled with factual errors, a betrayal of all that we stood for—and I read on the jacket that he now owns Swedlund's (renamed the Scene Shop), where he has "preserved the atmosphere of Momentism in all its raw brilliance and vitality." So a few weeks ago, on my way out to the Coast, I stopped off in St. Paul to see for myself.

I'm not naïve. I realize that the St. Paul scene became legendary after we left, that any number of artists have claimed the Momentist mantle, and that popular mythology links our movement to everything from rebirthing to "self-denial," to the work of such Incidentalists as Karen Johnson and Charles Shur, to the grab bag of the New Wave, No Wave, Now Wave, and Bye-Bye movements of the early eighties. I'm well aware that every year, on May 14, thousands assemble in Rice Park and jump into the fountain, to commemorate an evening of ours in 1962. And I'm not surprised. We Momentists fully expected to be misunderstood and exploited. I just never thought it would be done by one of us.

From the airport, I took a cab to our old block on Maple between Hyacinth and Sycamore, and I couldn't believe my own eyes. Three restaurants claim that we met there. *Two of them weren't even in business in 1962!* The Scene Shop is the third. As Swedlund's, it was a place where we met *occasionally—but not where they say we did!* They have a booth roped off that they say was *the* booth, but it wasn't. *The* booth was in the front by the window, and the table was linoleum-covered. This one is butcher block and they've set four places on it. (1) We never *ate* at Swedlund's, only drank coffee, and (2) there were always more than four of us—I mean, there were four of *us*, but some of us usually brought a friend.

Anyone who knows squat about Momentism can see this joint for the fake that it is. The same goes for the Four Friends, the Loft Bar, the Momentary Playhouse, Les Amis Gallery, and all the other tourist traps. None of us were playwrights or painters; we were Momentary artists. Permanence repelled us. Les Amis was a guy we *never* invited to our group. And yet there's Les, cranking out the same old trashy collages and claiming to be our heir! We have no heirs. We left nothing behind to inherit. That was the point of it.

What a dismal sight it is! The tony restaurants, the antique street-lights and paving blocks (all new since '62), the same dreary street-singers and sidewalk painters you'll find in the Village or at North Beach or the French Quarter—a scene of weary decadence where once we four were briefly young and hopeful, all artists together making something fresh and new and *momentary*. Now tourists wander in a carnival that claims us as inspiration for the cheap goods it sells.

In *Once There Was a Time*, Ed says he met Patty at the Four Friends, on the northeast corner of Maple and Sycamore. He offered her a Camel. She had never smoked, but she accepted it and said, "I am going to smoke one cigarette in my life. Only one. That way I

will always remember it." That led to Momentism. Later Patty
brought in Cheryl and Cheryl brought in me.

Untrue.

We four met on April 21, 1962. Patty and Cheryl got off work
at the Flameburger at 8:00 P.M. and went to Maple and Sycamore to
catch a bus downtown and go roller-skating. I was at the bus stop,
blowing my nose, a little upset, having just broken up with my
girlfriend Donna, who lived at 1987 Hyacinth and whose parents
forced us apart because we were getting "too serious" and they
couldn't stand the sight of me. I had gone to her house to return a
couple of photographs of her, including one of us standing beside her
dog, which she tore down the middle and gave me the half with her
in it and I promised to keep it forever, and we said goodbye and cried,
and I walked to the corner for the bus. Actually, the bus I wanted
was the westbound Maple bus, but, distracted by grief, I went and
stood with the two girls on the *southwest* corner of Maple and
Sycamore, and caught the eastbound. One of them asked if I was
all right. We talked. We sat in back, on facing seats. Ed was there.
He sort of attached himself to us. I thought at the time he was
a pushy guy.

In *Once There Was a Time*, Ed claims that the trip downtown
occurred much later, after he and Patty had laid the groundwork of
Momentism, but in fact it was something that just happened among
us three even before the bus came. We started fooling around, just
kidding, *improvising* things, and suddenly it clicked. We all knew it.
It was not any one thing that we said, and it wasn't like we were
thinking, "Hey, this is a movement!"—it *happened*. We got on the
bus together, we got off downtown at Fifth and St. Peter (with Ed in
tow), we walked around for several hours and talked a lot and did
things, and then we said, "Let's get together tomorrow."

I wish we hadn't. Looking back on it, I can see that that evening
was the high point, the apotheosis of what Momentism was all about.
If we had let it go at that and not made a movement out of it,

Momentism would have been *purely* momentary, but as it is Momentism became a self-contradiction—the Moment extended, recalled, amplified, and now commemorated. It's a shame.

*   *   *

People ask me, "But what exactly was *said* that night? What did you four *do?*" That's not the point. It was a feeling, more than anything specific. We were young and had fallen together accidentally and we shared a feeling that this was a brief moment in our youth when everything was iridescent and meaningful and charged with importance in a way it would never be again.

To write about it, however, the way Ed has ("The streetlights cast great cones of light into which we walked, the soles of our shoes clicking certain rhythmic changes that excited us, and we saw our own mystery in the great blank darkened windows, a mystery of unutterable poignance as cars swished by filled with persons whom we would never see again, and all of this happening on a night that we would never know again; no matter how much we might wish to recapture it, its essence was fleeting and would never be described, not even in this sentence"), is to make it trivial, a moment similar to moments in other people's lives. It wasn't similar at all! It was unique to us, and we knew it. A moment of art, perfect and complete, so why try to translate it into a work of art so that a lot of jerks could look at that and say, "Oh, yeah! I understand what you felt there! It's a lot like my own life in a way!" *No, it wasn't. They don't understand at all. How could they?*

Yes, we did climb into the fountain in Rice Park across from the St. Paul Public Library, just as in the legend, but it was not intended to be a legend at the time, it was only something we did. Patty said, "There will never be another night exactly like this one, so let's do something we've never done before," and the fountain was there and we got in—first Patty and then Cheryl and me, and finally Ed, who thought it was "dumb." (We were not arrested, as Ed says now, nor did he take off his clothes. We removed only our shoes and stockings. Nor did he recite Baudelaire. None of us recited anything or made any reference to a pre-existent work of art; we said what we were thinking and feeling *at the moment*.)

I don't mind that every year during Momentarily Week thousands of people jump into that same fountain, but I wish they would do it for their own reasons and not to celebrate something that happened one evening twenty years ago. If ever a movement resisted celebration, it was us Momentists. That was why I went back to St. Paul— to repeat the message that the world has misunderstood: Not Us but Yourself, Not That but This, Not Then but Now, The Answer Is Not on My Face. The moment is gone, now is the moment. We are gone, we will come back in a moment.

But I didn't have the heart to tell them. The crowds I saw milling on Maple were happy to think that the cheap imitation of Momentism they were buying was the genuine article, that a twelve-dollar T-shirt ("I Spent A Moment In St. Paul") made them members of a secret society of finer, more sensitive people, and that, strolling along this street, drinking burnt coffee in a room with burlap-covered walls and fishnet suspended from the ceiling, they were having an "experience" of a sort not so different from ours. I remembered what Patty said once after we had gone swimming at midnight and then sat around on the riverbank eating doughnuts. She said, "Don't tell anybody. Don't say anything, period. Don't ruin it."

She was right. It was Ed who ruined Momentism. First he insisted on writing "We Were Here" on walls and sidewalks with a piece of chalk, then he started taking hands off clocks. He wrote "Now" on his forehead. He talked to reporters. He wore strange clothes. He developed himself into a celebrity, a walking personal appearance, an event. Younger people started following him around; they shopped all over town for khaki pants, striped short-sleeved pullovers, white Keds, black horn-rimmed glasses exactly like his.

He looked so old when I saw him, there in St. Paul. I was disgusted. So sallow, flabby, *listless*. He sat in uniform at "the table" and allowed the patrons to stare at him. He was accustomed to being watched, I could see, and it had destroyed him. The Ed I knew was gone, his Edness all used up. I couldn't stand to look at him.

Thank goodness we true Momentists got out intact, leaving no work behind to be gawked at and eventually become dated and embarrassing and dull. Everything we created was in our heads and among us three, and only we know what it was, and so it exists outside of time and form and will be forever pure being just as it was at that moment. I walked away from the former Swedlund's and caught a cab to the airport, wishing I had never made the trip. And then something happened! In the airport! A woman in black was sitting at the shoeshine stand—the slap of cloth—a dime dropped!— a plane rose! It was such a brief thing, actually only a glimpse of something distant, fleeting, and so graceful that when it was gone I carried the image with me to the Coast, and it was worth going to Minnesota to see.

THE CURRENT CRISIS
IN REMORSE

R EMORSE IS A FAIRLY NEW AREA in social work so it's no wonder we get the short end when it comes to budget and staffing. Take me, for example. For three years, I was the *only professional remorse officer* in a Department of Human Services serving a city of *more than 1.5 million*, and not so long ago my supervisor Mitch (a man with no remorse background at all) told me I was "expendable" and that he would "shed no tears" if remorse was eliminated from the Department entirely. I had no office, only a desk across from the elevators, and I shared a phone with the director of the Nephew Program in Family Counseling. And it's not only me! Around the country, morale in remorse has never been lower.

We in remorse are a radical minority within the social-work community. We believe that not every wrong in our society is the result of complex factors such as poor early-learning environment and re-sultative dissocialized communication. Some wrong is the result of *badness*. We believe that some people act like jerks, and that when dealing with jerks one doesn't waste too much time on sympathy. They're jerks. They do bad things. They should feel sorry for what they did and stop doing it. Of course, I'm oversimplifying here, trying to state things in layman's terms, and I should add that we are professionals, after all, who are trained in behavioral methodology *including* remorse, but also a lot more—if you're interested, read "Principles of Deductive Repentance," by Morse and Frain, or Professor Frain's excellent "Failure and Fault: Assignment and Acceptance."

I did my training under Frain and graduated in 1976, just as remorse was coming to the forefront. People in the helping professions had begun to notice a dramatic increase in the number of clients who did terrible things and didn't feel one bit sorry. It was an utterly common phenomenon for a man who had been apprehended after months of senseless carnage to look at a social worker or psychologist with an expression of mild dismay and say, "Hey, I know what you're thinking, but that wasn't *me* out there, it wasn't *like* me at all. I'm a caring type of guy. Anyway, it's over now, it's done, and I got to get on with my own life, you know," as if he had only been unkind or unsupportive of his victims and not dismembered them and stuffed them into mailboxes. This was not the "cold-blooded" or "hardened" criminal but, rather, a cheerful, self-accepting one, who looked on his crime as "something that happened" and had a theory to explain it.

"I'm thinking it was a nutritional thing," one mass murderer remarked to me in 1978. "I was feeling down that day. I'd been doing a lot of deep-fried foods, and I was going to get a multi-vitamin out of the medicine chest when I noticed all those old ladies in the park and—well, one thing just led to another. I've completely changed my food intake since then. I really feel *good* now. I know I'm never going to let myself get in that type of situation again!"

It wasn't only vicious criminals who didn't feel sorry, though. It was a regretless time all around. Your own best friend might spill a glass of red wine on your new white sofa and immediately *explain* it—no spontaneous shame and embarrassment, just "Oh, I've always had poor motor skills," or "You distracted me with your comment about Bolivia." People walked in and stole your shoes, they trashed your lawn and bullied your children and blasted the neighborhood with powerful tape machines at 4:00 A.M. and got stone drunk and cruised through red lights, smashing your car and ruining your life for the next six months, and if you confronted them about these actions they told you about a particularly upsetting life-experience they'd gone through recently, such as condemnation, that caused them to do it.

In 1976, a major Protestant denomination narrowly defeated an attempt to destigmatize the Prayer of Confession by removing from it all guilt or guilt-oriented references: "Lord, we approach Thy Throne of Grace, having committed acts which, we do heartily acknowledge, must be very difficult for Thee to understand. Nevertheless, we do beseech Thee to postpone judgment and to give Thy faithful servants the benefit of the doubt until such time as we are able to answer all Thy questions fully and clear our reputations in Heaven."

It was lack of remorse among criminals, though, that aroused public outrage, and suddenly we few professionals in the field were under terrible pressure to have full-fledged remorse programs in place in weeks, even days. City Hall was on the phone, demanding to see miscreants slumped in courtrooms, weeping, shielding their faces while led off to jail.

Fine, I said. Give me full funding to hire a staff and I'll give you a remorse program you can be proud of. Mitch sneered. "Ha!" he said. He said, "Get this straight, showboat, 'cause I'll only say it once. You work for me, and I say remorse is Number Last on the list around here. Cosmetics! That's all City Hall wants and that's what we give them. A few tears. You can twist arms, step on toes, or use raw onions, but forget about funding."

His insensitivity shocked me. Remorselessness is a fundamental flaw, a crack in the social contract, and repair requires a major commitment. One man simply couldn't keep up with the caseload.

I spent two months on the president of AmTox, who was sent to me after his conviction for dumping tons of deadly wastes into a scenic gorge and killing thousands of trout and who took a Who— me? attitude toward the deed until finally I elicited a small amount of shame by requiring him to spend Saturdays panhandling in the bus depot, wearing a sign that said "Help Me, I'm Not Too Bright." But meanwhile hundreds of others got off scot-free. I'd put the screws to the guy who enjoyed touching pedestrians with his front fender, but meanwhile the guys who bilked hundreds of elderly women of their life savings walked out the door saying, "Hey, what's the big deal? So we exaggerated a little. No need to get huffy about it."

It depressed the hell out of me. Here I was, swimming in paperwork with my hands tied, and out on the street were jerks on parade: unassuming, pleasant, perfectly normal people except that they had an extra bone in their head and less moral sense than God gave badgers. And the ones I did put through remorse didn't improve a lot. Six months ago, thirty-seven former clients of mine filed a class-action suit against the state demanding millions in restitution for the ethically handicapped and arguing neglect on the state's part in failing to provide remorse counseling earlier. "We have suffered terrible remorse," the brief said, "as we begin to recognize the enormity of our sins, including but not limited to: pure selfishness, vicious cruelty, utter dishonesty, blind insensitivity, gross neglect, overweening pride, etc. And that's fine. But where was this program ten years ago? Nowhere to be found! That was the Me Decade! Is that our fault? Therefore, in consideration of the vast black abyss of guilt to which we have been suddenly subjected, we demand that the court order . . ." My heart sank as I read it. They had even quoted my speech to the Council on Penitential Reform in 1981:

> Criminal nonremorse is the tip of a very large iceberg, and unless we initiate broad-based remorse reforms on the community level and start talking about an overhaul of our entire moral system—church, media, education, the parental system, personal networking, the entire values-delivery infrastructure—and recognize that it requires major investment by private *and* public sectors in professional training and research

and that we're looking at a time frame of years, not months, and that we must begin now, we simply *must*, because, believe me, if we don't, that is a mistake we're going to live to regret!

The state, they said further, had failed to exercise due care in neglecting to warn them earlier and to inform them of the urgent necessity of changing their ways.

Three days later, the order came down that I was reassigned. By offering remorse assistance, it said, I had needlessly raised people's expectations of inner peace.

"That means you, lamebrain," Mitch cackled, leaning across his desk and poking an index finger into my rib cage. "Let's see how you like it in the basement." He assigned me to "assist in the assembly and assessment" of ancient and dusty ascertainment files in a dim, airless room deep in the bowels of Human Services—useless and demeaning work that left me weak and dispirited after only a day, but I held on and did the work and didn't complain. He plugged the ventilator, reduced light-bulb wattage, denied me a radio. I spent three weeks in that hellhole, reading lengthy case histories of clients long since deceased and sorting them into meaningless piles and attaching gummed labels that tasted like dead socks.

Suddenly, one afternoon, he appeared in the doorway, his face drawn, his eyes filled with tears. "I read Frain last night," he said. "All night. Why— I— You should have told me. Oh God, oh God! What have I done to you? How can I make it up? You want my job? Take it."

"No, thanks. That's all right. No problem," I said. "I'm quitting."

He begged me to stay. "I can't live with my conscience if you won't let me do something for you. Let me at least take you to lunch. There's a terrific little seafood place a block from here that I've been keeping to myself—"

"Don't bother," I said. "Come five o'clock you'll never see me again."

I was true to my word. I'm a vice-president of Yakamoto now, where I've designed a remorse program for assembly-line workers to build stronger emotional responses to poor workmanship, tardiness, false sick days, and excessive lunch breaks. The job is challenging, the people pleasant, the fringe benefits outstanding, and the salary is three hundred and ninety-five thou a year. The Japanese place a high premium on shame. You don't see them treating other people like dirt. They even feel contrition for things that someone standing next to them did! They treat me like a prince. I'm a lucky man. I'm extremely happy here.

THE PEOPLE VS. JIM

Q: Jim, I'd like you to look at this magazine article entitled "The Twenty Best Hash Browns in Town" and tell me if you wrote it.

A: Yes, I did.

Q: How about this? "Fifteen Great Ideas for Putting New Life in Those Dingy Stair Treads." Was that the second "list" article you wrote for a magazine?

A: No, that was my tenth. That was after "Eleven Restaurants You'll Remember the Rest of Your Life," "Ten All-Time Greatest Half & Halfs," "My Ten All-Time Favorite Racquetball Partners," "Ten Ways to Lose Four Pounds in Two Days," "Ten Celebrities Show Off Their Basements," "Eight Methods of Beating a Midlife Slump," "Seven Terrific Marriages," "Six Meaner Dogs Than You Ever Saw Before," and "Five Kids Who Make Your Kids Look Sick."

Q: What happened, Jim? Why couldn't you quit then? You knew it was wrong.

A: I know, but look at it my way. First of all, I think that—

Q: "Thirty People Who'd Like to Be Your Friend," "Ten Famous People's Breakfasts," "Eighteen Best Red Things," "Six Best Tops of Things," "Twelve Biggest Unnoticed Things," "Twenty-one Places Where Famous People Were Seen Doing One of Two Things"—the list goes on, Jim.

A: I had a house, I was married, we had two children, pets, a summer place, a boat, a membership in a health club, and a good investment program. But more than that, I found it satisfying. I was a child of the forties, and through the fifties, sixties, seventies, and into the eighties my life seemed confused, purposeless, ill defined. Lists helped to center me a little, calm me down. I took out a clean sheet of paper, numbered it from one to fifteen or twenty—I got a feeling of accomplishment.

Q: You went crazy, Jim. You wrote for sixty-eight different life-style magazines, including *Des Moines*, *The Boisean*, *The Orlandan*, *The Albuquerquer*, *The Wichitan*, *Los Angel*, *The Quad Citian*, *The Bethesdan*, *The Hobokener*, *The Duluthist*, *The Renoite*, *Oakland*, *The Queenser*, *Bismarck*, *The Baton Rougist*, *The Omahite*, *The Pittsburghast*, and you wrote lists of best artists, best music videos, best hamburgers, quiet restaurants, noisy restaurants, bourbons, aluminum foils, dining-room sets, wallets, American novels, cheese snacks, hotel lobbies, movies, women named Diane, burritos, "Ten Most Exciting Elevators," "Ten Cures for Winter Arghhhs," "Ten People Who Have Something You'll Never Have," "Ten Things That Look Very Unusual but Really Aren't," "Ten Things You Don't Need to Worry About," "Ten Places Nearby That You Ought to Drop Everything and Go Look At Immediately," "The Thirty-nine Most Successful, Restless, Desperately Unhappy People in West Virginia," "Fifty Top U.S. Businesses Run by Methodists"—surely, Jim, there must have come a point when you thought, That is enough. I can't do this anymore.

A: I had filled up sixty-one floppy discs by then. I wanted to reach a hundred.

Q: So you filled your hundredth disc, and you collected everything in a book, *The Fatal List*, and it reached No. 8 on the *Times* list, and then—?

A: I was ready to retire, but the editor of *Milwaukee* told me to cough up ten more, otherwise he would include me in "Fifty People Who Were Once Hot and Aren't Anymore for One Reason or Another." So I did them.

Q: Do you have any idea what damage you've done, Jim? You've made people more stupid. Some of your readers now find it hard to read paragraphs that aren't numbered.

A: How many? A lot?

Q: Jim, we're going to have to put you in a little room by yourself for a while, I think.

A: Will I ever write again?

Q: No.

THE YOUNG LUTHERAN'S
GUIDE TO THE ORCHESTRA*

To EACH PERSON God gives some talent, such as writing, just to name one, and to many persons He has given musical talent, though not as many as think so. For the young Lutheran, the question must be: Do I have a genuine God-given musical talent or do I only seem gifted in comparison to other young Lutherans?

If your talent is choir or organ, there's no problem. Choir members and organists can be sure their gift is from God because who else but God would be interested. Just like nobody gets fat on celery, nobody goes into church music for the wrong motives.

But for a Lutheran who feels led to play in an orchestra, the first question must be: Are you kidding? An *orchestra*?

In the Bible, we read about people singing and playing musical instruments, the harp, trumpet, psaltery, but always in praise of the Lord, not for amusement. We do not read that our Lord Himself ever played an instrument or enjoyed hearing others play theirs. The apostles did not attend concerts, or go to dances. *Are you sure this is what you want?* Do you know what you're getting into? Opera. Is that anyplace for a Christian? Don Juan and Mephistopheles and Wagner and all his pagan goddesses hooting and hollering, and the immorality—I mean, is anybody in opera married? You play in an

* With Randall Davidson.

31

orchestra, you're going to wind up in opera, and the next thing you know, you're going to be skipping Sunday mornings.

If you steer clear of opera and stick to orchestral concert music, where are the Christian composers? Modern ones are existentialists, the Romantics were secular humanists, the eighteenth century was all rationalists, and the seventeenth was Italians, except for Bach, and you can't make a living playing Bach. You go in an orchestra, you're going to be devoting your life to a lot of music that sort of swirls around in spiritual mystery searching for answers that people could find in the Bible if someone showed them where to look.

But if you're determined to play in an orchestra, then you ought to ask yourself: Which instrument is the best one for a Lutheran to play? If our Lord had played an instrument, which one would He have chosen? Probably not a *French horn*. It takes too much of a person's life. French-horn players hardly have time to marry and have children. The French horn is practically a religion all by itself. Should a Lutheran play the *bassoon*? Not if you want to be taken seriously. The name says it all: *bassoon*. Maybe you'd do it for a hobby ("Let's go bassooning this weekend, honey!") but not as your life occupation.

Many Lutherans start out playing *clarinets* in marching band and think of the clarinet as a Christian instrument, clear and strong and almost human, but a symphonic clarinet is different from the band clarinet: it's sardonic, skeptical, and definitely worldly. The *English horn* sounds Christian, maybe because we think of it as the Anglican horn, but it's so mournful, so plaintive. And so are English-horn players. They all have incredibly complicated problems, they're all depressed, especially at night, which is when concerts are. The *oboe* is the sensualist of the woodwind section, and if there's one wind a Lutheran should avoid, it's this one. In movie soundtracks, you tend to hear the oboe when the woman is taking her clothes off, or else later, when she asks the man for a cigarette. The *flute* is the big shot of the wind section. Jean-Pierre Rampal, James Galway, both millionaires (how many millionaire bassoonists are there?), because everybody knows it's the hardest to play. To spend your life blowing across a tiny hole—it's not really normal, is it. The flute is a temptation to pride. Avoid it. The last member of the woodwind family is the flakiest, and that's the *piccolo*. No Salvation Army band ever included a piccolo and no piccolo virtuoso ever did an album of gospel songs. This is not a devotional instrument.

We come now to the string section. Strings are mentioned in Scripture and therefore some Lutherans are tempted to become string players, but be careful. *Bass*, for example. An extremely slow instrument, the plowhorse of the orchestra, and bass players tend to be a little methodical, not inventive, not quick, not witty or brilliant, but reliable. This makes the instrument very tempting to German Lutherans. And yet, bass notes have a darkness and depth to them that, let's face it, is sexual. And when bass players pick up their bows, I don't think there's any doubt what's going on in their minds back there. The *cello* section seems so normal, and cellists seem like such *nice* people. The way they put their arms around their instruments, they look like parents zipping up a child's snowsuit. They seem like us: comfortable, middle-range. And yet there is something too comfortable, maybe too sensual, about the cello. The way they hold the instrument between their legs: why can't they hold it across their laps or alongside themselves? The *viola* section is not a place for a Lutheran and here you'll have to take my word for it. I know violists and they are fine people until, late at night, they start drinking a few bottles of cheap red wine and roasting chickens over a pit in a vacant lot and talk about going to Yucatan with a woman named Rita. Don't be part of this crowd. The *violin* is a problem for any Christian because it's a solo instrument, a virtuoso instrument, and we're not solo people. We believe in taking a back seat and being helpful. So Christians think about becoming *second violinists*. They're steady, humble, supportive. But who do they support? *First violins*. You want to get involved with them? The *first violins* are natural egotists. The conductor looks to them first, and most first violinists believe that the conductor secretly takes his cue from them, that he, a simple foreign person, gets carried away by listening to the violins and falls into a romantic, emotional reverie and forgets where in the score he is and looks to the concertmaster, the No. 1 first violin, to find out what's going on: this is what violinists believe in their hearts. If the conductor dropped dead, the rest of the orchestra would simply follow the violin section, while the maestro's body was carried away, and nobody would notice the difference. Is this a place for a Lutheran to be? In the biggest collection of gold-plated narcissists ever gathered on one stage? No.

Let's be clear about the brass section. First of all, the rest of the orchestra wishes the brass were playing in another room, and so does the conductor. His back is toward the audience, so they can't see what he's saying to the brass section; he's saying: You're too damn loud, shut the fuck up (in Italian, this doesn't sound coarse at all). The brass section is made up of men who were at one time in the construction trades and went into music because the hours were better. They are heavy dudes, and that's why composers wrote so few notes for them: because they're juveniles. The *tuba* player, for example, is a stocky, bearded guy who has a day job as a plumber. He's the only member of the orchestra who bowls and goes deer hunting. It's not an instrument for a sensitive Lutheran, and anyway there's only one tuba and he's it. The *trombonist* is a humorist. He carries a water spray gun to keep his slide moist and often uses it against other members of the orchestra. A Shriner at heart, he knows more Speedy Gonzalez jokes than you thought existed. The *trumpet* is the brass instrument you imagine as Christian, thinking of Gideon and of the Psalms, but then you meet a real-life trumpet player and realize how militaristic these people are. They don't want to wear black tie and play Bach, they want tight uniforms with shiny buttons, and they want to play as loud as they possibly can. Most of the people who keel over dead at concerts are killed by trumpets.

There are two places in the orchestra for a Lutheran, and one is _percussion_. It's the most Lutheran instrument there is. Percussionists are endlessly patient, because they don't get to play much. Pages and pages of music go by where the violins are sawing away and the winds are tooting and the brass is blasting but the percussionist sits and counts the bars, like a hunter waiting for the quail to appear. A percussionist may have to wait for twenty minutes just to play a few beats, but those beats have to be exact and they have to be passionate and climactic. All that the epistles of Paul say a Christian should be— faithful, waiting, trusting, filled with fervor—are the qualities of the percussionist. The other Lutheran instrument, of course, is the _harp_. It is the perfect instrument for a Christian because it keeps you humble. You can't gallivant around with a harp. Having one is like living with an elderly parent in poor health—it's hard to get them in and out of cars, impossible to satisfy them. A harp takes fourteen hours to tune and remains in tune for twenty minutes or until somebody opens a door. It's an instrument for a saint. If a harpist could find a good percussionist, they wouldn't need an orchestra at all; they could settle down and make wonderful music, just the two of them.

MAYBE YOU CAN, TOO

Janice Johnson was thinking computer software when she woke up last Wednesday morning, and when Bob and the kids came down to the kitchen she had scribbled three or four things on an envelope and was thinking some more. "I don't know what came over me!" she cried. "It's like a dream or something!" And two hours later she cashed in an insurance policy and started Janico. They make computer skirts. Cotton skirts with an elastic band to fit any console. "I saw computers in this dream," Janice explained, "and they seemed sort of *stark*. So I thought of dressing them up a little bit." A little bit! Janico was worth $2.3 million at noon today, and now she's bringing in a top management team from San Francisco "to handle the bills and checking account and all that stuff." They're due to arrive in fifteen minutes.

That's how fast things are moving nowadays—in computers, communications, quality control, the incentives field, all the hot spots in the economy. Friends of yours may be on their way to incredible first-quarter earnings—old chums you saw *last night!* You went out together to a little Australian restaurant for creamed onions and baked emu and sat around talking idle talk, and suddenly this morning, while you drank orange juice and read the funny pages, she was saying to him, "Earl, I had an idea about transceivers. Why not turn that little U-shaped gizmo around and put the little red things in from the other end?"

Why not, indeed! Tomorrow they'll be sitting pretty, their pictures in the financial section—a hundred thousand shares of ChumCo snapped up by hungry investors at $17.375—and you'll be wondering, "Why not me? Why didn't I think of that? Francine doesn't know *beans* about transceivers, she's in women's *shoes*, for heaven's sake! And yet here she's flipped the whole industry over on its ear! What's going on here?"

I know that feeling; it's exactly how I felt until ten days ago. I was in the slide business, cranking out those packets of color slides you see in souvenir shops—Yosemite, the Everglades, Homes of the Stars, Scenic Indiana—and going nowhere, while *Bam! Bam! Bam!* other people were hitting pay dirt. One day they were like anyone else and the next I knew they were off in another world. My racquetball partner, Bobby Lee, canceled a Friday match saying his head hurt, and the next Monday he was into soybean microchips and formed BLeeCo, and Tuesday he spun off two subsidiaries, BLInc and BLAmCo, to get into mood publishing and to shelter some of his earnings in forests. I had never even *heard* of mood publishing! On Wednesday, it was the old guy who lives across the alley from me and raises tomatoes and keeps about thirty-seven cats—one day a sad old duffer and the next thing he's chairman of the board of Down Home Video, and suddenly next to Ms. PacMan and Donkey Kong you see Ringalario and Kick the Can and Starlight Moonlight and Mumblety-Peg and Video Whist, and the old geezer is raking in the loot, sitting around with a noseful of quarters.

After a while, you get tired of being gracious and saying, "Gee! That's wonderful! I'm really happy for you!" You want to hide in Bobby Lee's bushes and wait for him to come out the door whistling. You want to jump on Bobby Lee and get his leg in a toehold and make him roll around in the dirt while you yell, "Tell me, Bobby Lee! Tell me fast! Tell me two or three good tips right now this minute or I'll bust your foot!"

That's what I did eleven days ago last night. He told me, too.

The next day I was in business as MeCo. We make a little ultrasonic thing that attaches to your dashboard and turns red lights to green in every state but Nebraska. Right now I've got more money than I know what to do with. You know what that's like? It's like breathing a different air. Like the law of gravity doesn't apply to you. Colors are brighter, food tastes better. You tell jokes and people laugh their heads off.

I'd like to share my secrets with you. Actually, one secret. It's so simple you'll wonder why you didn't think of it years ago. I'd like to blurt it out *right now*—at *no charge whatsoever*. You won't owe me so much as a *thank-you*.

"Why?" you're probably wondering. "Why would a rich guy be giving away his secret to people like us? There must be some hitch, some string attached. A guy like him isn't going to share secrets just like that! A guy like him isn't about to hand out the *secret inside information* that has earned him incredible sums these past ten days! Who is he trying to kid? Whom does he take us for? We weren't *born yesterday!*"

Okay, forget it.

That negative attitude wasn't the one Janice Johnson took when I told her a couple of things, but, then, she isn't suspicious and small-minded like a lot of people. She's Methodist, like me. Our church is well known for having a generous nature. Sunday morning, Janice slipped a hundred thousand dollars into the collection plate. Now, that's stewardship! We're like that. We're not stingy and mean. We don't hold with the idea that America is slipping and the economy is drying up and everyone will have less and hold on to it tighter and tighter. We think the opposite. Fabulous possibilities are all around us! Wealth abounds, if only we open ourselves up to new ways of thinking!

That's why Janice, Bobby Lee, and myself formed the Birds of the Air, Beasts of the Field Foundation over the weekend. BOTABOTFF believes that animals have much to tell us, that they *can* communicate with people and *do*—on a daily basis!—and that these important messages are lost simply because we are not receptive to them. BOTABOTFF will be spending more than six million dollars in the next few weeks on research aimed at training people to hear messages, verbal or telepathic, from the animal world.

"What sort of messages?" you're probably wondering. "Might they include business advice or investment tips?"

Sure, they might. It all depends. Depends on the animal, too.

Janice is very high on cats right now, which she sleeps with two of and claims they speak to her in dreams, sitting around a long dark walnut conference table. Me, I don't trust cats, and if a cat walked up to me this minute and said, "Mutual fund," I'd pay no attention. If I heard it from my dog, Buster, I'd listen, but not from a cat and not from snakes. Bobby Lee swears by snakes. He keeps three of them under his bed.

We all agree on one thing, though. Whales are the smartest creatures on earth, smarter than dolphins. A dolphin's ideas are ideas that whales had months ago. Humpbacks communicate halfway around the world, emitting a vast range of sounds, most of which concern food and sex, but some are about marketing and development. Of course, most people can't profit from interspecies exchange because they're too dumb. They don't have the sense that God gave geese, to use an extreme example.

Let's take a purely hypothetical case. Let's say that your dog, Buster, had an ear infection, so you put him in the car and drove to the vet's. Let's say Buster was agitated and stood on the front seat with his forepaws up on the dashboard and made this strange whining sound. Let's say that you drove 6.5 miles through busy streets and never had to stop for a single red light. In addition, a pain in your left elbow went away and your car radio started picking up ship-to-shore from off the coast of Portugal. Let's say you happened to have a cassette recorder in the car with you. Would you press *Record* and capture Buster's vocal secrets while sailing through intersections where long lines of cars on the cross streets wait for you to pass? Or would you pull over to the curb, stifle the mutt, and wait for the lights to turn red?

Let's say you do the first thing and a week and a half later you become a multimillionaire. You decide to tell someone else about it. Now let's say you're that other person. Someone tells you he got rich and offers to share the secret for free and you don't believe him, but then he tells you more and suddenly you sort of do but now he is asking $239.50 for the secret, postpaid.

How long do you think that offer will stand? Is it too late already? Is that your dog? Is that a smile on his face?

A LITTLE HELP

Ellen in Wichita was troubled that her husband, Jim, and three boys (eleven, fifteen, and sixteen) took advantage of her cheerful nature, expecting her to put a good dinner on the table every night, and not spaghetti but things like stuffed pork chops and creamed potatoes, and also to keep their three-bedroom home bright and attractive, and to be a warm and funny person—all of this on top of her full-time job in sales! She resented their expectations, which, being unspoken, were hard to argue with—especially for Ellen, who believed that love is meant to be given without reservation.

Then the phone rang one night after dinner, while Jim was watching the finals of a professional fishing tournament on television and Ellen was up to her elbows in dishwater. It was Richard Gere. "I want to speak with Jim, please," he said.

Jim was on the phone for twenty-three minutes and all he said was "Uh-huh" and "Sure, I can see that," and when he hung up, he was pale and shaking. The young star of *Breathless* and *An Officer and a Gentleman* had given him a dressing-down he would never forget, pointing out his insensitivity to Ellen's needs. If she had told him about it, he would have shrugged it off, but coming from Gere, it made a deep impression on him, and he decided to change. Thanks to one film star who cared, a family started to function as a team.

*　　*　　*

The call was no random shot in the dark but a carefully planned and researched project of Hollywood Calls, an organization of screen luminaries who want to use their influence to do good. Of course, movie celebrities have always been active in good causes—endorsing charities, appearing at fund-raisers, speaking out on public issues—but many of the younger stars feel that they can have more impact on a personal basis, and dozens of them spend as many as three hours daily on the phone, speaking up for persons like Ellen, whose problems tend to be overlooked by the Red Cross and other major organizations. Unlike the older Hollywood idols, who plunged into well-publicized humanitarian efforts in order to assuage intense guilt for amassing fabulous wealth and fame, the young stars feel that they are "actors, no different from anyone else" and prefer little unsung acts of charity; as one says, "How I spend my time is my business." Few outsiders are aware of the good these celluloid giants do.

It is known that Tom Hanks and Harrison Ford work tirelessly in behalf of young victims of misunderstanding—teen-agers regarded by friends and family as "ordinary" although they are filled with deep longings, passionate feelings, and inexpressible thoughts; Meryl Streep and Diane Keaton devote countless off-screen hours to women suffering from poor self-image; Dustin Hoffman is working to get men more involved in early child care; Clint Eastwood is on the phone every night with men who have lost their individuality in large corporations.

"He cares deeply," a source close to Mr. Eastwood says. "The corporate lifestyle is so all-encompassing that after a few years a man who fails to acquire real clout feels terribly diminished. Many of these men relate to Clint, and a few minutes on the phone with him can really turn things around. It's nothing that he tells them necessarily but just the fact that he's there, listening, sharing feelings, responding as one man to another."

"Acting is not an expository skill, it's an illuminative art," says one Hollywood Caller, "so an actor can sometimes clear up a problem with one phone call when years of intense therapy haven't helped. I dial a number and say, 'Hello, this is Warren Beatty and I want to talk about you and Janice,' and instantly they *see* the importance of the relationship, they *see* where they're at with it, it's almost electric."

Beatty is referring to Janice and Mike's relationship, a marriage of ten years that was threatened by her training in auto mechanics and karate and his inability to accept a shift in sexual roles. Why? Mike didn't know. He knew it was right for her to expand her skills, that his feeling of inadequacy came from fear and was trivial compared with the incredible richness she brought to the relationship, and yet he couldn't get beyond it—until Hollywood called. A top box-office draw saved a marriage. It's as simple as that.

A top draw, it should be said, who himself had failed thus far to make a lifelong commitment to another person. A top draw whose multiple romances filled gossip columns but never gave him the sense of bonding he sought in the shallow, fast-moving film world.

"When I call up these people, ordinary people, middle Americans, and assist them with a problem, I always receive more than I give," he says.

Beatty had no idea how much he would receive until a month ago, when the white phone rang in his Malibu hideaway—the ultra-secret phone, the number of which was known only to six persons—and he answered it. "Warren, this is Julie Dittman, in Muncie, Indiana," said a soft and yet incredibly strong voice. "I want to talk."

His first thought was to hang up, but something—her sincerity, perhaps—attracted him to her, and he sat down and listened for almost two hours as she poured out her concern for him, not as a screen star but as a human being.

"You're defensive, and of course you have to be, with so many unscrupulous people trying to get a piece of you, and yet it has left you hungering for real intimacy in a relationship built on absolute trust," she said, and instantly he knew she was right. She sounded wonderfully close and real as she said, "I hate to intrude on your privacy, and yet, when I sense hurt, how can I distance myself? How can I pretend that it's not my problem, too?"

He was moved by her concern, moved in a way he had always wanted to be moved and yet had never dared to ask to be moved, and instinctively, not taking even one second to think about it, he asked her to marry him.

She hesitated, wondering if at this point in her life her own growth as a person might be threatened by marriage to the sexual fantasy of millions of women, and then said yes.

It turned out to be the best thing either of them had ever done in their entire lives.

In the fuzzy photograph of them emerging from a Santa Monica laundromat that appeared in *People* recently, Julie Dittman appears to be no starlet but a fifty-one-year-old divorced mother of three who could stand to lose a few pounds. Yet to Warren she is a woman of fantastic vitality, a deeply caring woman, a woman who loves sunsets and children and laughter and long conversations and cats and quiet dinners and going barefoot and listening to Vivaldi, and he nurtures her, accepting his half of all household chores—even though she protests, "No, darling! You have commitments, multi-picture contracts, development deals, artistic obligations!" The forty-five-year-old screen idol scrubs floors, shops for fresh vegetables and fruits, repairs appliances, even cleans the oven.

"Warren has thrown away his career," says one old pal, but has he? Or has he found a new one? One thing is sure: no pal of his dares criticize Julie to his face. Jack Nicholson called her "dumpy" once, and he and Warren didn't speak for days. To Warren, she is the source of happiness. She now takes all his calls, and even if you're a top producer, if she thinks you're phony or stuck up or only trying to use Warren and not really caring about him, you may as well say goodbye right then and there.

A LIBERAL REACHES
FOR HER WHIP

O<small>UR MOTHERS BROUGHT US ALL UP</small> to be nice people. We all knew what it meant. Around the age of fifteen we may have thought niceness was too uncool and was retarding our development as sex symbols and we may have bumped around in the dark for a while, being nice and trying to hide it, but eventually we came out as a *very nice* person, or *basically nice*, or *nice once you get to know him*. Or *not so nice*.

Nice people are quiet and responsible and don't make you pay a big price for their presence. They don't beg or threaten, they are self-effacing, and they do what they can to make human life smooth and enjoyable. The fact that there are no flies on you doesn't qualify you as nice, nor the fact that you never burned the flag or that an independent prosecutor has decided not to seek an indictment. It's who you are that counts, not your reputation. So it's unfortunate that nice people are so sensitive about vicious slander.

When your Aunt Hazel, the Mother Teresa of Bonhomme, Iowa, hears via the Methodist grapevine that a neighbor named Mildred has told numerous Bonhommeans that she, Hazel, isn't as nice as everyone thinks but is "selfish" and has a "glorified opinion" of herself, it knocks your poor aunt flat on her back. Stunned, she leaves the community outreach luncheon in tears, drives straight home, and spends the afternoon lying weeping on the couch, bewildered by hostility from a woman she has gone out of her way to be nice to.

She imagines Mildred cutting her up all over town with lie after shabby lie, but this cruel injustice does not make your aunt angry, it fills her with sadness, and she feels depressed for days, imagining the terrible things people are thinking about her. It does no good to tell this wonderful Christian woman, "Ignore that slut. She's a tramp, a liar, a piece of baggage. She drinks big tumblers of sherry in the morning, her house is filthy, her cucumbers are puny, her begonias are all eaten up with bugs. Don't let the bitch get you down." Hazel is unable to think in those terms. She's all torn up over it.

Of course, who can blame Mildred that Hazel's extreme niceness invites disbelief? Hazel's reputation suffers from a lack of interesting negatives. Her faithful service to the church, the library, the Girl Scouts, the 4-H, the park board, the Bijou Theater renovation committee, the soup kitchen and shelter where she volunteers two days a week, her Sunday visits to the county jail, the parade of damaged children she has taken under her wing, her lifetime of Christian charity and hopeful good humor in the face of drought and illness and death—people are hungry to hear a bad word about her. Some Bonhommeans suspect that Hazel suffers from occasional depression and that she may take medication for it. They speculate about this from time to time. If on the other hand, she were a professional wrestler named Olga the Mistress of Death & Whore of Babylon, a three-hundred-pound witch with black lipstick and green-and-purple hair who spits big gobs on the flag and carries a whip and waggles her boobs at the referee and gouges her opponent Betty Anderson's eyes and screeches weird obscenities into the darkness, she'd have a million fans around America, including many in Bonhomme, who'd say, "You know, in real life Olga's really a nice person. She knits and cooks and is devoted to her husband and children." But as Hazel the Soul of Kindness she has a hard row to hoe: after her three decades of good works, people say, "I hear that she may have seen a psychologist at one time."

America is a big two-hearted forgiving country. If Hitler was alive today, he'd be on the "Today" show, talking about his new book, *My Struggle*. Around the country, people would turn away from the toaster and stare at the little screen: *Hitler*. "A lot of people still have hard feelings toward you because of that whole Auschwitz thing, you know," the host is saying. "What do you say to that? How do you deal with animosity on that level? I mean, personally, you and Eva. Is it rough on your marriage? How do you explain it to your kids?" The former Führer speaks in rapid German and we hear a woman's voice translate: "Bryant, a person can't look back. I live in the future. People who still carry a grudge from forty—what was it? *fifty* years ago—that's a tragedy. The stories about genocide are so old and worn out and threadbare and the people who repeat them are—I'm very sorry to have to say this—they're to be pitied. I feel sorry for them. Life is a garden, a summer day, a fragile butterfly, the smile on the face of a child. Why would I kill millions of people when I myself love life so much?" Some dogfood is then sold, followed by instant coffee, and then we're back for the weather. Coming up in the next half hour, a report on St. Luke: did he steal some parts of his gospel from other sources without attribution?

People can forgive anybody for just about anything but they don't respect *nobody*, and so a miserable sinner with one redeeming virtue is equal to a righteous person with a secret fault. Maybe better. The prodigal son's brother learned that lesson one day about 6:00 P.M. in St. Luke's gospel when he stumbled through the back door bone-tired from another ten-hour day hoeing corn and heard happy voices and found a crowd of family friends on the patio, the fatted calf on the spit, the band warming up, the beer on ice, and the honored guest, Donnie, dressed in rags and smelling of pig shit, and his dad hugging him. His dad had never hugged *him*, hardly even squeezed his hand, his dad wasn't a hugger, but he was all wrapped around the prodigal. The brother said, "What's happening? Oh, hi, Don. Nice to see ya, fella. *What's going on, Dad?*" Then he caught the gleam on Donnie's finger. "The *emerald*? You're giving him the emerald ring that you told me— Dad, you promised me that ring. Two years ago. This isn't right, Dad." Hot angry tears filled his eyes, but, nice person that he was, he also felt darn guilty about making a stink when everybody else in the parable was jumping up and down.

His dad said, "Look! it's Donnie! he left and now he's back! be happy! we're having veal tonight!"

So he smiled and had a beer, but with a certain contrary inner resonance. *Great. Wonderful, Dad. Terrific. I'll be hitting the sack now. Back's killing me, but never mind. Night-night. Maybe I'll sleep in the pigpen, seeing as how you go for that. See ya later, Don. Help yourself to my stuff. Clothes, jewels, shekels, just take what you need, Don. Take my room. Want me to introduce you to my fiancée, Sheila?*

Soon afterward, the brother joined a humane society opposed to cruel practices in the meat industry, e.g., calf fattening. Poor dumb animals kept chained up in cramped dark pens and force-fed, to produce pale tender beef for a feast to honor a jerk. The brother was a liberal, or Samaritan, as liberals were known in those days, and while there were a few bad Samaritans, about ninety-five percent of them were nice people who would have stopped to lend assistance to anyone who needed it—a man set upon by thieves, for example. But most Samaritans would draw the line at the sort of boondoggle enjoyed by the prodigal son. You run off and waste your substance on riotous living with a fast crowd in Galilee, you shouldn't expect to come home and get a feast and a ring and a big hug.

The Old Story: jerks rewarded, nice people abused.

Take the liberals that George Bush, the Willie Horton of American politics, spent the 1988 campaign kicking down the stairs, the one or two that Ronald Reagan hadn't kicked already. These aren't Iranian liberals, they're a bunch of extremely nice American people. Call them reformers, progressives, New Dealers, or call them the Great Satan of Massachusetts and his hounds of hell: liberals are fundamentally democrats with a quick social conscience who carry water for a million good causes from here to 123 Maple Street, Anywhere, U.S.A. They are teachers, boosters, and inveterate instillers of social obligation. Call them schoolmarms, goody two-shoes, busybodies, or bleeding hearts: basically a liberal is a person who knows you very well and loves you very very much, perhaps more than you deserve.

Who wanted you to be aware of the hungry children in China as you played with the food on your plate?

Who taught you to take turns on the swings and share your cake with other children and made you feel guilty for being such a greedy selfish little child?

Who taught you to be decent to children whom you *despised*?

Who, when you lost the game and incurred the silent wrath and contempt of Dad, took you into her arms and said she loved you?

Who could possibly be more liberal than that?

> M is for Minorities and helpless,
> O is Obligation to the poor,
> T is Taking money from the greedy,
> H is Helping beggars at our door,
> E of course is Eleanor our Mother,
> R is Reagan's mom, the lovely Nell.
> A fine old Christian liberal and a lady—
> He kicks her down the stairs, but what the hell.

The old lady lay face up on the dank cellar floor, stunned and dizzy. A Sunday afternoon and she had been fixing pot roast and potatoes in the kitchen and then— It all happened so fast: the sudden blows from her two sons, the long terrible fall backward down the steps like in a nightmare, her hands grasping for the railing as she slid half sideways and then turned a complete somersault and banged headfirst on the concrete. She couldn't see. Her neck felt like it might be broken, and also her right wrist. She could taste blood. There seemed to be a loose tooth in her mouth. Her head started to pulse with pain. She lifted her left hand and touched her forehead. A dent there, and something wet. A radio was playing upstairs. She could hear loud breathing. Her dress was gathered up above her knees, and as she tried to straighten it she saw, standing in the light at the top of the stairs, arm in arm, Ron and George, laughing.

"Guess we showed you!"

She raised her head. What had she said to make them so angry? She certainly was sorry, whatever it was. Had she been too hard on them about how they ought to attend church? Had she nagged them too often about doing their homework and their Boy Scout projects? She didn't mean to be a scold. She moved her lips, *Ronnie, George,* but no sound came out. She struggled to her knees. George took two steps down and spat at her.

"Ptew. Guess *you* learned a lesson! Guess you won't be buttin' inna *my* bidness, Ma! Huh, Ron? Guess you won't be tellin' *me* what to do for a while, huh!"

The pain in her head was deafening, and the words wouldn't come out. *Oh my dear boys forgive me for provoking you to anger. But no matter what you do—if you kill me and throw my body in a ditch and rip out my heart—remember that with the last beat of my heart I will always love you. A liberal's love can never be less. Never, no matter what you do.*

"Kinda weak on defense, ain't ya, Ma? Ha ha ha." With the last ounce of strength in her battered aching body, she hoisted herself to her feet.

"Mother! Your dress!"

She looked down and saw that her blue knit dress had fallen down in a heap around her ankles, leaving her clad in a black one-piece spandex bodysuit she didn't know she possessed and also a pair of black knee-high steel-toe kangaroo combat boots with white laces and red and blue sequins. Her hair was long and snarly, not in a bun like she usually wore it, and in her right hand she held a long riding crop. Across her bosom were silver-lamé letters two inches high that spelled "ONE HELLUVA WOMAN."

"Mother?"

"Don't say another word," she said, "or I'll bust your heads."

"Mom?"

She placed her right foot on the first stair, keeping her weight nicely balanced, her eyes fastened on the bottom youth as he shrank back whimpering. She shook her head slowly and smiled and licked her lips. She grabbed both banisters and rocked up and down on the balls of her feet. "Liberal," she said. "I'm going to liberate you boys from ignorance or die in the attempt." She took three long deep breaths, and sprang like a tiger, her hairy arms outstretched, her eyes burning bright red, and the sound she made deep in her throat was one they had never ever heard before.

HOLLYWOOD IN THE FIFTIES

Q: I understand that the frankest book yet about life in Hollywood has been written by someone named Mark Van Doren. Who is he? What is the title of his book?—K.L., LITTLE ROCK, ARK.

A: Mark Van Doren (1894–1972) was a famous poet, literary critic, and professor of English at Columbia University. You undoubtedly are confusing him with Mamie Van Doren, 56, a singer-actress fairly well known in the Hollywood of the 1950s and '60s.

—"Walter Scott's Personality Parade," in *Parade*.

FOR MARK VAN DOREN, famous poet and literary critic, the fifties in Hollywood were a confusing time, especially after he met Mamie at the home of his friends Donna and John Reed. Mark had just left RKO to go with Columbia after scripting Donna's *It's a Wonderful Life* (based on John's *Ten Days That Shook the World*), he was exhausted and disillusioned, and the buxom young star of *Untamed Youth* and *Born Reckless* clearly offered something powerful and natural and free.

"Show me things. Tell me. Touch me. You know so much, you're a poet. I'm a child in the body of a woman. Show me," she said, as they sat on the railing, looking out across the merciless sunbaked valley toward the Pacific Ocean shimmering like a blue-green afterlife beyond the used-car lots. Just then Donna called from the kitchen, "Do you want a slice of lemon in your nectar?" John was gone— who knew where? The moody hazel-eyed revolutionary had never lived by other people's rules, not even after marrying Donna. And he hated Mark, after what Mark had done to his manifesto. He vowed to punch Mark in the nose if he ever saw him.

You all know Donna Reed. Well, she was like that, except more so—the World's Most Nearly Perfect Wife and Mother. She set her clock by her son, Rex, and after he ran away with Vanessa Williams, Ted and Esther's girl, Donna grieved openly. Her pain hung around her like an old black bathrobe.

Ted's uncle, William Carlos Williams, could sense Donna's need to be loved, but he was in town to adapt his epic *Paterson* for Twentieth Century–Fox, and was writing a large body of water into the script so that Esther, a swimming actress, could be featured. The poet was crazy about his ballplayer nephew's gorgeous wife. He hung his cap for her. The sun rose and set on her. Whenever Ted was in Boston, W.C. flew to L.A. Esther liked him as a close confidant, but he wanted to be more, much more, to her, so his sudden boyish desire for Donna confused him.

"I'm bad news for any woman I touch," he told Jeanette and Dwight Macdonald. The former Trotskyite, author of *The Root of Man*, tugged at his beard as the famous poet stood poised on the tip of the diving board. Burt and Debbie Reynolds looked up at him and so did Carlos and Carroll Baker. Williams held his arms over his gray head, his knees slightly bent. He didn't notice Lassie and Malcolm Cowley, who had just returned from a walk and stood half shielded by a clump of sumac. "Blouaghhhhh!" W.C. cried as he dove, splitting the water like a fork.

It troubled Mark that Mamie couldn't swim an inch. He watched gloomily as Esther Williams plowed up and down the length of the pool, just as she did in Williams' poem "The Singing Swimmer" ("the row of maidens/beside the cool water/and the splashing fountains when/suddenly you/sing in your democratic American voice and plunge/deep below the surface, your white mermaid arms held out to me").

"Esther swims, why not you?" Mark whispered, but Mamie only laughed. Bertrand Russell glanced up from his chaise longue. "Jane swims circles around Esther," said the tanned white-haired philosopher in his clipped English accent. The author of *Principia Mathematica*, from which *Peyton Place* was adapted by Edmund Wilson's brother Earl (both of whom made a play for *Peyton* star Lana Turner after Frederick Jackson Turner, the historian, took a shine to Shelley Winters, Yvor's ex), laughed harshly as he stood and stripped off his light-blue terry-cloth robe. "And I can take any son of a bitch in the joint," he snarled, his icy eyes fixed on John and Ford Madox Ford, whose wives, Betty and Eileen, had vanished into the white stucco bathhouse with Danny and Dylan Thomas. "Anytime you like, gentlemen," he added.

The silence hung in the pale-yellow air like a concrete block. From far away came the mournful hum of rubber tires on the burning highway, a viscous sound like liquids splashing on the grass, and also there was an odor like raisin bread burning in a toaster, except worse. It was a Wednesday. John Ford squinted against the hard light. He cleared his throat, like buckshot rolling down a black rubber mat. But it was Williams who spoke.

He stood, water dripping from his white swimming trunks. "Look at us. Fighting each other like starving rats, while the people we ought to be fighting sit in their air-conditioned offices and laugh their heads off," he said. "I'm talking about the bosses, the big boys, the playboy producers, the fat-cat choreographers, the directors, the dream-killers. Those are the bastards we ought to be battling, Bert."

"You sound just like John."

It was Donna. Dylan stood behind her, blinking, with D. H. and Sophia Loren. And Andy Williams. "Hi, Dad," Andy said softly. Doris Day, C. Day-Lewis, Jerry Lewis, Lewis Mumford, Neil Simon, Simone de Beauvoir, Patti Page—everyone was there: the whole Rat Pack, except Bogart. Before Bacall, the wiry little guy had been with Bardot, Garbo, the Gabors, Candy Bergen, Bergman, Clara Bow, Teri Garr, but none of them were quite right. They were too different.

"You're right, Bill." Mark let go of Mamie's hand, and she sank like a wet sponge as the trim critic climbed out of the pool. "We're writers, artists, literary men, not messenger boys," he said, lighting a pipe. "And just look at us. Look at us."

"You look like writers," said Ted Williams, squinting and spitting in that special way of his that his brother Tennessee had tried to copy until his mouth was dry and torn. "You can't help but look like writers. Because that's what you are. Writers."

"I'm as bad as any of the rest of you," said Dylan sadly. Everyone knew his story, how the sweet voice of the poet was swallowed up in the silent, violent world of gray suits and men with blank empty faces and the watercoolers and the flat beige walls and the uncaring woman behind the desk at the dentist's who looks up with that empty vinyl expression and says, "Next." She doesn't know about your pain. How can she?

"Let's walk," said Mark.

Mamie whispered, "Wait. Please."

"No," he replied, and the writers left, marching down the long driveway into the dark, the lovely dark, and across town to the airport and back east to teach in college, all of them, and somehow they knew in their hearts and nobody had to say it that when they left, the women they loved would find new men and Hollywood would forget them and never mention their names again, and they did and it has and it doesn't, and that is the plain honest truth, you dirty bastards.

LIFESTYLE

T HE MAN THEY ONCE CALLED The Mayor of South Roxy was Jabbo
O'Brien, who ran a news shop in a storefront on Eleanor Avenue,
which the O'Briens had run since back when T. B. (Sweet Tommy)
O'Brien stepped off the boat from Tooralooraloora in 1892. But then
Coronet magazine died and *Collier's* and *Look*, and all the great
columnists, like Hector Timmy, and Jabbo lost interest in journalism.
One day in 1982 he missed winning a million dollars in the lottery
by one numeral, a six instead of a seven. He sold the storefront to
his nephew Butch for $75,000, and he and Maggie split for Parma,
Florida—a studio apartment only two miles from the beach—to collect
shells and sharks' teeth.

The next year Butch sold the building to a developer named Rob
Niles for $630,000. Jabbo's younger brother Francis called him up at
11:00 P.M. and told him. "Franny," Jabbo replied, "you're drunk.
Go to bed. That whole street isn't worth the powder to blow it to
hell. It's nothing but heartache. We got out in the nick of time."

The false-aluminum front of O'Brien News was ripped off and
the underlying brick was tuck-pointed and natural wood window
frames installed. The downstairs became a yarn shop called The Yarn-
ery. Upstairs were The Candlery, The Bookery, and The Pottery-
Wottery. B&B Plumbing Supply next door in the Trischka Building
was bought by the law firm of Payne, Batten & Noyes, and Mickey's

Last Call Lounge, on the other side, became the office of Robert
Niles Ltd.

Together with Payne, Batten & Noyes, Rob Niles formed the
Market Square Corporation. The neighborhood had always been
known as South Roxy, or Luigitown, and there was no square anywhere in it, but six months later St. Jude's Church was designated a
National Architectural Wonder, and Market Square was named a
National Living Cultural Resource Neighborhood and a Genuine
Treat. Within weeks, old dark apartment houses with purple acrylic
carpeting in the halls were selling for fabulous sums of money. The
carpeting was ripped up and the floors sanded and lightly varnished,
walls were painted white. Boxes of bright-red crockery were brought
in, and pale pastel drapery, Hockney prints, steel-tube chairs, and
slender cats.

Rob Niles and his wife, Nancy, a therapist at a center for men in
life-change situations, and their children Randy, fifteen, and Sue,
fourteen, moved into a gorgeous three-bedroom loft with white walls
and gray carpeting and new Swedish furniture, on the fourth floor
of what used to be South High School, approximately where the
home-ec classrooms had been. The building, on Eleanor at Willow
Street, had been restored to its early-1920s neo-Castilian splendor;
the parking lot became a cooperative garden. The new high school
was located off to the east, somewhere beyond the Interstate.

The handsome old South High was named Market Square South,
with twelve shops on the ground floor (The Cat's Pajamas, Wines
'n Stuff, Big Boy's Toys, Liz Johnson, Frank's Fruit Pudding, The
Shirtery, The Phonery, The Fudgery, The Wrappery, The Toolery,
The Suitery, The Computery) and sixteen spacious condominiums
above.

Randy and Sue complained that there was nobody their age in
the building or anywhere around the neighborhood, and they were
right—the old South gymnasium, now the Market South Athletic
Club, rang with the voices of men and women in their late twenties

and early thirties, who jogged counterclockwise around the gym and conversed without panting about the rapid upward fluctuations of the real-estate market in the Market Square area. It was going gangbusters:

Virg 'n Rollie's Meats, $1,125,000.

The Beauty Spot, $900,000.

The Bijou, $2,450,000, converted to the South Market Racquetball Club.

Trischka Bowlerama, $3,110,000, now The Greenery.

Marilyn's Cozy Cafe, $600,000, renamed The Eatery.

And many more.

*   *   *

"I hate you," Sue Niles told her parents one evening at the dinner table. "I absolutely hate both of you, you're the most boring odious disgusting people I ever saw. You think you're cool, but you're not, you're just ridiculous."

Randy looked up from his plate. "She's right, you know, you are," he said.

Nancy smiled at both of them and set down her fork. "Rob and I have something we want to share with you," she said softly.

"It's taken us a long time to face up to this, but you two are just not the right children for us. It's not your fault, any more than it is ours. Please try to understand. You're a constant source of aggravation—the mess, the endless clutter and noise and confusion and hostility. It makes for a stifling atmosphere for mine and Rob's relationship. We're all the time being parents, we don't have time to grow. I choose not to accept that."

Rob took Nancy's hand. "I don't know if our marriage can survive your adolescence," he said. "We've come to a decision. We have to do what's best for us. We're going to sell you."

They decided to work out this change in the family through The Family Place, a private agency upstairs from Wings 'n Things. "Our society still attaches some guilt to the idea of selling kids, but not so much as in the past," said Bart, the counselor at TFP. "There's been this gradual demystification of blood relationships, which is allowing people to admit openly what was known all along, that some work and some don't."

"That's interesting. How does it affect the kids?" Rob asked.

"We're finding more and more that an outright cash sale actually boosts a child's self-esteem. I mean, for a lot of kids, this is exactly what they need—we handled a fat boy last week who went for almost $300,000. Eight years old. That really changed that kid's whole . . ."

"Three hundred? For one little fatty?" Nancy was stunned.

TFP placed the children with a younger couple named Scott and Lainie for $185,000. (Randy and Sue were a little older than what the market wanted, and Randy had bad skin.) Scott was the heir to an insect-repellent fortune, and he and Lainie owned a big ranch, La Bamba, in the Crisco Mountains a hundred miles from the city, where the kids would have horses, a Porsche, their own bunkhouse.

Saying goodbye wasn't easy. Sue asked, "Can we come and visit on weekends?" as the cab honked, and Rob and Nancy cried and promised to feed Gipper the guppy, and Randy said, "Take care of yourselves, you two. Have a good life." Rob and Nancy both felt an incredible emptiness for days afterward.

But slowly they rediscovered some basic values from earlier in their marriage, such as self-expression and having fun. The childless lifestyle made them feel youthful, even giddy, and soon they were spending their evenings at the Amalgamated Trucking and Storage Company, the new bar that opened up where Pripicsh Bros. Transfer used to be, mingling freely with persons half their age.

One spring they went to a little resort in Biafra which nobody had ever been to or heard of, a gorgeous deserted peninsula where they spent three weeks in pure silence eating only bok choy and something like rutabagas, and they came back deeply emerged in selfhood in ways they couldn't explain. Nancy, tired of listening to weeping men, quit her job at the life-change center, and Rob sold his business to two architects named Sharon and Karen, and Rob and Nancy went into partnership as resource persons.

Their first client was St. Jude's Church. Father Quinn had retired (he was deaf and stayed in the rectory and was unaware of changes in the parish) and Father Todd, a tall, angular man who dressed in blue jeans, a white shirt, and a tweed jacket, wanted to get a dialogue started between the church and what he called "the development community."

One night, arriving for dinner at The Buffalo Wingery, Rob and Nancy ran into Randy and Sue sitting at the bar. Rob and Nancy struck up a conversation and talked for forty-five minutes before they identified themselves. Their former children couldn't believe their eyes! "Mom? Dad?" they cried. "You seem so—so interesting, so alive, so . . ."

"Young?" smiled Nancy.

"Yes!"

Sue said, "Mom, it's so good to see you."

"Call us Rob and Nancy," said their ex-parents, hugging them. They ate dinner together, and Rob and Nancy were glad to hear that the children were just as happy with their new lifestyles as they were with theirs. The four of them formed a much stronger bond that evening than they had had as a family, perhaps because it was based on mutual respect and not on the accident of birth. "Let's get together again, *soon*," they promised. Everything was great.

*   *   *

Then came the stock-market crash in October, and though everyone said the next morning that it meant nothing really and was a natural correction and not a crash, nevertheless life seemed shakier around Market Square and South Market. One cool morning a runner was heading south along Eleanor Avenue past all the new little trees in their brick pots on the sidewalk when the Velcro strip on his left shoe caught the Velcro strip on his left wrist. He fell heavily and broke his right leg so badly it almost had to be amputated.

Word got around fast in The Eatery among the breakfast croissant crowd: *Marc almost lost his leg.* People walked around thinking about it, a wonderful man in his early forties tripped up by himself and almost crippled.

Same day, The Wokery shut down. Bankrupt.

Next afternoon, 2:00 P.M.: a woman, thirty-two, gasped in mid-sentence and pitched forward into her wilted spinach salad at The Coffee & Tea-ery and had to be pounded back to life by the Vietnamese dishwasher. Choking on salad? You think it's impossible and yet it seems that a leaf of lightly oiled spinach can form a tight seal in your throat, a deadly green diaphragm that hard coughing only makes tighter. People sat down to dinner that evening and thought about her, a beautiful slender woman almost slain by nutritious food.

Father Todd, of St. Jude's, disappeared one day, gone to Minneapolis to become the head of a conference center, leaving a note: "I hate goodbyes, so simply left last night. Good luck." And then a masseuse at The House of Touch was loosening up a muscle in Nick's neck (Nick of Nick's Book Nook) and accidentally hit a nerve and the plump young entrepreneur stiffened and let out an *eek* and was paralyzed for two days, hung up in the hospital like a side of beef. People felt stiff just thinking about him. When he got out of the hospital, he and Tad sold their two-bedroom apartment in Market House for $94,000, about half what they had paid for it in 1983. A fifty-percent loss; fifty.

Within minutes, the news spread. Men stood ashen-faced around the deli counter at Barnes & Fields. At The Little People Preschool, children stopped their games and stood gripping the fence and weeping, the bitter wind in their faces. Next day a studio went for $50,000, and then a *seven-room apartment with 16-foot ceilings and three WBF's and an FDR* went for $98,500. That night, in The Market Inn, people were getting plastered on a very light, slightly fruity New

Zealand *pinot noir* and singing old Simon and Garfunkel songs and trying to be brave.

The bottom dropped out of the resourcing market. Rob and Nancy lost the St. Jude's dialogue job when the new priest, Father Quint, arrived and fired them on the grounds they were not Catholic. Unable to keep up mortgage payments on the loft, which had been valued at $528,000 and was now worth approximately squat, they were forced to move to a dumpster behind The Greenery, subletting the loft to a couple named Trish and Nat for $210 a month. Nancy did a nice job paneling the garbage bin with cardboard from Swedish furniture cartons; they had a futon and kept their clothes nice, had nice haircuts, and took showers at the health club; their magazines were forwarded to them; they kept their two cats, F. Cat Fitzgerald and Meow Tse-Tung; *and yet:* the place was a dump. That was where Randy and Sue found them last Thanksgiving, huddled with the cats in the dumpster, wrapped in down quilts, listening to the Grateful Dead.

"You're coming home with us," the kids said, helping their former parents up over the high sides of the dumpster and into Randy's black Porsche.

"The $185,000 is all gone," Nancy wept.

"That's all right. You're with us now," said Sue. "We'll take care of you."

"Why?" asked Rob.

Randy said, "We respect you, that's why." The kids were great. They talked to their new folks and convinced them to hire their ex-parents as domestic servants. Rob and Nancy came to live at La Bamba in a studio apartment over the garage, and they worked in the kitchen and cleaned the bedrooms. They and Randy and Sue grew even closer to each other, and Scott and Lainie got to be close to them, too. There was no jealousy, no recriminations, just a very good relationship all around.

The only problem was that Rob and Nancy were terrible cooks. After two solid weeks of frozen enchiladas, it was clear they weren't doing the job they were hired to do. Randy confronted them one morning and told them that because he loved them he expected them to measure up. It wasn't easy for him or for them either. There was a lot of tension the next two weeks, but soon Rob and Nancy were producing acceptable soups, casseroles, stews, sandwiches, light meals, and that's where things stand right now. Macaroni and cheese, Sloppy Joes, fish sticks. Not great but okay.

HE DIDN'T GO TO CANADA

JUST AS I WAS FINISHING COLLEGE in 1969 and was about to join the Marines, the Indiana National Guard made me a wonderful offer, via my father, to join their public-information battalion, and so, despite a lingering affection for those fighting in Vietnam, one bright June afternoon I drove my old Mustang to Fort Wayne to enlist along with my best friend, Kevin. A few miles out of Muncie, he lost his nerve and went to pieces. "I'll never make it," he said. "I'm sorry. I thought this could remain my secret, but I'm afraid that the stress of Guard training would crack me like a nut. You see, I have a flaw inside me, a dark place in my soul—something painful and unnameable that can only be eased by alcohol. Let me out of the car. I'm going to Canada." I let him off at the bus depot and never saw him again. Years later I heard that he became very wealthy up there selling amphetamines but then ate a bad piece of meat and got worms and died an extremely painful death.

I went to Fort Wayne and reported to the address that the recruiter had given to my dad over the phone, a haberdasher's called Sid's Suit City, upstairs from a trophy plant in a cinder-block building. A little bald guy with a tape around his neck who looked like his feet hurt stuck out his hand. I showed him my papers, and he showed me a nice green knit shirt (short-sleeved), a pair of yellow slacks, and white buck shoes with red tassels and sharp cleats.

"Those are golf clothes," I said.

He grabbed me by the neck and threw me up against the mirror and shoved his grizzled face within an inch of mine. "Don't tell me anything I don't ask you for first, you chicken doo. I own you, Mister. If I tell you to play golf, you reach for your clubs, Mister, and if I order you to order two big pepperoni pizzas and a six-pack of Bud, you jump to the phone and do it, Mister, and if I tell you to sit down and watch 'Andy Griffith,' 'Huckleberry Hound,' 'Leave It to Beaver,' and 'American Bandstand,' I don't want to catch you with a book in your hand. You're in the Guard, understand? Good. Now take your face out of here and get it over to the Alhambra apartment complex, on West Cheyenne Drive. You're in 12C. Beat it, you booger, and take your convertible with you. You're gonna need it."

He wasn't kidding about the golf. The next Monday morning, forty of us reported bright-eyed and bushy-tailed to Burning Bush Country Club and were each issued a set of Wally Hammar golf clubs and an electric cart and sent out to play. We were assigned to foursomes. Randy Qualey, Keith Quintan, and Dennis Quintz were in mine, and in the next couple months we got to know each other like real buddies. We went out drinking together and everything. We shot eighteen holes every morning—sunny or cloudy, warm or cool, it made no difference.

Two months later, I was fed up. I'd been promoted to Corporal, but why wasn't I doing the job I'd joined the Guard to do: inform the public? Was it because of poor grades in college and a low score on the Guard entrance exam? Was it because of my inability to type? If the Guard didn't have confidence in me, why hadn't they permitted me to go to Vietnam?

I talked it over with my dad, and he promised to look into the matter. Meanwhile, I met my wife at a dance. It was love at first sight. The next three months were the happiest of my life. Then one day I was called into Colonel Mills' office at ComInNatGu—the secret Guard command center housed in a complex of deep bunkers around the ninth hole. You entered the center through a tiny tunnel via a door marked "HIGH VOLTAGE: EXTREMELY DARNED DANGEROUS!" The door was in the janitor's closet of the men's room off the Bee Bee Lounge, in the clubhouse basement. Before I reached the men's room, though, I heard a big, booming voice say, "Sit down, trooper."

It was the Colonel, looming up behind the bar in a green-and-yellow Hawaiian shirt with a bolo tie made from bullets, shaking up a batch of Bombardiers, his face hidden by a broad straw hat with long loose fronds.

"Understand you got some questions, son. Let's talk."

I climbed up on a stool and leaned forward and started to tell him that I was trying to figure out why the heck I was in the Guard and what I was supposed to accomplish.

"Mmmmhmm," he said. "Uh-huh, uh-huh." And then, in a split second, before I could move a muscle, he grabbed me by the neck and hauled me across the bar and had me flat on my back on the pop cooler and was holding a blender to the side of my head.

I'll never forget the cold animal anger in his green eyes as he stared down at me, unblinking, for the three longest seconds of my life. Then he helped me to my feet and offered me a drink.

"Sorry about losing control like that," he said. "I guess I got angry because I see in you so much of myself. I get fed up with waiting around, too. It's the hardest part of being in the Guard. And it's twice as hard in the ING. You want to know why?"

I did.

"Because we're not even supposed to exist."

He put a big ice cube in his mouth and ate it like a cherry. "You see, Soviet spy satellites in low orbit are reading Indiana right now like a children's book, and we have to make sure they see us as a bunch of civilians in one-bedroom apartments who happen to like golf a lot. You see, at peak strength, mobilized, the Indiana National Guard numbers fourteen million men. It's the biggest secret army in the free world. And one of the best equipped. We're one ace the

President's got that they don't know about—maybe the only one. Get in my car, Dan."

The Colonel's beige Buick Electra was moored in a secret parking space under an aluminum roof beside the kitchen. Aluminum confuses the heck out of radar, he explained, and beige is the hardest color to remember afterward. The car shone. A good wax job, he pointed out, prevents a person or persons from leaving messages in the dust. When he turned the ignition key, the car sprang alive, antennas rose, the radio came on, the seats themselves hummed with power, ready to go forward or back at a finger's touch. "Always fasten your seat belt," he said. "It's one thing they'd never expect us to do." We cruised west into the warehouse district, and he pointed out long, low aluminum ING buildings where the hardware was kept. "We have more than four thousand forklifts, fifty-two hundred portable biffies, eighteen bulk-milk trucks, and four thousand rider mowers," he said. Those were the figures I wrote down. There were more than six hundred infrared cluster-type thrusters with uplink/downlink/intercept capability. "Only two thousand fifty of those puppies in the whole U.S.," he said. "So, you see, we're sitting on top of one of the larger secrets in the defense community. Our job: keep it that way. It's tough to sit tight, no buts about it, but when we get the word to go, I want the other side to find out about us all of a sudden. Bang, we're there. INDIANA GUARD HITS BEACHES, TAKES TOWNS AND MOUNTAINS, SWARMS THROUGH HANOI. I don't want the enemy general to be studying us for three years and getting a Ph.D. The big secret of the ING is that we could take ninety percent casualties with no effect on our capability. I don't want him to know why. When the time comes, I want to be able to get in there, search, destroy, interdict, capture the flag, and bring the boys home for Christmas."

"Count me in," I said softly as the big car nosed homeward. "I want a piece of it."

"Just don't forget who you are," the Colonel said. "Look relaxed, but don't be relaxed. Smile, but don't make a point of it. Drink vodka. Lots of ice. Lemon, not lime. Not too many peanuts. Always turn the conversation to the other person. Pace yourself. Always take the end urinal in the men's room. Sunday morning, take a side pew. Don't wash dishes; always dry. Remember: you're a killer, a professional killer. Your stereo has a sharp needle you could poke a man in the eye with. You know how to take an ordinary putter and beat somebody senseless. With your skill, even an ordinary golf ball is lethal. Killers are what we are. And by the way, always choose Thousand Island."

He pulled up in front of the Alhambra. Music drifted out from behind the closed windows, shadowy figures moved behind the drawn shades. "So for now, trooper, your orders are to stay low: play good golf, drink cold beer, and make love to beautiful women. And let's just hope the Russians aren't doing the same."

He came around to open the door for me, but I was ready for him, and when he tried to kick me I got him by the ankle and flipped him up on the roof of the Buick and pounded him twice, hard, in the pancreas. "Good," he said. "Darn good."

His lecture changed my way of thinking, and for the remaining two months of Guard training I tried to act as normal as humanly possible. It wasn't easy. A guy looks down at his typewriter knowing it can be switched over instantly to invisible ink simply by typing "Hoosier" (a word that even Russians fluent in English would not be familiar with), and he finds it hard to relax and have a cool time. (I kept my typewriter set on invisible most of the time in case I forgot the password.) We had to remember to always use electric golf carts on the course, for fast response in case of a Code Green alert. The signal would be two longs and a short, either on a horn or a saxophone. In case telephone communications should become unreliable, the alert would come by radio—either on "The Don Davis Show" on K-Wayne or on my own "Dan the Man Show," on the Gentle Giant 101 (2:00–6:00 P.M.)—either "Mellow Yellow" by Donovan or "Circle

Game" by Joni Mitchell. The song would be played and then the
word "Skeezix."

Being an information officer meant that I knew a great deal, and
having a popular radio show meant that I was in a position to sway
minds, and so, in the event of enemy capture, I was prepared to take
cyanide. On the golf course, I kept it hidden in a fake ball (I always
used my dad's Top-Flites, but one ball, which could be pried open to
reveal the deadly white pill wound with string in the core, was marked
"Top Flight"—a discrepancy a Russian would never notice), and in
the radio station I kept the cyanide in a tiny slit cut in the foam
rubber around the microphone. All I had to do was lean forward and
bite. It wasn't easy playing music knowing that death was always
two inches from my lips, but I did it. And then one day the war was
over. I was out of the Guard and in Congress.

All of us knew that if the President had pursued an all-out strategy
to win the war and had unleashed the ING against the Vietcong, the
outcome would have been very different, but we were never allowed
to go. We never blamed the President for it—his hands were tied by
the press and the protesters—but the tragedy is that we never got
the chance to get over there and get the job done.

Twenty years later, millions of Indiana National Guardsmen suffer
from postwar regret, waking up in the middle of the night with an
urge to go out in the rain and hunker down in the mud, to hold a
gun and use a walkie-talkie, and for a while I felt bad like that, too,
and made a point of playing golf in extremely hot weather and not
drinking enough liquids, deliberately pushing myself toward the edge.
It was on a real scorcher of a day, playing the Gary Country Club,
that I met Colonel Mills for the last time. He was dressed in regulation
green and yellow, blasting out of a sand trap and up a steep hill to a
small green sloping to the back and surrounded with boulders and
accordion wire. He made a perfect shot and turned and saw me and
we exchanged the traditional National Guard wink. (Russians do not
wink and therefore would fail to comprehend this signal.)

"How's civilian life treating you?" he asked. I told him how I felt and he stood there and gave me a dressing-down that I'll always be grateful for.

"You should be proud, soldier," he said. "You served honorably. You never went AWOL. You didn't go to Canada. You didn't burn the flag. You never embezzled money while on duty, never aimed a loaded gun at a crowd of innocent bystanders, never looted a town in a disaster area (though there were plenty of opportunities), never raped a helpless woman. No prosecutor ever returned an indictment against you. Accept the rewards of a grateful nation." And he turned on his heel and went straight up and over the hill and I never saw him again. About three years after that, I actually did go to Canada for a weekend. It was my first time, a fact-finding trip. It was okay, but based on what I saw I was glad that I hadn't gone there previously.

HOW THE SAVINGS AND
LOANS WERE SAVED

T HE PRESIDENT WAS playing badminton in Aspen the day vast hordes of barbaric Huns invaded Chicago, and a reporter whose aunt lives in Evanston shouted to him as he headed for the clubhouse, "The Huns are wreaking carnage in Chicago, Mr. President! Any comment?"

Mr. Bush, though caught off guard by news of the invasion, said, "We're following that whole Hun situation very closely, and right now it looks encouraging, but I'm hoping we can get back to you in a few hours with something more definite." The President appeared concerned but relaxed and definitely chins up and in charge.

As he spoke, the good citizens of Chicago were fortifying the Loop and organizing scalding-oil brigades, but their caldrons never got hot enough, and soon the hordes broke through, miles of them—wave after wave of squat, flat-nosed horsemen on their ugly steeds galumphing through the streets, waving their hairy fists, rolling their little red eyes under their long black eyebrow, grunting and blatting and howling, bellowing at women in a coarse, unintelligible tongue that sounded like irate geese.

Over the next three days, as additional hordes of Ostrogoths, Visigoths, Hloths, Wendells, and Vandals swarmed into the Windy City with relentless, locustlike ferocity and burned churches and performing-arts centers and historic restorations, and dragged away monks, virgins, associate professors, and postal employees to be sold into slavery, and seized great stores of treasures and heirlooms and sacred vessels, and tore down libraries and devastated three-star restaurants and traded away the Cubs and Bears, Mr. Bush was said to be conferring with John Sununu, meeting with the Cabinet, weighing his options, on the verge of taking some kind of dramatic action. To those close to him he appeared burdened but still strong, upbeat but not glib, and then in came Robert Teeter with a poll that showed that seventy percent of the American people thought the President was doing an excellent job with the barbarians. Mr. Bush was seen as confident and in charge but not beleaguered or vulnerable or damp under the arms, the way Jimmy Carter was. Most Americans admired the way George Bush played down the story and wasn't weakened or distracted by it. They felt that he was doing exactly the right thing, and they viewed Chicago as a place where a lot of pretty rough stuff goes on most of the time anyway.

So the President didn't make an address to the nation on television but simply issued a statement that barbarianism is a long-term problem and must be met with patience and wisdom, and the answer is education, and everything that can be done is being done and will continue to be done. It called for bipartisanship. That evening, a White House croquet tournament went on as planned. The President appeared calm but interested.

The barbarians made their squalid camps in the streets and took over the savings-and-loan offices. ("Savings and loan" sounds the same as the Hun word *chfnxnln*, which means "henhouse.") They broke out all the windows and covered them with sheepskins, they squatted in the offices around campfires built from teak and mahogany desks and armoires, eating half-cooked collie haunches and platters of cat brains and drinking gallons of after-shave. Their leader, Mogul the Vile, son of Generic, squatted down beside a speakerphone on the thirty-eighth floor of American National and called the White House and babbled and screeched for more than twenty minutes. His English was horrendous. He seemed to be demanding a ransom of three chests of gold and silver, six thousand silk garments, miscellaneous mirrors and skins and beads, three thousand pounds of oregano, and a hundred and sixty-six billion dollars in cash.

The President, who did not speak to him personally, pondered the outrageous demand. He appeared quiet but wakeful, thoughtful but not grumpy. On the one hand, a major American city was in the hands of rapacious brutes, but, on the other hand, exit polling at shopping malls showed that people thought he was handling it OK. So he flew to Kennebunkport for a week of tennis and fishing. He appeared relaxed but hearty, animated but restrained.

A few days later, the Hun sacking of Chicago was old news. It had already happened. Mr. Bush, in striking a note of determination right at the beginning and then refusing to be stampeded into action, had outflanked the entire story and avoided any loss of public support. The press covered the pillaging up north, but most of the press was in Washington, not Chicago, and what could you say about Huns that everybody didn't already know? Huns perspire heavily; they despise agriculture and don't eat vegetables, only meat and gravy and desserts, and they drink bad sweet wine; their clothes are ill-fitting and covered with lint; they smell bad and their hair is limp and dull, and they're ugly as a mud fence: short, flat-faced, thick-lipped, illiterate, grunty people with heavy brows, hairy backs, and no necks. And their relationship with the press is very, very poor. Everyone knew that a long time ago. On the other hand, collie haunches can be very tasty if you braise them with plenty of garlic over a trash fire, and some reporters who tried collie wrote long Sunday pieces about Hun lifestyles that concluded they were barbaric, heck yes, but thrilling and possessed of a drop-dead visceral authenticity.

The President decided not to interfere with the takeover attempts in the savings-and-loan industry and to pay the hundred and sixty-six billion dollars, not as a ransom of any type but as ordinary government support, plain and simple, absolutely nothing irregular about it, and the Huns and the Vandals rode away, carrying their treasure with them, and the Goths sailed away up Lake Michigan. Gothic boats are hard to handle, though, being built of stone with great high arches that make them tippy, and they all sank in Lake Michigan in a light breeze, carrying half the loot to the bottom, but not before the President's chopper landed in Grant Park. A serious-faced George Bush stood at the water's edge, hair blowing from the backwash of the rotor, and announced that the barbarians had left. He said that the savings-and-loan industry was sounder than at any time in its history. He announced that he was deeply moved by the heroism of the people of Chicago and reiterated his opposition to barbarianism of any kind whatsoever.

2

THE LAKE

LETTERS FROM JACK

JACK'S AUTO REPAIR WAS THE FIRST SPONSOR of "A Prairie Home Companion." Jack always thought it could become a good show, but his advice was ignored. "The show had great guests, and all it needed was an Ed Sullivan or a Ted Mack to say 'Here's Wanda Wonderful' and get out of the way, but instead they hired a humorist (that's a man who does comedy in slow motion) who stood there and talked, while the talent sat backstage and played cribbage and read the want ads," he wrote. "But that's all water under the bridge now that you retired. Congratulations on the job you did all those years. You certainly earned the chance to quit." That letter and the following were written on old Jack's Auto Repair letterheads, the ones with the slogan "Friendly, Reliable, Clean" and the old JUniper 2014 number.

* * *

April 1980

Dear Sir:

I read with interest that your radio show will be beamed by satellite to a number of radio stations around the U.S. I've advertised on the show for six years, and would have done better writing my phone number on barroom walls, so hope we won't be paying extra to be ignored in distant states, no matter how big a thrill this is for you. People won't drive a thousand miles for an oil change and you know it. And your public-radio audience is a pain in the wazoo. Before they buy a dollar's worth of gas, they have to know your feelings about Central America and make sure that the kid who mans the pumps is earning minimum wage. So don't tell me what a great opportunity this is.

*   *   *

December 1980

Dear Sirs:

Thanks for the May listenership data. The copy you sent is faint, as if typed with lemon juice, but not so faint as the impact of your show, I'm afraid. This creation has burst upon the scene like coffee spilled on the carpet. People look away out of politeness. My opinion is that you need an emcee. Do you remember Danny Olsen who you went to high school with? Everyone said he was fun to be with, but I guess he didn't know the Right People, because he'd have won that host job hands down if they held auditions, which obviously they didn't dare do. Here in the Midwest, having a real good time is considered okay provided you don't let it happen again. People think if they let go, they might fall off. Your show sure proves that pretty well, not that I hold this against you personally. I am aware of your religious beliefs which hold most types of entertainment to be immoral. But couldn't you just compromise those beliefs a little bit and go to hell?

*   *   *

June 1981

Whomever Is In Charge Down There:

I tuned in your show out east with interest. (Or is it "back" east? I say "out" west so maybe so, but I suppose it's all a matter of how you look at it.) Anyway, the audience sounded unduly excited, far more than the material warranted. It was the sort of heat I recall from when the Saxophone Pals swung into "Ring Dem Bells" at the old Night Light Club on the Beltline. I used to go there on Saturday nights when the small-town virtues you celebrate were driving me nuts, and as soon as I sat down and ordered a Bombardier and saw the Pals swaying back and forth onstage playing fornicating music in their white tuxes, why, Lutheranism'd leave me like a bad dream. So it's odd to hear Eastern sophisticates whoop it up for a guy who talks slow. My Uncle Emmett has some unfinished sentences that go back to the Hoover Administration, but he never claimed to be a humorist. I guess it just goes to show that when it comes to entertainment it's hard to tell. In my day, we went for flash and pizzazz, but one of these days, a guy who hums to himself and spits in the dirt will be the big phenomenon. If so, congratulations. I take nothing away from you, because frankly there isn't that much. Cordially,

*   *   *

April 1982

To Whomever Is In Charge Down There:

Believe me, I could do without the "News from Lake Wobegon" in its present epic form, but if forced to hear it, I'd prefer to hear it without all the sighing and wheezing and chuffing on the part of the announcer. I don't know if his problem is a deviated septum or nasal growths or what, but if he can't learn to breathe more quietly, then he ought to make anonymous phone calls like all the rest of them. Radio is intimate enough without him putting his nose right in our faces. I hope the country doesn't take this show as an indication of who we are in Minnesota. If so, somebody ought to pull the plug on his bathtub. It's sad that a person with ambition and a powerful disregard for the facts can go a long way in the world, whereas the more conscientious slog along in the same old rut. As the poet said, "The best lack all conviction, while the worst are full of passionate intensity." On the other hand, you don't have much passionate intensity either. What's the problem? Cordially,

*   *   *

January 1983

To Whomever Is In Charge:

I continue to be amazed by your appeal. Sylvia and I were in Chicago, staying up past ten o'clock, and met several people who, when they heard we're from Minnesota, asked about "Prairie Home Companion." They reminded me of you: you know the type—people of the sixties, who think honesty is the main thing and if we all got to know each other better we'd like each other more than we do. And maybe that's your appeal. You're honest (you never claimed to be good), and people listen to you thinking that if they get to know you real well, maybe eventually they'll like you. Well, I've been listening for years and must admit that its appeal is sporadic. We listen to it at low volume, and when something good comes on we jump up to turn it up loud, but it never lasts long. There is just too much simple heartfelt sincerity, which I hear enough of from customers who are late with their payments. Wish you'd say something funny. Just remember we're listening at low level. If you think of something good, speak up. Cordially,

* * *

August 1984

To Whomever:

Couldn't help but notice that Walter Mondale plunged downward in the polls the week after attending your show Saturday P.M. even though he tried to fix the damage by visiting a Presbyterian church Sunday A.M. Presbyterianism was a good choice, a solid well-known religion a candidate can attend without fear that people will suddenly start hollering and prancing around and woofing like dogs. You'd think a candidate's staff would show the same caution in selecting a show for him to attend, one that all Americans know and love, like "Sesame Street," and not one that raises questions in people's minds about his judgment. A Minnesota Norwegian minister's son has got three strikes against him in the charisma department, and if on top of those problems he is the sort of guy who gets goosebumps from hearing extremely slow jokes, then he can kiss charisma goodbye. Sincerely,

* * *

November 1985

To Whomever Is In Charge Out There:
It's interesting to think of you out there on tour. Last week Seattle, and now Hawaii, and next week Los Angeles. Ordinarily a person stays in one place and works hard and builds a reputation but show business is different: you want to leave the jurisdiction as fast as you can. This week, I imagine you could no more sell "Prairie Home" tickets around Puget Sound than you could peddle bottles of swamp-water labeled as Peruvian Youth Tonic: people have tried a bottle already and their tongues turned white and scaly. If you attempted an encore, they might kill you. So you remove to Hawaii, a few thousand miles beyond the Seattle city limits, and feel pretty lucky. Well, don't count on it. Show business makes for a grim biography; it just doesn't take long to go from being Up and Coming, a bright magical talent in this dark world, a source of love and laughter, to wallowing in deep shit looking for the ladder. Suddenly you go from talent to star, which is a guy who sleeps all day and wanders around a tasteless mansion at 3:00 A.M. looking for someone to talk to and have a burger with. Let me give you one word of advice before you take one step too far. On second thought, I gave you that advice two years ago. Forget it. When are you coming back to Minnesota? Your friend,

* * *

January 1986

To Whomever:
Before you rent a tux for the grand reopening of the World Theater, maybe you ought to check the plumbing. This is a wise word of

caution. Pay attention. There have been countless other projects to
restore historic theaters to their former elegance and grandeur that
ended badly because the money was spent on thin-waisted young
men in designer coveralls talking about lighting concepts, meanwhile
the historic water pipes burst and restored the theater to the grandeur
it had before the world was created, when there was only mist upon
the waters. You would know this if you were in a town with a decent
newspaper. You fritter away funds on the visual aspect of things and
ignore the underlying realities such as drainage—suddenly, as the
star is about to sweep down the golden staircase and into their hearts,
the folks in Radioland hear a sound effect that seems strangely out
of place on a program about glamour and wealth, a sound effect that
suggests a story from Scripture about God's dealings with Pharaoh.
Anyway I hope you got a good plumbing contractor but I suppose
by now it's months too late. Good luck,

*   *   *

February 1986

Great Hairy-Legged Leader:
We got your invite to the Grand Opening of the World Theater and
Sylvia and I decided to stay home and shell peas or something. I hate
these big glittery events, the velvet ropes, the cheese and wine, the
unctuousness and bootlickery, the small fry craning their necks to
see Who's Here, and what's more, you fixed up a perfectly good 1905
theater so that it looks fake. It was old and you made it Olde, like a
set in Disneyland. Frankly, I liked it better when my shoes stuck to
the floor. I remember sitting in the balcony in 1938 and observing
Deluna DeMars in four consecutive performances of *Romany Maidens*, an operetta that was mainly interesting for Deluna's deep bows.
We fans clapped and clapped for her until she had no choice but come
forward and bow and then we clapped until she did it again, taking
curtain call after curtain call, no doubt convinced she had found an

audience that appreciated her gifts, and we did, especially her gorgeous balcony.

I mention this to remind you that in your business (the one that there is no business like), cheap trash and light froth predominate, and if you let the Methodists take over and turn entertainment into something wholesome and thoughtful, you will lose your shirt. This happened to Deluna's husband, Ernest DeMars, a St. Paul broadcaster sometimes referred to as "another Nick Portland," which apparently was a superlative at the time. Ernest got it in his curly head that he was cut out for interpretive reading and booked himself into the World for an evening of Shakespearean sonnets entitled *Love's Not Time's Fool*, which drew a big crowd expecting a bedroom farce in which dukes chase the dairymaids in and out of closets, but instead they got a stageful of one man in a blue serge suit interpreting poetry at an oak lectern. He launched into "Let me not to the marriage of true minds admit appliances" and at line 5 somebody yelled, "Start the show, ya jerk!" The tumult built up over the next four sonnets. When he got to "When in disgrace with Fortune and men's eyes," he was in real trouble.

This was in the days when theaters sold fresh fruit in the lobby, back when more men played baseball, and performers had to keep an eye on the crowd. Nowadays, the average theatergoer couldn't hit the broad side of a soprano from the royal box, but in those days, a thespian learned to keep moving onstage and to use other actors as a shield at the sign of a sudden movement in the cheap seats. An actor delivering a long soulful monologue would flit about the stage, ducking, reversing direction, trying to throw off the customers' aim. Even death speeches had a furtive, restless quality, the dying person even as he orated keeping a weather eye on the house. This was before television taught the American people to appreciate dreck, and a cast had to stay on its toes in a play that stank. Sometimes if a patron merely stood up to remove his coat or cocked his arm to scratch his ear, the actors dove for cover. Oftentimes, this improved the play. People clapped and the cast did it again.

Ernest, however, was a serious man and like most serious men he was slow to recognize what was happening around him. He plowed ahead, assuming that the commotion beyond the footlights was an emotional response to his art, which in a way it certainly was, and it also was the crowd responding to a man in the back row holding a Beacon apple in his right hand as he stood and judged the distance. He was only eighty-five feet from stage, closer than home to first base, an easy pick-off. The Beacon caught Ernest in a spot vital to his artistry and put him out of commission. He slithered to the floor, and Deluna dodged out from the wings and bent down to revive him and got a standing ovation. She stood and smiled at the crowd that had decked her husband. They clapped louder. She stepped over his prostrate body to the front of the stage and bowed deeply, and they all went crazy.

That's show business, pal. I hope you enjoy it, because if you don't then it's not worth it, not even for all the Beacon apples in the world. Cordially,

*   *   *

April 1986

To Whomever Is In Charge Down There:
What you are heading for in making your TV debut is, of course, a disaster, so it's good it'll be on television, where we can all see it for ourselves. Radio is the medium of imagination, but it's hard to imagine something as awful as this will be. That's what TV is for. Maybe you'll see I was right when I told you: you look good on radio, better than most.

Perhaps you are too old to remember the radio personality of the forties, Sidney Cedargren, who held forth at 12:15 daily with humorous homespun observations on human foibles on "The Old Bean Walker." (One of Sidney's foibles was a weakness for expensive threads, and at 12:25 every day, after hollering "Hooo-eeee," his signoff, he slipped out of his Oshkosh bib overalls into two-tone shoes and a silk suit and strolled to the Minneapolis Club to lunch with nabobs. A real swell.) In the summer of 1947, overcome by personal vanity, Sidney agreed to be on television, then an experimental device. There were 659 sets in the Twin Cities, each one the size of a refrigerator, with a screen as big as a tea saucer, but big enough for those 659 viewers to see Sidney clearly that August afternoon when he stood in the Dairy Building at the State Fair to talk about why folks should never never never use vegetable margarine. A cow named Martha stood next to him, which he didn't enjoy, and he flinched when she lowered her head and sniffed around in the vicinity of his pockets, and he stepped backward into something the cow had left there. Sidney knew what it was but he just kept smiling and talking, but, believe me, nobody looks as dumb as a man in two-toned shoes standing in cow flop and pretending it's Easter lilies. You see this all the time on TV but people never get tired of it. So we will all tune in. Hope you bring an extra pair. Cordially,

* * *

May 1986

To Whomever Is Down There:

I watched your show on television last week and can assure you that, considering what it was, it wasn't as bad as it could have been. Some parts were better than others. Beyond that, I won't comment. There are times in a man's life when his self-esteem is paper-thin and he can't bear derision no matter how richly deserved. Nonetheless, I would suggest in re the "News from Lake Wobegon" segment that thirty minutes of a man speaking in a flat Midwestern voice about guilt, death, the Christian faith, and small-town life is not what people look for in a stage performance. People don't attend the Ringling Brothers Circus and after an hour of tigers and ladies in tights yell at the ringmaster to talk more, do they? You don't see them stand up and stamp their feet and chant, "Share your experiences! Share your experiences!" No, they are having a good time and hope to continue.

So many radio announcers have plunged into these same pitfalls. I can't help but recall Erwin Wombat, the Silver-Tongued Boy Wonder of the Airwaves, also known as The Voice of Minnesota Livestock, who anchored the 11:45 futures report from the stockyards. Like you, Erwin was tall and slightly pretentious and had good enunciation (which you need to have if you're going to say, "Prices were $1.25 to $1.75 weaker on No. 2 and 3 275–330-pound barrows and gilts," and have your audience understand you out in Aitkin County where reception is poor and not have some 220–245-pound farmer arise at 5:00 A.M. and drive 260–275 miles expecting a windfall profit from his load of 18–25-pound tabby barn cats). Erwin was a good reader of livestock prices. Unfortunately, he also spoke at a few church suppers, where, from all the chuckling, he got the impression he was a great untapped talent. He didn't stop to consider that Lutherans are brought up to be appreciative come hell or high water. He just assumed that his tales of a prairie boyhood in bygone days was hot stuff. He began inserting warm humorous anecdotes into the market prices. "Barrows and gilts, $1.25 to $1.75 lower—and speaking of barrows reminds me of the spring day many years ago when Dad and I planted crabapple trees alongside the old asparagus patch," he'd reminisce in his rich baritone voice, and soon his fifteen minutes was up and people didn't know if prices were up, down, or sideways. But Erwin was happy. He stood there at the stockyard, microphone in hand, and expressed himself. One day, while reminiscing about his old Aunt Deborah, he felt the ground shake and heard the pounding of thousands of cloven hooves and turned to see all the No. 2 300–375-pound barrows and gilts galloping straight toward him. Someone had left a gate unlatched, offering the animals a choice between death and Erwin. Erwin's listeners, who were following the tale of how he had learned to stop feeling sorry for himself by visiting elderly relatives, suddenly heard a gasp and a plop and a distant yell as Erwin dropped the microphone in the dirt and dove over the fence into a pile of lumber. That was the end of his career. He went into television soon afterward, sitting in a tiny booth and saying, "We're sorry. Due to technical difficulties we have temporarily lost the picture. Please stand by." When the union agreed to allow this to be recorded on tape, Erwin became a parking-lot attendant, sitting in a tiny booth, saying, "I'm sorry. I can't change anything larger than a five-dollar bill."

As I mentioned, this must be a hard week for you, so I will stop now. Please say hello to your wonderful family and tell them that they may be seeing much more of you in the very near future. Cordially,

* * *

January 1987

To Whomever Is In Charge Down There:

The awards committee of the World Order of Old Fishermen (WOOF), of which I am a charter member, met this month to award the Old Spellbinder trophy for Best Storyteller of 1986 and I am writing to you because someone said you thought you were going to get this coveted prize and I want to be sure you know that you are not. No point in you making the long drive up to the lodge, rehearsing your acceptance speech behind the wheel, talking about what a big surprise this is and a thrill although you can think of many who deserve it more than you—we can, too, so we're giving it to one of them. This year, the trophy, the battered old bait box emblematic of storytelling prowess, will go to Bob Jablonski. "What?" I hear you remonstrate. "Old Bob! Why, he couldn't narrate his way out of a sheet of waxed paper—why, he couldn't describe a flat surface—why, he couldn't tell you the story of his own life in thirty seconds or more." And of course you're right. But one thing Old Bob *has* got and that is a lovely heated fish house and that's where the World

Order of Old Fisherman (WOOF) intends to spend its Saturday nights starting in a few weeks. The moon and stars in the high winter sky, the dazzling snow, the silence across the lake, the distant lights of town, and the sweet aroma of woodsmoke and whiskey and old fishermen—in a paradise like this, you don't want a guy going on and on with a story. Winter casts its own spell, and when you get to the age of an old fisherman, you've heard most of the long stories already. You want the short sudden story of a fish. A handsome large fish and its tragic mistake and short struggle and then it is hauled up through a hole in the top of its world into the afterlife and, *voilà*, that fish discovers that heaven is a dark place full of old men in warm clothing chewing tobacco and sipping whiskey and stepping outside once in a while to piss and look at the stars. That is the story we care about, OUR story, and we intend to go on repeating it over and over. Have a good winter. Cordially,

THREE MARRIAGES

MRS. ROY TOLLERUD
TO
MR. AND MRS. FLOYD C. OLSON

Dear Floyd and Eleanor,

As you can see from the postmark, we got to Texas, though by the time you read this we'll probably have left Brownsville and gone I don't know where. We're searching for that resort the Larsons recommended, on the Gulf. The ones we've seen don't have weekly rates or else are not too clean, and the one the Larsons said was so nice, and half the price of what you'd pay in Florida, called Sea Drift or Sun Drift (or maybe it was Spend Thrift), we can't find it where they said it would be. They said it was right on the ocean and a lot of seniors from Minnesota stay there, so Roy wants to keep looking. I'd be just as happy to stay at a Holiday Inn and just not stay so long but he's set on finding this resort the Larsons liked, whether it exists or not. The weather is good along the coast and Roy is getting some color. We have met some very nice people in their own way, they are just like anyone else except for being Southern of course. It floors me the way they come right up to you the way they do and talk a blue streak. One minute it's Hello, how are you, and the next thing they're telling you about their daddy. I couldn't tell my life story to complete strangers if you put a gun to my head but they think nothing of it.

You would get a kick out of seeing Roy down here when the waitress walks over and says, "What can I dew for yew, honey?"— he just turns to jelly and when he kids her a little she throws her head back and laughs like he was Red Skelton. I never saw anything so comical as him when his little remarks are laughed at by a young woman, and I've never seen him leave a twenty-five-percent tip before either. Oh well.

You know he was here in Houston during the war and then Corpus Christi. I came for a couple months after Richard was born. In fact we talked about staying in Texas because everyone said it was going to have a big boom as soon as the war was over, which of course happened. I reminded him of this the other morning and he didn't remember it. I know that we talked about living here but he says no, that he would never've left Minnesota. But it was on the beach one afternoon, we had the baby with us, we were eating fried chicken, and he said, "How would you like to stay here?" or something very close to that, it was the fall of 1944. He says, nonsense, he wouldn't have lived here for anything, but I remember. What happened was that we decided to stay here, and we'd both go to work, but then his dad was feeling bad and so Roy thought we should go back for a few years and help them out, and that was that. I'm not complaining, but I do know it was what we talked about. He said to me, "How can you even imagine us living here all these years? We wouldn't have our friends, our church, nothing would be like what we got, who knows what it would've been like, we might not've had five kids. Is that what you want?" That is just ridiculous. If we had stayed we would have found something else. Anyone can see that. I think I could live here pretty well. There is a lot more to the world than what we have at home and a lot more perfectly good ways to live than what we're familiar with, but it was a mistake to say so. He said, "Maybe you would have been happier with someone else. Go ahead. Say it." Now he'll be mad the rest of the day and half of tomorrow. Anyway don't tell the Larsons we couldn't find their resort. I am going to write to them and say it was beautiful all right but all booked up.

Love,
Gladys

Mrs. Ruth Luger
TO
Mrs. Joanne Lienenkranz

Dear Joanie,

This is being written Monday night outside of Bakersfield somewhere, a nice motel but right on the highway and the truck traffic sounds like the Russian army. Bob says to say hello. Tomorrow down to San Diego to Francine's and Sunday we come home which I wouldn't mind doing right now though I suppose we are having a pretty good time considering what has happened to us. We have spent practically the whole trip looking up Bob's old buddies who he hasn't seen for ten years and when we meet one of them I suddenly see *why* it's been ten years but then it's too late, we're already there. Gruesome. His friends, they invite you to stay the night at their place and they just don't stop to think that you might like a room with a door or a bed—they say, "We've got plenty of room, it's no trouble," and you don't know what they mean until you get there and then all the trouble is yours. We were at his friend Dave's in Rapid City and they (Dave and Sharon) gave us some cushions and two army blankets. Real South Dakota hospitality. Slept on the living-room floor and a clock ringing every hour and woke up at 6:00 and her two kids were sitting two inches away with messy pants watching the Flintstones on TV. They are her kids and Dave has some of his own somewhere and he and she aren't married but I guess none of that bothers them. Dave says, "I've been meaning to go see my little girl for weeks now," as if she was a movie he had read was supposed to be pretty good. I said to Bob, "I can't stay two nights here," but he said it had been ten years since he saw Dave and this was his only chance— Well, those are the ten years since we were married so it's not like he's been without company. But these are people I wouldn't have around my house so I guess you got to travel if you want to see them.

We saw Bob's cousins Denny and Donny, they live outside Las Vegas where they race cars on weekends at a racetrack and the rest of the time I think they drink beer and say, "Hey, all right." We had to drive like crazy to get there Friday night in time for the race and then Bob went down in the pits and left me up in the bleachers with some people whose names I didn't get, a fat lady in a white jacket that said "Bad Girls Get To Go Everywhere" and her boyfriend who weighed three hundred and had a big beard with food stuck in it and a sad wispy woman who smoked up a storm, and afterward we had dinner at a drive-in with Denny and Donny and these people and they talked two hours without saying a single sentence I was interested in and never asked how I was (or who, either)—women out here are supposed to just sit outside in the dark and wait to go home, I guess. Denny's girlfriend Luanne sat and looked at him like he was the world's most wonderful man which you didn't have to know him very well to see that he isn't. I was glad they lost the race. It's a terrible thing to say but I hoped they'd crash and maybe knock some sense into themselves. They are almost forty and still in their teens and I doubt they will know much more until the day they die, though the day after that they may find out a lot of things.

After dinner it was midnight and Bob and I went to go look at Las Vegas which, just as they say, it never stops, and 4:00 A.M. is the same to them as 4:00 P.M. I know because we stayed up until 4:00 A.M. gambling at the San Remo. Farmers are milking cows now, I thought, and I am playing cards and winning money. In fact, I am getting more money than they earn in a week. Bob wanted to go see

Lola Mazola or somebody, some dancer, I said go ahead enjoy yourself. I was hot. I played Blackjack which was the only game I knew how to play (they didn't have Hearts or Rook, ha ha) and I went along pretty well, Bob hanging around and offering dumb advice, and then about 3:30 I had a great feeling and put everything on the table, a bucket of chips, and he almost got a heart attack right there. I won $4,864. Bob was out of the room at the time, sulking in the bar. I cashed in my chips and went and sat down in the booth with him and had a rum and Coke. He just about went crazy when I told him I won and he wanted to know how much. I wouldn't say. A lot. Well, then he wanted some of that to play with and I said, no. I said I had promised that it was going to the church. He didn't believe me but I was telling the truth, but he said it was his money to start with. He said, you don't earn no salary. Those were his exact words, spoken to his wife who keeps his house clean and raises up his children. "You don't earn no salary." It was the wrong thing to say to me at that time of the morning. I sailed out through the lobby and down the street. He said he didn't care if I left because he knew I'd come right back but he was walking along behind me as he said it. I walked six blocks in a cold fury with him trotting along behind. I got on a bus, he got on, too, and we rode to the end of the line, out in a regular neighborhood with churches and a school and ranch houses with green lawns and gardens. We walked all the way back as the sun came up and had breakfast at a nice place and slept all day and drove last night and here we are.

The money is in my makeup bag wrapped up in a scarf. Bob says, "That'd completely pay for this trip and leave us plenty for the next trip and then some. It's good luck, we're supposed to enjoy it, not give it away. It's for us, it's like a big wave that comes and lifts us up and off we go to bigger and better things. It could change our whole marriage." He says to me, "Did you promise to God that it'd all go to the church or did you only promise yourself?" To him there's a big difference.

God must've set this trip up so I could learn something. He sure didn't intend it to be fun because it isn't. I found out that I love my husband but I don't really like him very much right now but I'm sticking with him. You look at Sharon and Luanne and you see what happens to people whose word doesn't matter, their lives are a mess. I don't like Bob because he's so weak I think he'd even steal money out of my makeup kit so when he goes to sleep tonight I'll sew it into my dress, forty crisp new hundred-dollar bills, and carry it home and slip it into the collection plate. That'll be nice. Tomorrow we see the zoo and visit one last long-lost friend and then back home to our own house. I hope the kids are behaving themselves.

Love,
your sister Ruth.

CLARENCE BUNSEN
TO
HIS WIFE, ARLENE

My darling Arlene,
You were right, it is nuts to come to Saskatchewan to go ice fishing. Forty-six below zero today (minus a zillion windchill), and when you spit on the ground, it sounds like you dropped your car keys. But we aren't alone so there must be a reason for being here. Four in our party, plus four optometrists from Kansas City, and believe it or not, two California guys. Plus the Canadians. Twenty-seven fish houses all told here on the ice on Moose Tail Lake, like a regular little village, and for all I know they could issue bonds for long-term street improvements, it's that cold.

Fishing is lousy but then it wasn't good last year either so it's not a big surprise. It's nice to sit in a warm fish house and think. A person could probably do this in his living room, sit and hold the end of a string, but then you couldn't spit. I'm trying out a plug of Day's Work which makes me lightheaded as perhaps you can ascertain. Cully is talking a blue streak, all about himself and the war and the price of gas and whatnot, says he lost twenty pounds by only eating things he doesn't like. Still drinks a pint of whiskey a day. I asked him why and he said: my wife is angry at me no matter what and why would I want to listen to her sober? He has turned in for the night, he's had enough for this trip. He's a fly fisherman at heart and it goes against his nature to sit, back to the wall, and watch a drop line in a hole in the floor. It eliminates the skill and judgment and only leaves the religious aspect of fishing, but that is enough for me. A man needs to contemplate his sins and decide which ones to repent of and which to be more patient with and see if they might not cure themselves. Women don't need this because women are better than men.

It's midnight now and toasty warm in here and I can smell Bernie's bait, which he is secretive about but I believe it involves rancidized chicken parts, anyway it reminds me of when all the kids had stomach flu. Remember you called me at the garage and said Quote Come home, the kids are throwing up Unquote. Well, I didn't drive as fast as I could've.

That's one sin I want to get off my chest, and another is that Christmas about 1971 when the squirrel got in the bird-feeder. The one I made with a system of counterweights so if a squirrel got aboard it'd collapse under his weight, like the dropleaves on a dining-room table, which took me two weeks to design and the squirrel figured out in 8.2 seconds. And it was such a jerk squirrel, a real loudmouth.

This was Christmas Eve day. I got out the nozzle and garden hose and rigged it up on a two-by-four frame by the garage, aimed dead at the feeder, and I sat by the damn faucet in the laundry room and waited for a half-hour and finally nailed the bugger. A laser beam of ice water right smack beneath the tail, and he exploded into mid-air . . . flew across the snow, leaving a trail of turds . . . and sure enough, came back an hour later and I got him again! The second time you could *see* that squirrel yell "Oh shit!" and took off with his wheels spinning and tore up a tree and sat and wept for the plight of the

Irish people. I had a glass of whiskey and sat and felt pretty smug and after a while Barbara Ann came in, tears running down her cheeks, saying that something was wrong with Chuckie, he was hurt. Well, you know who Chuckie turned out to be. Her favorite squirrel. (I'd thought of him as Nick, but never mind.) He was in the yard under her bedroom window, limping around on the crusted snow. A fake limp, meant to win sympathy from a child. A *cynical* squirrel. "He's hurt," she said. "Can't we bring him in? It's *cold*, Daddy." My little girl. I explained why it'd be bad for Chuckie to remove him from his natural habitat. Big tears in her little brown eyes, pools of tears with Christmas lights reflected in them. I carried her up to our bed and tucked her in and told her a story, "The Squirrel Family's Christmas," which was pretty listless because as I began it I noticed, on your bedside table, a Christmas card that you'd stuck halfway into a book. I wondered why hadn't you put it on the mantel with the others so I looked at it (still telling about Mr. and Mrs. Bushy Tail and their kids) and it was postmarked San Francisco, and when I saw a letter inside the card and saw David Danielson's name, I felt sick inside. My stomach turned to stone. I felt betrayed. But she lay there, all awake, smiling, and Sammy and Sylvester and Sandy Squirrel all were waiting for Santa Squirrel to come shinnying down their old hickory tree with some walnuts and candy for Christmas, so the story droned on, and with one hand I held the letter down below bed level and quietly unfolded it. Jealousy!

You knew him as a good-looking boy who squired you to dances and drove you around in his daddy's Pontiac, but I knew him from football team, where he was the left halfback and I was a tackle. He was light and strong, built like a swimmer, graceful, the golden boy, and I was a squat little guy with stumpy legs, too small for the line really but they didn't know where else to put me, so in I went. I got the stuffing knocked out of me, my hands walked on, my face scratched, just so Dave could lope around end and into the end zone without anyone touching him, while I lay in the mud spitting up turf. You dated him for most of our junior and senior years and then he went to Stanford and you went with me. We were sitting in my car one night, I asked you about him, my heart pounding, and you thought for a *long* time and said, "I liked talking to him. He was smart. He was good to talk to." So for years, whenever you and I didn't have much to say, I'd look at you and imagine that you were thinking about him. Maybe writing letters to him. All the times I felt I wasn't much fun to be with, which was about half the time, Dave was there in the shadows, a handsome man who was good to talk to. I guess I wished you would say what a terrible person he was, which is crazy—why would I wish that a woman I love had spent all that time being miserable? but there you are.

I read the letter. It wasn't about joy in our hearts at this joyous season. It was about feelings from the past becoming stronger with the passage of time and closeness between old friends getting deeper and richer even though far apart—a real California Christmas letter. I could imagine a guy with slim hips and big shoulders in a blue pinstripe suit and red bowtie, a very youthful forty-year-old, not like your old tackle. I put Barbara Ann in her bed. I went to bed. You came up after a while. We lay in the dark. I wished that I could extend my influence out into the joyous world and find David and kill him. I got up and prowled around and looked out and saw Chuckie ensconced on the feeder, feasting on sunflower seeds without a worry in the world. I felt like something was eating my heart. We went to church in the morning and I imagined that Dave Ingqvist was winking at you from the pulpit. Why was he talking so much about love?

I am sorry! It was a miserable Christmas and you kept asking what was wrong, I should've said. I know you could've straightened it all out so well as you've straightened out so many things, but I let it eat at me. We had been talking about taking a vacation trip to California in June and I announced over Christmas dinner that we couldn't go, we'd spent too much money this year already. The look of pain on your faces, the blank uncomprehending pain.

It's years later. I'm still jealous. I still worry that if he'd asked you maybe you'd have chosen him. I imagine that one day you walk out the front door and there he is parked in a blue Thunderbird in the driveway and you have a choice, to stick with me and be yourself or go with him and be seventeen and get to live your youth over again.

Well, that will be your choice, of course. I want you to choose me. Nothing makes me feel emptier than the thought of losing you. I would wish you were here right now except that it wouldn't be nearly so wonderful as it will be when I come back to you tomorrow night.

Your loving husband,
Clarence

THE BABE

OUR LAKE WOBEGON TEAMS DID not do well in 1986, the Whippets with no pitching finishing dead last, the Leonards pitiful and helpless in the fall even with a 230-pounder to center the offensive line, and now it's basketball season again and already the boys are getting accustomed to defeat. When they ran out on the floor for the opener versus Bowlus (who won 58–21), they looked pale and cold in their blue and gold silks, and Buddy had the custodian turn up the heat, but it was too late. These boys looked like they were on death row, they trembled as their names were announced.

It's not defeat *per se* that hurts so much, we're used to that; it's the sense of doom and submission to fate that is awful. When the 230-pounder centered the ball and it stuck between his tremendous thighs and he toppled forward to be plundered by the Bisons, it was, I'm sure, with a terrible knowledge in his heart that he had this debacle coming to him and it was useless to resist. Two of the basketball players are sons of players on the fabled 1958 squad that was supposed to win the state championship and put our town on the map, but while we looked forward to that glorious weekend our team was eliminated in the first round by St. Klaus. None of us ever recovered from that disappointment But do our children have to suffer from it, too?

As Harry (Can O'Corn) Knudsen wrote: "In the game of life we're playing, people now are saying that the aim of it is friendship and trust. I wish that it were true but it seems, for me and you, that someone always loses and it's us."

Can O's inspiration came from playing eleven years for the Whippets, a humbling experience for anyone. The team is getting trounced, pummeled, whipped, and Dutch says, "Come on, guys, you're too tense out there, it's a game, go out there and have fun," and you think, *This is fun? If this is fun, then sic your dogs on me, let them chew me for a while, that'd be pure pleasure*. But out you trot to right field feeling heavyhearted and not even sure you're trotting correctly so you adjust the trot and your left foot grabs your right, *you trip on your own feet*, and down you go like a sack of potatoes and the fans in the stands are doubled up gasping and choking, and you have dirt in your mouth that you'll taste for years—is this experience good for a person?

Some fans have been led to wonder if maybe our Lake Wobegon athletes are suffering from a Christian upbringing that stresses the unworthiness angle and is light on the aspect of grace. How else would boys of sixteen and seventeen get the feeling that they were born to lose, if not in Bible class? And the uneasiness our boys have felt about winning—a fan can recall dozens of nights when the locals had a good first half, opened a nice lead, began to feel the opponents' pain, and sympathized and lightened up and wound up giving away their lunch. Does this come from misreading the Gospels?

Little Jimmy Wahlberg used to sit in the dugout and preach to the Whippets between innings, using the score of the ball game to quote Scripture; e.g., John 1:1: "In the beginning was the Word, and the Word was with God, and the Word was God," or Matthew 4:4: "Man shall not live by bread alone, but by every word that proceedeth out of the mouth of God." That was fine except when he was pitching. God had never granted Little Jimmy's prayer request for a good curveball, so this fine Christian boy got shelled like a peanut whenever he took the mound, and one day Ronnie Decker came back to the bench after an eternal inning in centerfield and said, "First Revelations 13:0: Keep the ball down and throw at their heads."

Ronnie is Catholic, and they have more taste for blood, it seems. (Was there ever a *Methodist* bullfighter?) In St. Klaus, the ladies chant, "Make 'em sing and make 'em dance / Kick 'em in the nuts and step on their hands." The boys are ugly brutes with raw sores on their arms and legs and with little ball-bearing eyes who will try to hurt you. A gang of men stands by the backstop, drinking beer and talking to the umpire, a clean-cut Lutheran boy named Fred. Fred knows that, the week before, Carlson called a third strike on a Klausie, dashed to his car, the men rocked it and let the air out of the tires but couldn't pry the hood open and disconnect the spark plugs before he started up and rode away on the rims. Fred hopes to keep the fans happy.

For a Golden Age of Lake Wobegon Sports, you'd have to go back to the forties. The town ball club was the Lake Wobegon Schroeders, so named because the starting nine were brothers, sons of E. J. Schroeder. Nine big strapping boys with identical mops of black hair, big beaks, little chins, and so shy they couldn't look you in the eye, and E.J. was the manager, though the boys were such fine ballplayers, he only sat in the shade on a white kitchen chair and grumbled at them, they didn't require management.

E.J. was ticked off if a boy hit a bad pitch. He'd spit and curse and rail at him, and then R.J.'d go up and pound one out of the park (making the score 11–zip) and circle the bases and the old man'd say, "Boy, he put the old apple right down the middle, didn't he? Blind man coulda hit that one. Your gramma coulda put the wood on that one. If a guy couldn't hit that one out, there'd be something wrong with him, I'd say. Wind practically took that one out of here, didn't even need to hit it much"—and lean over and spit. When the Schroeders were winning every game, E.J. bitched about how they won.

"Why'dja throw to first for, ya dummy?"

"But it's the third out, Dad. We won the game."

"I know that. You don't have to point that out to me. Why'ntcha get the guy at third?"

"It was easier to go to first."

"Easier! *Easier??!!*"

The tenth son, Paul, had a gimpy right leg but still tried to please his dad and sat in the dugout and kept statistics (1.29, for example, and .452 and .992), but E.J. never looked at them. "That's history," he said, spitting, "I am interested in the here and now."

So his sons could never please him, and if they did, he forgot about it. Once, against Freeport, his oldest boy, Edwin Jim, Jr., turned and ran to the centerfield fence for a long long long fly ball and threw his glove forty feet in the air to snag the ball and caught the ball and glove and turned toward the dugout to see if his dad had seen it, and E.J. was on his feet clapping, but when he saw the boy look to him, he immediately pretended he was swatting mosquitoes. The batter was called out, the third out. Jim ran back to the bench and stood by his dad. E.J. sat chewing in silence and finally he said, "I saw a man in Superior, Wisconsin, do that a long time ago but he did it at night and the ball was hit a lot harder."

What made this old man so mean? Some said it happened in 1924, when he played for the town team that went to Fort Snelling for the state championship and in the ninth inning, in the deepening dusk on Campbell's Bluff, Lake Wobegon down by one run, bases loaded and himself the tying run on third, when the Minneapolis pitcher suddenly collapsed and writhed around on the mound with his eyes bulging and face purple and vomiting and foaming and clawing and screeching, everyone ran to help him, including E.J., and he jumped up and tagged them all out. A triple play, unassisted. *What a rotten trick*, but there they stood, a bunch of rubes, and all the slickers howling and whooping their heads off, so he became mean, is one theory.

And he was mean. He could hit foul balls with deadly accuracy at an opponent or a fan who'd been riding him, or a member of the fan's immediate family, and once he fouled twenty-eight consecutive pitches off the home-plate umpire, for which he was thrown out of the Old Sod Shanty League.

"Go! Hence!" cried the ump.

"For foul balls?"

The umpire and the sinner were face to face. "Forever!" cried the ump. "Never again, so long as ball is thrown, shall thy face be seen in this park."

"Foul balls ain't against any rule that I know of!"

The umpire said, "Thou hast displeased me." And he pointed outerward and E.J. slouched away.

So he coached his boys. He never said a kind word to them, and they worked like dogs in hopes of hearing one, and thus they became great, mowing down the opposition for a hundred miles around. In 1946 they reached their peak. That was the year they disposed easily of fifteen crack teams in the Father Powers Charity Tournament, some by massacre, and at the closing ceremony, surrounded by sad little crippled children sitting dazed in the hot sun and holding pitiful flags they had made themselves, when E.J. was supposed to hand back the winner's check for $100 to Father Powers to help with the work among the poor, E.J. said, "Fat chance!" and shoved away the kindly priest's outstretched hand. That was also the year Babe Ruth came to town with the Sorbasol All-Star barnstorming team.

The Babe had retired in 1935 and was dying of cancer, but even a dying man has bills to pay, and so he took to the road for Sorbasol, and Lake Wobegon was the twenty-fourth stop on the trip, a day game on November 12. The All-Star train of two sleepers and a private car for the Babe backed up the sixteen-mile spur into Lake Wobegon, arriving at 10:00 A.M. with a blast of whistle and a burst of steam, but hundreds already were on hand to watch it arrive.

The Babe was a legend then, much like God is today. He didn't give interviews, in other words. He rode around on his train and appeared only when necessary. It was said that he drank Canadian rye whiskey, ate hot dogs, won thousands at poker, and kept beautiful women in his private car, *Excelsior*, but that was only talk.

The sleepers were ordinary deluxe Pullmans; the *Excelsior* was royal green with gold-and-silver trim and crimson velvet curtains tied shut—not that anyone tried to look in; these were proud country people, not a bunch of gawkers. Men stood by the train, their backs to it, talking purposefully about various things, looking out across the lake, and when other men straggled across the field in twos and threes, stared at the train, and asked, "Is he really in there?" the firstcomers said, "Who? Oh! You mean the Babe? Oh, yes, I reckon he's here all right—this is his train, you know. I doubt that his train would go running around without the Babe in it, now, would it?" and resumed their job of standing by the train, gazing out across the lake. A proud moment for them.

At noon the Babe came out in white linen knickers. He looked lost. A tiny black man held his left arm. Babe tried to smile at the people and the look on his face made them glance away. He stumbled on a loose plank on the platform and men reached to steady him and noticed he was hot to the touch. He signed an autograph. It was illegible. A young woman was carried to him who'd been mysteriously ill for months, and he laid his big hand on her forehead and she said she felt something. (Next day she was a little better. Not recovered but improved.)

However, the Babe looked shaky, like a man who ate a bushel of peaches whole and now was worried about the pits. He's drunk, some said, and a man did dump a basket of empty beer bottles off the train, and boys dove in to get one for a souvenir—but others who came close to his breath said no, he wasn't drunk, only dying. So it was that an immense crowd turned out at the Wally (Old Hard Hands) Bunsen Memorial Ballpark: twenty cents per seat, two bits to stand along the foul line, and a dollar to be behind a rope by the dugout, where the Babe would shake hands with each person in that section.

He and the All-Stars changed into their red Sorbasol uniforms in the dugout, there being no place else, and people looked away as they did it (nowadays people would look, but then they didn't), and the Babe and his teammates tossed the ball around, then sat down, and out came the Schroeders. They ran around and warmed up and you could see by their nonchalance how nervous they were. E.J. batted grounders to them and hit one grounder zinging into the visitors' dugout, missing the Babe by six inches. He was too sick to move. The All-Stars ran out and griped to the ump but the Babe sat like he didn't know where he was. The ump was scared. The Babe hobbled out to home plate for the ceremonial handshakes and photographs, and E.J. put his arm around him as the crowd stood cheering and grinned and whispered, "We're going to kill ya, ya big mutt. First pitch goes in your ear. This is your last game. Bye, Babe." And the game got under way.

It was a good game, it's been said, though nobody remembers much about it specifically, such as the score, for example. The All-Stars were nobodies, only the Babe mattered to the crowd, and the big question was Would he play? He looked too shaky to take the field, so some said, "Suspend the rules! Why not let him just go up and bat! He can bat for the pitcher! Why not? It wouldn't hurt anything!" And nowadays they might do it, but back then you didn't pick up the bat unless you picked up your glove and played a position, and others said that maybe it wouldn't hurt anything but once you start changing the rules of the game for convenience, then what happens to our principles? Or do we change those, too?

So the game went along, a good game except that the Babe sat sprawled in the dugout, the little black man dipping cloths in a bucket of ice and laying them on the great man's head—a cool fall day but he was hot—and between innings he climbed out and waved to the fans and they stood and cheered and wondered would he come to bat. E.J. said to Bernie, "He'll bat all right, and when he comes, remember the first pitch: hard and high and inside."

"He looks too weak to get the bat off his shoulder, Dad. He looks like a breeze would blow him over. I can't throw at Babe Ruth."

"He's not sick, he's pretending so he don't have to play like the rest of us. Look at him: big fat rich New York son of a bitch, I bet he's getting five hundred dollars just to sit there and have a pickaninny put ice on him. Boy, I'd put some ice on him you-know-where, boy, he'd get up quick then, he'd be ready to play then. He comes up, I want you to give him something to think about so he knows we're not all a bunch of dumb hicks out here happy just to have him show up. I want him to know that some of us *mean it*. You do what I say. I'm serious."

It was a good game and people enjoyed it, the day cool and bright, delicious, smelling of apples and leather and woodsmoke and horses, blazed with majestic colors as if in a country where kings and queens ride through the cornfields into the triumphant reds and oranges of the woods, and men in November playing the last game of summer, waiting for the Babe, everyone waiting for the Babe as runs scored, hours passed, the sky turned red and hazy. It was about time to quit and go home, and then he marched out, bat in hand, and three thousand people threw back their heads and yelled as loud as they could. They yelled for one solid minute and then it was still.

The Babe stood looking toward the woods until everything was silent, then stepped to the plate and waved the bat, and Bernie looked at him. It was so quiet you could hear coughing in the crowd. Way to the rear a man said, "Merle, you get your hands off her and shut up now," and hundreds turned and shushed *him*. Then Bernie wound up. He bent way down and reached way back and kicked up high and the world turned and the ball flew and the umpire said, "BALL ONE!" and the catcher turned and said, "Be quiet, this doesn't concern you," and the umpire blushed. He knew immediately that he was in the wrong. Babe Ruth was not going to walk, he would sooner strike out and would do it himself, with no help from an umpire. So the umpire turned and walked away.

The Babe turned and spat and picked up a little dirt and rubbed his hands with it (people thought, Look, that's our dirt and he's putting it on his hands, as if the Babe might bring his own) and then stood in and waved the bat and Bernie bent way down and reached way back and kicked high and the world turned and the ball flew and the Babe swung and missed; he said *huhhhhnnnn* and staggered. And the next pitch. He swung and cried in pain and the big slow curve slapped into the catcher's mitt.

It was so still, they heard the Babe clear his throat, like a board sliding across dirt. They heard Bernie breathing hard through his nose.

The people were quiet, wanting to see, hear, and smell everything and remember it forever: the wet fall dirt, the pale-white bat, the pink cotton candy and the gentlemen's hats, the smell of wool and the glimmer of a star in the twilight, the touch of your dad's big hand and your little hand in it. Even E.J. was quiet, chewing, watching his son. The sun had set beyond right field, darkness was settling, you had to look close to see—Bernie took three steps toward home and pointed at the high outside corner of the plate, calling his pitch, and the Babe threw back his head and laughed four laughs. (People were glad to hear he was feeling better, but it was scary to hear a man laugh at home plate; everyone knew it was bad luck.) He touched the corner with his bat. Bernie climbed back on the mound, he paused, he bent down low and reached way back and kicked real high and the world turned and the ball flew and the Babe swung and it cracked and the ball became a tiny white star in the sky. It hung there as the Babe went around the bases in his famous Babe Ruth stride, the big graceful man trotting on slim little feet, his head down until the roar of the crowd rose like an ocean wave on the prairie and he looked up as he turned at third, he smiled, lifted his cap, strode soundlessly across home plate looking like the greatest ballplayer in the history of the world. The star was still in the sky, straight out due northwest of the centerfield fence, where he hit it. The ball was never found, though they searched for it for years.

"Did you see that?" your dad says, taking your hand.

You say, "Yes, I did."

Even E.J. saw it and stood with the rest and he was changed after that, as were the others. A true hero has some power to make us a gift of a larger life. The Schroeders broke up, the boys went their own ways, and once they were out of earshot, E.J. sat in the Sidetrack Tap and bragged them up, the winners he produced and how they had shown Babe Ruth a pretty good game. He was tolerated but Babe Ruth was revered. He did something on that one day in our town that made us feel we were on the map of the universe, connected somehow to the stars, part of the mind of God. The full effect of his mighty blow diminished over time, of course, and now our teams languish, our coaches despair. Defeat comes to seem the natural course of things. Lake Wobegon dresses for a game, they put on their jock-straps, pull on the socks, get into the colors, they start to lose heart and turn pale—fear shrivels them.

Boys, this game may be your only chance to be good, he might tell them. You might screw up everything else in your life and poison the ones who love you, create misery, create such pain and devastation it will be repeated by generations of descendants. Boys, there's plenty of room for tragedy in life, so if you go bad, don't have it be said that you never did anything right. Win this game.

HOW I CAME TO GIVE THE
MEMORIAL DAY ADDRESS
AT THE LAKE WOBEGON
CEMETERY THIS YEAR

IT ALL BEGAN BACK IN MARCH, the month that shows people who don't drink exactly how a hangover feels, when the snow started melting in the yards facing south and flowed east downhill, and the chairman of the Lake Wobegon Memorial Day Committee, Clarence Bunsen, heard water running in his basement, dripping from the walls, and noticed a fifty-foot lake in the empty lot between him and the Lutheran church where Benders' house burned down in 1955, in the winter. I was thirteen years old that winter and remember it well. Right before the sirens went off, I had wished something exciting would happen in town, so I felt ashamed to go running up there and see hellish flames in every window flashing in the black smoke and bursting up through the roof and high in the air, the whole nice house burning to smithereens and those extremely nice Benders, including Charles, my classmate, standing by in stone-cold shock and confusion, but it was interesting to see, a real catastrophe similar to the miniature ones we made in the mud in the ditch every spring. All around the little town of Sandville and its square squat earth houses bunched around Route 66, the Hell River ran fast and furious through Sandy Canyon toward the Devil's Culvert, carrying barges loaded with various things and also fast skiffs and yachts, the biggest yacht belonging to the old rich guy Henderson who lived in the sand castle and who if he knew what we had learned in Sunday school would be darned nervous about his future, though that Sandville levee seemed to be protecting the folks pretty well. Men stood in a row along the top, cowpokes and blue and gray soldiers, and looked at all the water rushing by and said, "I ain't never seen her as high as this, not in a coon's age." "Yup. But the levee feels sure enough solid, by cracky." Over the roar of the river, how could they hear the Luftwaffe heading their way? They couldn't, of course, and when the gigantic mud bombs dropped out of the cold gray sky and their comfortable little world vanished under globs of the very substance from which it was made (cruel irony), I could feel the sadness come up from the ground under my feet. There is no love or justice in this life, my friend, just a passel of illusions on a sunny spring day that is shattered by sudden brutal death. *Alas! poor Sandville!* The Benders didn't die, though, they just left Lake Wobegon and the ashes behind and went to live in a town named something-field in Connecticut where her brother was a chiropractor, and the next September Charles wrote a letter to our class saying Connecticut was a swell state, they lived in a very big brick house, and he had his own sailboat, a lie if I ever heard one. I wished there were someone I knew faraway who I could lie to and say that *we* were rich. Everyone I knew knew us too well, our junky yard with lumber stacked in the mud, our half-finished house, our worn-out furniture, and what is the benefit of lying to impress people you don't know? I could put palm trees and passion flowers in that empty lot and make the lake of melted snow into a fifty-foot pool where long-legged naked girls skinny around in the clear blue water, and I could pick your name out of the phone book and send it to you, but where does that get us? All it was was a big cold puddle in the empty place the Benders left to go to Connecticut and get happy, but it worried Clarence sick, so he passed the Memorial Day chairmanship to his brother Clint, the Mayor of Lake Wobegon, who already was chairman of so many things he didn't think about it until a few weeks later.

The next day was warmer, the first of a series of warm ones. The Norwegian bachelor farmers sat on their board bench in front of

Ralph's like a jury, watching and listening, chewing and spitting, bundled up tight. They saw Clifford appear in the front window of the Mercantile and take Lorraine's dress off and—she had no underwear on underneath, only pale-pink wooden skin, a shapely woman but the paint on her left breast was chipped and there were deep nicks in her slender waist—tack a blue cotton skirt to her and slip a white jersey over her head. Some boys came along from school at 2:30. There'd been a rumor in school that someone was hit by a car and killed in front of the Sidetrack Tap, but the bachelors said no. Ridiculous. To get hit by a car in this town, you'd have to wait awhile and then try to jump in front of one, but it'd probably just stop and they'd ask, how are you doing. What happened was that Mr. Berge walked out of the Sidetrack after lunch and, blinded by sunlight, walked into the side of Florian's car. Florian was driving slow. No harm done. Berge went back and had more lunch to calm himself down, and Florian proceeded out of town to St. John's to visit his friend Father O'Connell. Disappointed, the boys went to church and found the dam they had built to hold the lake was busted open, the lake had drained, the ships run aground, the story was over.

Memorial Day didn't pass Clint's mind until one evening in April when Mr. Berge said to him, "I wouldn't be surprised if we got more snow." They were in the Sidetrack. Clint had dropped in to use the phone. He had a beer while he waited. He was calling Irene to say he'd be home in a minute but the number was still busy, so he had another one. "Hard to snow when it's sixty-five degrees out," he said.

Spring is a miserable time of year for the mayor of a town that runs on the weak-mayor, stupid-Council system of government: the roads crumble under the wallop of warm weather and the uncompleted sewer construction thaws out and trenches collapse and pipes crack, costs rise, the sewer company sulks in its tent in Millet, and the Council sits and talks about whether or not to discuss whether to talk about when to discuss a way of deciding where and how to talk about making a decision, Yes or No, Now or Never, on the one obvious way to solve the age-old problem of shit, and the worst one was his sister-in-law Arlene Bunsen, elected in 1984 to fill the seat of the senile A. B. (Cully) Tollerud. A bad year. For years Clint had voted the old man like a dummy, but Arlene is independent, which is fine in theory but whenever she sees a page full of big numbers she gets all fluttery and yammers about whether it's *really* necessary and couldn't we *discuss* this further, get some advice, maybe find a book in the library, call someone at the University, send for an expert, have a referendum, form a special committee, and how do you explain to this lovely Christian lady that a community septic-tank system is going to cost $2,400 per household plus $150 annual usage fee, including construction, materials, and the $97,000 to Mr. Hansen for twenty acres of land for the drain field? Clint had spent hundreds of hours in agonizingly dull meetings negotiating with Hansen, his lawyer, two real-estate men, the assessor, two Mist County commissioners, the state pollution-control agency, the waste-control board, a consulting engineer, and some weasel at the EPA—and Hansen's property was where the drain field had to go and $97,000 was what they had to pay for it, so when Arlene asked one night, in a sweet and helpful tone of voice, "Wouldn't it be worth it to look for alternatives that might be more economical?" and the idiots in the folding chairs actually *clapped* for her, it weakened his faith in representative democracy. The second bottle of beer represented some faith restored.

"You're a good man, you know that?" Mr. Berge said wearily. "I mean that. You're a good man." Clint smiled. You don't say thank you for a compliment from a drunk, he thought, you endure it. "No, it's true!" said Berge. "Look at you. Got a wunnerful fam'ly, a beertiful house, own your own gas station—"

"It's a car dealership. Not a gas station."

"Car dealer, then, and you're the mayor of the town, and look at me, wouldja. Just look at me. I'm your same age—we're the same— I'm seventy-two, you're about seventy, arentcha—"

"Sixty-one."

"Like I say, *look* at us! What happened? I'll tell you what happened. It was the war. Guys who weren't there, they'll never know what it was like. I'll tell you what it was like: it was hell. You never forget a thing like that. I lost a buddy in France. We were there together and I turned to say something to this guy who asked me a question and I turned back and his head was blown off. You ever see a guy's head blown off? I tell you, if you had, you never forget it. There isn't a day goes by I don't see that like it was right now."

It was so quiet, like a phone was about to ring or the door open and someone say, Hi, everybody, the jukebox wake up and hum and clunk, and Willie sing "Blue Eyes Crying in the Rain," but nothing happened, just pure stupid silence until Wally unleaned off the back bar and walked up to the sink and ran himself a glass of water. "I remember when Johnny Paul, that spring he—" Berge said, "*Everybody* remembers that, don't tell me about him. I was there, too. That's not the same."

Johnny Paul worked for Mr. Ray Fredricksen. He was about sixty-six or so, the last of those old-time hired men who worked alongside you all year long and lived on the place in a little shack except for a week or two in February or March when they went off to cure their cabin fever, rode the bus to Duluth, spent a couple hundred bucks on old whores and whiskey, and walked along the shore yelling and singing, cursing you to hell, and drank themselves an inch and a half short of death, and came home carrying their head under their arm, and were nursed back to respectability to spend another eleven months in sobriety and good work, but one year that old man skipped his annual visit to Duluth, threw his system out of whack, and one April day fell off the tractor while plowing Mr. Fredricksen's eighty over by his sister Rose's and was killed pretty badly.

"He was a nice old guy," said Clint. "If only he hadn't tried to straighten out, he'd still be here, I bet," said Wally. Mr. Berge said, "I din't mean to insult'm— Here! let's drink to'm. To his memory and the memory of all of'm. To all m'buddies!" Clint stood up. "How'd you like to be chairman of Memorial Day?" he almost said, before he went home. On the way home, he thought, "Why should Memorial Day be so prim, like it was lady schoolteachers who went ashore at Normandy? Why not let Mr. Berge and his friends run it? It was their war." But instead he fobbed off the chairmanship on Clifford Turnblad the next week, the first week of May.

That was after Lorraine's eyes were repainted by Clifford's cousin's boy, Mark, an art student, who tried to correct her walleyed look by making her slightly crosseyed. A few days later, arriving to open the store, Clifford's sister Miriam noticed certain dark shadows under Lorraine's house dress. She was too embarrassed to mention this, afraid it might be what in fact turned out to be exactly what it was, two large aureoles and a triangle of pubic hair. Every Boy Scout in Troop 12 had come for a look before Clifford finally caught on. "Poor old Lorraine, I'm so used to looking at her, I didn't even see how sexy she'd got," he told Clint and Clarence Bunsen. Clint wanted to dump Memorial Day on him right then but felt inhibited with Clarence there. They were eating lunch and talking about Clifford's idea of planting pine trees along the alleys so that in fifteen years the town will look green year-round. Clifford also thinks a March festival would be an original idea, maybe a John Philip Sousa festival. Or we could paint a happy face on the water tower and nickname ourselves "The Town With a Smile." There's no end to the ways a dying town like ours can lift itself up by its broken bootstraps, is Clifford's way of thinking. He said, "Look." He showed them a drawing of Bunsen Motors and the Mercantile and the empty storefront between them where the paint store used to be: a new sign in front said "Tan My Hide."

"A leather works?" asks Clarence. "The trappers are gone, Cliff. Years ago." Clifford said, "It's a tanning parlor."

"For who? I don't know anybody over the age of twenty who gets tan in the *summer*. We Lutherans are a pale people. We keep our clothes on. Even if we *did* have a tan, you'd never know it to look at us, because we don't undress, so there's no way we could ever show it off, so we don't bother. So why do it?"

"For a sense of well-being, Clarence. A sense of confidence. Confidence is what we need around here." Another Clifford idea.

Mr. Coleman, who once owned the paint store, lacked confidence and good ideas, thinks Clifford, and either one could've saved him from the bad word of mouth the summer that twelve houses in town broke out in blisters, but most people say it was his sardonic way with his customers: he simply couldn't understand or tolerate their utter lack of information about paint, a subject he knew quite well. Paint ignorance made him shake his head and sigh. "Let me start at the beginning," he would say in a dry amused voice. He soon cured people of coming in and asking him questions. The blisters made him furious. The people had not followed directions, so what could he do? He couldn't go paint the houses for them, could he? So why did they stop patronizing him? A direct descendant of the Coleman surveying team that misplaced the entire township in 1866, he brooded all that fall, a dark face peering out from between the bathroom tile displays, and after Christmas he opened, in addition to his paint line, a line of imported gift items that didn't sell either. He was filled with anger and frustration, which he tried to relieve through fishing, but an angry man can't catch fish, and after thirty or forty minutes of nothing, not even a nibble, Coleman would suddenly lash out at the water with his pole and throw things overboard. He had a prodigious temper. One hot August day, fishless, biteless for more than forty minutes, he unclamped his Johnson outboard, disconnected the gas line, hoisted it overhead, and heaved it in the drink, followed by the gas tank, one oar, a life vest, the minnow bucket, the second oar, and the pole itself. That cleared out his system for a few months, but in January he went out one night, fished all night in his little green fish house, Coleman's Fancy, and nobody heard him yelling and pounding on the ice and nobody saw him come back to his apartment over the paint store at 6:00 A.M. and get the dynamite, otherwise they would've offered him a bigger stick. He drove back out to the fish house in his Chrysler station wagon, carrying two small sticks, a waterproof fuse, and a big plastic bag to carry all the fish home in after he had stunned them. He prepared the charge, lit the fuse, dropped the dynamite down the hole in the ice, and then saw that he'd forgotten to tie on the lead sinker. The dynamite floated up and sat, a dark shape under the ice beneath his feet. He reached down the hole and tried to pull it out with his pole but only pushed it farther away, and then he heard a crack and suddenly he got a warm feeling in his pants. It wasn't ice cracking—it was lovely Patricia Peterson on shore in her dad Pete's duck blind, practicing her sharp-shooting for the Tri-County Queen Contest, where, though she wasn't sure the rules allowed her to fire a shotgun for the talent segment, she figured if she shot well enough, they'd make an exception—but Coleman panicked, thinking his time was up. He tore out the door and aimed himself toward shore, any shore, and eighty yards away a beautiful young woman, who had removed her unattractive glasses to see if she could sharpshoot instinctively at the beauty contest, pumped and aimed at the blurry lake and blasted both barrels at about the same moment his charge went off. It opened a broad hole of cold water into which the Chrysler plunged and sank like a green whale, and when Patty's dad came out and peeled Coleman off the ice, he was a changed man, placid, mute, almost spaniel-like. His anger was gone, and without it he had no reason to remain in retail sales. He locked up and left for Minneapolis, leaving on his paint-shop door a telephone number that turned out to be no longer in service at this time, which in a way people had known about him for a long time. It was hard, Clarence thought, to imagine that good ideas would have saved him.

Ideas! Clifford kept trying. At the City Council one Tuesday evening he stood up and talked festival. "This town needs a real event to put us on the map! Toast & Jelly Days is all well and good but it

isn't going to do the job when it comes to bringing new people in."
Bob Bauser looked sick. His mother gave her heart and soul to Toast
& Jelly Days for thirty-two years, died as a direct result of exhaustion
from driving around town returning all the borrowed toasters. How
could Clifford say these things? "We need something," Clifford said.
"Duluth has Lake Superior, Rochester's got the Mayo Clinic, St. Paul
has the state capitol, Minneapolis has Dayton's—what do we have?"
People thought long and hard. Val stood up. "Maybe we could es-
tablish some kind of Bible camp. One that's open year-round, where
people could come whenever they liked. People of all denominations.
Have dormitories and of course there'd be recreational opportunities
but mainly it'd be where you could come for a week or two and really
dig deep into Scripture."

Clifford was thinking along the lines of an all-night bingo casino
and greyhound track, not a major-league Bible camp. "In a better
world," he said, "I'm sure that Bible study would be a wonderful
tourist attraction, but meanwhile—" "The Bible teaches us to believe
in a better world," said Val.

Clint smiled at them both. "You're both right, and I think we've
heard some very interesting proposals here tonight that we can all
think about and discuss and maybe bring in a consultant from the
university, but right now, Cliff, I need to ask you to take on a big
job that I think only you are the person with the imagination and
the ability to do and that is to run Memorial Day this year. It's only
a few weeks away and I know that you can come up with an excellent
speaker, an excellent program, an excellent . . ." Clifford sat down.
He felt a need for oxygen to awaken him from this sad dream. Clint
talked about the sewer project, using a crude chart showing flow rates
and system capacity. After adjournment people filed out like sheep
down a chute. The next morning the Chatterbox had to close up due
to a yellowish fluid seeping from the front wall and onto the sidewalk—it smelled bad. Nobody knew where it came from so they
waited for it to stop.

So much bad news, and none of it in the newspaper. Ella Anderson has emphysema and was seen by Myrtle wearing an oxygen tank on her back and a mask like a scuba diver, bending over her flower beds, and poking a stick down around the tulip bulbs—to do what? let air in the ground? Dr. DeHaven was ill, too, and went to St. Cloud to consult with specialists, and returned home in the same condition except more tired. "He is dying of a brain tumor the size of a fist," Myrtle said calmly, a prognosis based on what had happened to her mother. Another sinkhole opened up on the football field, the third in the past year and the largest, almost fifty feet across—it sank three feet. "It's an isolated problem," say Clint and Bud, which they said about the first two. Three sinkholes in one small town can't be sheer coincidence, can it? Is the entire municipality built atop a honeycomb of caves that now collapse one by one and our lives collapse with them? The soil is sandy; it isn't hard to imagine how underground rivers or something—pigs perhaps, the wild boars of Norwegian bachelor-farmer legend who got lost in vast caverns years ago and burrowed and fed on roots and grew immense and blind and vicious, digging like fiends through the soft ground every spring, zeroing in on the warmth of our homes and the smell of frying pork, grunting up through the soil against our basement floors, cracking the concrete, breathing their sour pig breath into our cellars—something could make hundreds of channels through the soft earth and sandstone that a century of well-digging and drainage has made spongy with huge hollows where dry brittle columns bear the weight of overburden, Our Lady Church and the high school and all our most splendid edifices held up by slender filigrees of sand that one shock such as a semi on Main Street or a new sewer system could shake loose and the thin crust break, a mushroom-shaped dust cloud rise up and obliterate the town, and when the dust blows away, we see a gargantuan pit between Adams Hill and the shore, a half-mile long, full of bricks and wooden wreckage and cars.

But we won't see it. Other people will: the State Highway Patrol, the Red Cross, reporters from the *Pioneer Press*. We will be down deep in the pit, dying in that hot black hole lying crushed under Ralph's frozen-meat case and a Bunsen Motors gas pump trickling lead-free regular around our ears as we hear thumping in the sky overhead the Channel 4 and 5 and 9 and 11 news helicopters circling for a good angle and then a spot to land so they can cover the press conference with Sheriff Anton (Huffer) Hoffman. This old gasbag is from Millet, and he is secretly glad to see us gone. "There was nothing to be done," he says, trying to look solemn, drilling for earwax, "they were all killed instantly. They didn't have a chance. I can't send in searchers until we can stabilize the wreckage. May take us weeks to recover the bodies. Worst thing of this type I ever saw."

The reporters lean over the edge. "Anybody got a child's toy we can toss in there for a good picture? a little red wagon or a doll? something to humanize all that rubble? Naw, a baseball glove isn't gonna work. Looks like a cow flop. Something brighter. How about a dollhouse? Fantastic! A little wooden dollhouse perched atop the debris, undamaged, a child's fantasy survives while the real world collapses around it— Somebody run into St. Cloud and get a goddamn dollhouse!"

We lie with dirt in our mouths, gasoline leaking around us and meat juice, and hear their voices echo in the hole and assume that we are in hell. A life of faithful attendance on Sunday morning did not work in our case, and God in His infinite wisdom has chosen to hurl us down into everlasting torment. We hunger and He crushes us with frozen food, we thirst and He gives us gasoline, we despair and He sends the press. What indignity is left, dear Lord? Pain and misery all too evident, redemption hidden and all the good works of faith, friendship gone, love gone, children grown up and gone and no word comes back from them or anyone else we gave our lives to, life is over, it's Memorial Day for all of us: what can we do but get up out of bed, make coffee, fix breakfast, and tune in WLB.

Bea Lady does the kitchen show six days a week plus "Looking

Up" on Sunday morning, and on Wednesday morning at 10:15 Ella Anderson listened to her give out a recipe for three-bean salad, and just before the women's club news Bea said, "Here's a tip for how to relax. Did you know that sighing is a proven way to let tension out of your body? Try it. Three deep sighs in a row." To Ella this was wonderful news, to hear that what she'd been doing all her life was good for her. She sighed. It did feel good. And three deep ones felt better. She couldn't remember a single bean of the three-bean salad, but she had gotten something to call up and tell to Arlene Bunsen: sighing is good for you, it helps you relax and it relieves the effects of beans.

Immediately before the Bea Lady show is Orville C. Ball and "The Wall of Hope Gospel Hour" on tape from Grand Rapids: fifteen minutes including two of music, three of the mailing address, and ten minutes of Gospel preaching that could pulverize concrete into small chunks. You listen to O.C.B. and you wish for his sake that he *is* a hypocrite who goes out to motels and howls every Saturday night, the thought of a heart so sincerely unforgiving is too awful. His poor listeners, you can tell who they are as they drive by, heads slumped, arms limp, mouths open like beached fish. Orville says: "Oh, you can fool everyone else with your sweetheart ways and your big grin, you can be a wonderful friend, a good parent, a steady worker, a member of the church, and a true neighbor who everyone *likes and trusts* but you can't fool me, I look in your heart and see a filthy rotten stinking *cesspool* of evil thoughts and shameful desires that if those people knew you were thinking along those lines, they'd turn away from you in *disgust!* Oh, yes! it's true!"

Down the road they go, slumped behind the wheel. *If people really knew us, they'd hate us.* He says, "Look here in the book of Romans, Chapter 3!" They're driving and can't look but they know the verse. They've heard the message before, many times, from their parents, and to hear Brother Ball now is to hear their father, in cold fury forty years ago, withdraw his blessing and prophesy a worthless unhappy life for them that they have suffered forty years trying to elude. He nails three more verses in them, gives the mailing address, the organ weeps a lonely pitiful hymn, and then Bea Lady is there in her sunny kitchen. "Good morning," she says, like your favorite aunt, your third-grade teacher, "it's so nice of you to join us again. Today we'll be giving out a wonderful recipe that Virginia Ingqvist sent in for a salad you can make now and freeze for later—it only takes ten minutes to thaw—and we'll talk about sighing. Did you know it helps you to relax?" It's no wonder she's so popular all over the county.

Arlene Bunsen wasn't home when Ella called. The phone rang eight times, exactly enough time for Clarence to step out of the shower, grab a towel, navigate the stacks of old clothes and curios and boxes of books in the upstairs hall, where Arlene was preparing a glacial contribution to the rummage sale, and clamber carefully down the bare wood stairs (being aware of where the two sharp nailheads stuck up) and trot demurely into the kitchen and reach for the phone as it stopped ringing. His midday shower was due to a mishap at the garage involving a quart of motor oil he hadn't known was open, and he assumed the call was from Clint to apologize for what he said. This cheered Clarence up right away. Arlene was driving to Lutheran Women's Circle lunch, which Bea mentioned right after she was done sighing. She said, "The lunch will be by Arlene Bunsen and you know that's always something to look forward to. Mmmmm, yes." Bea didn't know Arlene from a bale of hay but still it was nice of her to say that, Arlene thought, listening to WLB as she drove past the school. Charitable. Arlene was also leading the devotions: maybe she'd mention charity. For lunch she was making a soup that Bea Lady had given out the recipe for last April, Primavera Soup. A white-bean soup with celery, bacon, two big onions, garlic, salt and pepper, oil, and bouillon, and Arlene was going early to church so she could prepare it in private and put red wine in. Devotions would be the love chapter from First Corinthians. She wheeled the big Fairlane up next to the back door, put the wine under her coat, and went to work. The kitchen was chilly. She kept her coat on. She put all the ingredients into the big soup kettle and poured in a cup of wine—two cups—three (the alcohol burns off, you know). This spring she is going to blow some life into Women's Circle, bring up important topics at devotions, assign books by exciting authors, and maybe bring in speakers who know something we don't. The Primavera Soup was bubbling along—meanwhile Arlene was distracted by thoughts of her new job as chairman of Memorial Day, which Clifford with a burst and a flourish had presented her with the day before, a tremendous honor, but who could she get to speak?—she tasted the soup, which needed more salt, and she took down the big tin shaker and salted the soup and the top fell off so that all the salt fell in the soup, a cup and a half or so, and dissolved instantly. It was 11:15. She dumped the Primavera down the drain and rinsed out the pot with a blast of scalding water. The only canned soup they had was cream of mushroom, twenty gallons of the stuff. Lutheran manna, it's called. A food group all by itself: cream of mushroom. Some ladies put it in half the dishes they make—meatloaf, tuna hotdish, meatball delight, even chow mein. Mrs. Tollerud once poured it as a sauce over prime-rib steaks at the mister's seventieth birthday.

Arlene cranked open ten cans, dumped the grayish glop in the pot and ten cans of water, stirred, drank the rest of the wine, and wrapped the empty bottle in a paper bag and stuck it in an empty soup can as the women came trooping in. She looked tired but game as she read to them, "Though I speak with the tongues of men and of angels and have not charity, I am become as sounding brass or a tinkling cymbal." She felt dizzy. She said grace with her eyes open to keep the horizon in sight. She served up the soup with a tin dipper and sat down at the end of the table. In thirty-five minutes she could go home and cry and take a nap. But as the twenty-six women tasted it, they each gave a little cry of pleasure and turned to her and said, "Oh, Arlene. This is the *best soup*. What did you put in this?"

"It's straight out of the can."

"It can't be. What did you—what kind of mushrooms did you put in?"

"They came with the soup."

"Don't be silly, this is *so delicious*—is this a French recipe? Doesn't this taste French to you, Marilyn?" Yes, Marilyn thought it had a *sort* of Frenchness to it but nót heavily French, not so spicy and rich like so much French cooking tends to be. A suggestion of spice, a delicacy, a hint of mushroom, a very *light* French quality. They ate up every last spoonful and afterward they sighed, which made the soup seem even more delicious. Arlene excused herself. The others heard a report from Judy Ingqvist about Lutheran Lyceum, all finished for the season except the final performance (Mr. and Mrs. Ernie Lundeen and Their Performing Gospel Birds) on May 20, but even not counting the popular Lundeens, Lyceum was a big success, the December concert with George Beverly Shea and the Concordia Choir packing more people into the church than anyone thought possible: *nine hundred*, including the overflow in the basement and Sunday-school annex and the crush in the cloakroom and furnace room, and that didn't count the choir and singer and conductor and pianist and bus-driver/harpist. An outstanding musical event, and when he sang "How Great Thou Art" people wept, and when he invited everyone to sing "Silent Night" and the entire building sang and then softly hummed the old Christmas lullaby, the tears flowed freely, people just fell apart in pieces over it. It was good they were packed in tight. The Lyceum series had also brought in a gymnastics act called the Five Tumbling Pastors and Little Wally Holmberg the World's Tiniest Evangelist (4'2"), which Judy mentioned briefly. The choir concert was wonderful enough. You don't need to be wonderful all the time.

(Did I mention that, when Arlene left, she asked Judy Ingqvist to step outside for a moment and there, weeping, she begged her old friend to take the chairmanship of Memorial Day because after the soup disaster and what with all the pressure she was under at the Council with this sewage thing, she didn't think she could handle another thing, and that Judy said, "Yes, of course"? No? Well, that's exactly what happened.)

Before May 20 *or* Memorial Day rolled around, however, Judy got a letter saying that the Performing Gospel Birds were indisposed and that a Lutheran flamenco troupe, La Pasionaria del Norte, would come instead. She was concerned about the birds, and phoned the Lyceum office in Chicago and talked to a man named Em who tried to sign her up for next season. He said there would be a Christian magician and also a troupe of firewalkers from the Ecuadorean jungle, former headhunters who were thought to possess a shrunken missionary—the entire body, not just the head. Em's voice dropped to a whisper: "There's an outside chance they might take the body with them on tour. I hope not, and we're doing everything we can to stop them, but they're not easy to deal with, and frankly they scare me."

The *only* reason Lake Wobegon Lutheran had signed up with the Lyceum, she told him—the single solitary reason—was to get the Concordia Choir and Mr. Shea, those two, nothing else, and an Ecuadorean troupe would be a tough ticket to sell, so if he was thinking of raising his prices on that account— "No, of course not," he said. He was hurt. "I do this work out of my *basement*," he said. "Maybe you think I'm a big promoter up in a swanky office suite, but I can assure you I'm not. I barely clear my expenses." His voice cracked. "I went into this work twenty-three years ago, when my friend Dr. Wallace Graves Peterson told me he was considering giving away glassware and tableware to get people into church for midweek services. That was the situation. Churches empty. Lutheran Lyceum is bringing people in for entertaining programs that also preach the Word, and once you get them in, you can get them back. That's our motto." She asked about the Gospel Birds and he said that one of the doves had flown into a stained-glass window at a performance in Ashland and broken a wing. "You're going to love the flamenco group," he said.

La Pasionaria del Norte was six Lutherans from Monte Olivetta Church, near Madrid, in the suburb of Brookdale, three olive-skinned slim-hipped *caballeros* with dark flashing eyes and three black-haired *señoritas* in flaming red dresses: passionate and extravagant, and yet Lutheran. They traced their faith back to a ship en route from Norway to England in 1783 that was caught in a nor'wester and blown off course. It landed on the Spanish coast, where kind Spaniards took them in and fed them rice in tomato sauce with green peppers and hamburger (what we know as Spanish rice) and in return the Norwegians gave them the Epistle to the Romans.

Val Tollefson was supposed to meet La Pasionaria at the St. Cloud bus depot at 5:45 on May 20 and drive them to church in his van but unbeknownst to Judy he had forgotten. He and Florence had found their cat, Magic, dead in the alley early that afternoon, not a mark on him, poisoned (they were pretty sure) by a resentful neighbor, and when they tried to think just who might've done it, everyone seemed a plausible suspect. Everyone had some grudge against them. It was depressing. They put Magic's body in the freezer to await an autopsy and after a while Val, upset, thinking about sneaking downstairs for a glass of whiskey, said that maybe they'd feel better if they worked outside for a while. He figured she'd get busy digging around her flowers and he could have a snort, but when he got to work hauling down storm windows she insisted on helping him, and at approximately five o'clock he dropped one on her. She reached up, not knowing how heavy it was, and it conked her on the forehead and knocked her dizzy.

She sat down on the grass, bleeding. Blood ran down her face. "I'm all right," she said. "You go without me. You go and enjoy yourself and have a good time."

He helped her indoors, put an icebag on the bump, and laid her out on the couch. "I'm all right. You don't need to fuss over me." Her right eye was swollen and turning black. "I'm sure it's going to be a lot of fun. You go. I'll be all right. You go and I'll just stay and have some quiet time with the Lord." Her tongue was bloody.

Val ran to get Dr. DeHaven, first stopping in the basement to settle his nerves with a pull of Old Crow from the workbench drawer. He drove to the doctor's house, where a note on the door said: "At Cabin All Day." He drove like a bat out of hell six miles to Lake Malene and banged on the cabin door. A dog snarled inside. He let it out. "Find Ernie, Rex!" he said. The dog looked confused. Was its name not Rex or was it a guest dog who had no idea of the doctor's whereabouts? Or did it know him by his last name?

"Find Dr. DeHaven!" The dog turned and raced to the lake and ran into the water up to its chest, and barked. A red boat sat far away, a speck with two men in it. Val, imagining Florence in convulsions, ran back to the cabin and grabbed an old blue fiberglass canoe by one end and hauled it into the water, ran back for a paddle, ran out to catch the canoe floating away, and boarded it in four feet of water, which wore him out. Nevertheless, he paddled hard toward the fishing boat, yelling "Hey!" over and over, trying to steer and paddle, his fist scraping the side on every stroke, his breath coming harder and harder, the Heys weakening, until he stopped to rest for a moment and felt his heart convulsing and took out a pen to write a message about Florence in case he should die. The only paper he could find was his checkbook. He thought: oh, what an ironic end to a life too much spent as a church treasurer and member of the building committee. He wrote in big black letters: "HELP FLORENCE AT HOME, SHE'S HURT BAD. DON'T WORRY ABOUT ME. I'M ALL RIGHT." He signed it, "Love, Val," and then, thinking of his children, he added, "With All My (Love, Val)." He felt limp as a dishrag. The red boat seemed to be moving off to another spot. Val slumped down into the canoe and set his head on the seat and dozed, the little craft rocking on the waves of Lake Malene. Meanwhile, it was 6:30, and then 7:00, there was no flamenco troupe at church, though twenty-seven people came and waited around, including Mavis, whose last name Judy forgets

(Thorsen), who kept asking, "Can I help?" Judy was trying to raise Val on the phone. Finally she ran up to his house and pounded on the door.

Florence answered. She had an icepack on her head and looked dazed and weepy. "Val hit me," she said. "With a storm window. He was up on the ladder—" She started weeping in earnest. "I was trying to help—I didn't know it was so heavy." She leaned and Judy caught her and walked her in and sat her in the big blue easy chair covered with clear plastic. A photograph of their daughter Sherry sat in a gold frame, the poor girl whose life was ruined when she was elected Senior Homecoming Princess, missing out on Queen by (it was said) three votes, losing to a girl who had despised her since they were five.

The haunted blond face made Judy forget about La Pasionaria. She perched on the arm of the blue chair and held Sherry's graduation picture in her hands, wishing she had the power to change that tragic life that kept going wrong. Wrong college (Concordia in southern California, full of successful Lutheran girls) and then the stigma of dropping out after a month, then a bad job (secretary in a Lutheran Life & Auto office where she sat staring out at the empty parking lot), then a bad relationship with a basketball player, finally a bad marriage to his younger brother, and three little whiny children and a messy little house and a problem with Bailey's Irish Cream, and now she hardly ever washes her long blond hair, all because she couldn't be Queen.

"How's Sherry?" asked Judy.

Florence said, "She's just fine. She's very happy." Florence's left eye was swollen shut and there was dried blood around her lips. Judy thought: *That bastard. Storm window my foot. Why does she lie for him?* She wiped off Florence's face and went to get her more ice and then she found the cat's body in the freezer. Yes, it was a cat all right. On the plastic bag, written in black grease pencil, was the word "MAGIC." Judy shuddered. She shut the freezer door. *Magic*. The man certainly made no attempts to hide his tracks. Odd for a Lutheran. The first priority was to protect Florence from seeing this, assuming she hadn't already. One thing to be beaten by your church-deacon husband but quite another to know the man kills pets and uses the bodies in cult rituals. Judy shuddered to think of what she had to do, but she got out a grocery bag and was about to open the freezer when the phone rang. It was Mavis, asking if she could help. Judy thought. "Yes," she said. "Tell them there's no show. Just lock up the church and go home. Can you do that?" Then she put the cat in the grocery bag and carried it out and put it in the trunk of her car. She was going to confront Val with it directly, no tiptoeing around. *Explain this. And then explain why you're belting your wife around. What sort of secret group are you in and what activities are they engaging in? And exactly how many other members of the church are involved? Tell the truth.*

She found Val when the red boat towed him to shore and Dr. DeHaven (who had been in his basement, not at the cabin, which was now his son Jim's anyway, whose dog it was, an old fishing dog named Bruno, now deaf) gave him a couple antihistamines on general principle and drove him home. Judy drove all around town looking for him and there he was sitting on his own back step, bewildered. He told her the truth about his poor cat Magic. She felt sorry for him, but not so sorry that she couldn't pass on the Memorial Day chairmanship. "I hope that, in all this confusion, you haven't forgotten that you're the chairman of Memorial Day," she said. "We're all counting on you for something good." He was too weak to resist, and he was so worn out that he went to bed and slept twelve hours and forgot all about Memorial Day until the morning of the 30th, when he saw flags all over town. He panicked. Then he saw me and thought, *Speaker.* I was heading into the Mercantile to buy a white shirt. I was in town visiting my Aunt Myrna and Uncle Earl, two of the greatest people in the world, so I was in an amiable mood. We'd just eaten chocolate cake and ice cream for breakfast. That's how wonderful they are. Val took my elbow and told me how wonderful I was and then and there, on the sidewalk outside the Mercantile, under Lorraine's seductive glance, he popped the question.

Well, I'd once recited the Gettysburg Address at Memorial Day and heard Aunt Eleanor afterward declare it the finest performance of the spoken word she had ever heard, so I said okay, and two hours later I was in procession behind the Sons of Knute honor guard, heading up the hill to the cemetery, full of magnificent oratory about home and community and family and friends, about life and death and the price of coffee, a lovely extemporaneous speech that as I hiked up in the hot sun and stood in the hot sun in front of the GAR obelisk and listened to the Ladies' Sextette sing "Abide With Me" and young Ben Tollerud recite "O Captain! my Captain!" seemed to expand larger and larger in my head until it came to include the entirety of all essential truth about our existence on earth. For a minute there, facing the crowd of familiar faces that looked like a Monet painting when I took my glasses off, I was in possession of a vast brilliant message, a gift of the Holy Spirit, and felt like Jeremiah must have felt when God said, "Here, say this." And then somehow it came loose. Maybe it was the note the ladies hit on "foil the tempter's power"—Arlene had quit the group a week before, saying she was too old and her voice was ruined and she couldn't sing anymore: a blow to the other five because she was their best singer, and Florence was no prize as a replacement—or it might've been the Lord's Prayer coming on the heels of the Address and making me think, "Our Father Who art in heaven, hallow this ground so that I shall not die in vain," but die I did, in plain view of everyone in town, including the ten or twelve I've wanted all my life to impress. I gave a horseshit speech.

What I wanted to talk about was whether the boys of the First Minnesota Brigade, including the one buried here, who made their heroic and brutal counterattack on July 2, 1863, at Gettysburg against Longstreet's army that had found a great vacancy in the Union line and was swinging into position against its flank to roll up Meade and run him straight to Washington and win the war for the Confederacy—whether those boys thought of us in the future and what the country would come to, what they were fighting for and who would keep their memory—would they have *liked* us? or would our America horrify them? And how all two hundred of them jumped up off the grass and ran toward the smoke. They could've run for the river but they ran into the smoke, because that's where everyone else was running and they were loyal to each other, loved each other, so in some way they loved the nation and us and our life that owes so much to them. Only forty of them came back out of the smoke; the rest were dead or wounded. Young men in the spring of life. A hot day, thick smoke, horses shrieking and men screaming horribly in that unbearable cannon fire around the peach orchard and meadow. But they all ran into the smoke, and how this somehow changes everything. The citizens of death. Our duty to honor them, a *lovely* duty. It's a civic duty to look at death and thus see life clear, and how life—the furtherance of life—is the purpose of the state and community—parenthood—the value of storytelling—our connection to each other— It was a long horseshit speech, stumbling around in the thickness of my mind and trying to seem profound by saying dumb things and pausing after each one, and when I talked about loving each other, all of my neighbors looked down in the grass and waited for it to stop.

I soon obliged them. There was applause. They all congratulated me afterward and said it was wonderful, except Clint, who put his hand on my shoulder and said, "One nice thing is that when it's done, it's all over," and he was right. I am so sorry about all of them lying dead on the hill, the trooper from the First Minnesota and all the old women and the farmers, all the kids who died of diphtheria and influenza, and now my classmate Corinne, and I wish my speech had been great, just as I wish we could bring them all back to life, but it's over and now summer can begin. School can let out. Baseball gets going and the sweet corn begins to get serious. Soon the very first ear will appear—on Aunt Myrna's good china platter one Sunday after church, a faint yellow ear of corn, steaming hot, glistening with butter and crystals of salt—and then the life to come will start to begin.

WHO DO YOU THINK
YOU ARE?

Hey

IT HAS BEEN *a quiet week in Lake Wobegon, my hometown* was
such a sweet line all those years on the radio, the standard opening
of each week's story, a pleasant, modest, *useful* sentence, considering
how many writers stew over their opening lines (e.g., "Ray opened
the refrigerator door and bent down to look for the margarine"), and
most stories stop there and wind up in the wastebasket, brilliant stories
wasted because the first sentence wasn't as brilliant as what would
soon follow, so the writer quit and his masterpiece, his *In Our Time*,
his *Great Gatsby*, his *Collected Stories of John Cheever*, never got
written because the first sentence opened like a rusty gate, and is it
so different for you and me? The marvelous work we could do if only
we didn't have to *begin* it but could start in at the middle. The things
we could accomplish if only we didn't know what we are doing until
later.

It has been a quiet week in Lake Wobegon gets you right in there,
into the dim recesses of the Chatterbox Cafe, the air lit up with the
smell of hot caramel rolls, where three heavy men in dark-green
shirts hunker in the back booth under the Allis Chalmers calendar
("Krebsbach Farm Implement / New & Used Since 1912 / JUniper
5610") and drink black coffee, refilled by Dorothy in her big pink
uniform, who doesn't ask if they'd like more (Do bears pee in the

132

woods?), she just pours, as they commiserate on the lousy world situation and console each other with a few beloved old jokes about animals in barrooms. There was this man who trained his dog to go around the corner to Bud's Lounge with a dollar bill under his collar and get a pack of cigarettes and bring them home, until one day the man only had a five, so he put it under the dog's collar and sent him down, waited an hour, and no dog, so he got mad and went to Bud's and there was the pooch sitting up on a stool drinking a vodka gimlet. He said, "You've never done this before!" The dog looked straight ahead and said, "I never had the money before."

One problem with *It has been a quiet week in Lake Wobegon* is that you couldn't go straight from that into talking about dreams of boundless grandeur and the many-rivered generosity of life, but, then, it was that way when I lived there, too. Dreams we did not discuss, they were embarrassing in normal conversation, especially big ones. We sat at supper, Dad at one end, Mother at the other, children in the stanchions along the sides, and talked quietly about the day's events. We might discuss the immediate future such as a history test the day after tomorrow or Bible camp next June, but the distant future, 1964, 1980, was inscrutable, due to the imminence of the Second Coming. And there was to be no grandeur. Once, just to see how it would sound coming out of my mouth, I said I was going to college someday. "College" rhymes with "knowledge." I was ten years old and words were as good as food in my mouth. I chewed my food fast so as to clear the way to be able to say more. "I'm going to go to college," I stated. My sister laughed: Who d'ya think *you* are? She was right, I didn't know.

What I didn't dare mention was my other dream of going into the show business, a faint dream because we were Christian people and wouldn't dream of doing immoral things, though I hoped to find a way around this. I mentioned S.B. to Mrs. Hoglund, the piano teacher, and she told me the story of the famous Swenson Sisters, who hailed from nearby Kimball, a girls' quartet who sang at summer resorts including Moonlite Bay and who, one cold winter day in 1954, won the St. Paul Winter Carnival Outdoor Talent Contest, and the next week boarded the morning Zephyr to Chicago and then the Super Chief to Hollywood. They signed a contract with Fairmont Pictures to make a movie called *Minnesota Moon* but then the producer, Leo Lawrence, took a deep drag on his stogie and growled, "Kids, I love this script, it's beautiful, I loved every bit of it except the cows and the lakes and the farmers—we're going to change them to camels and desert oases and thousands of Bedouins galloping hard over the desolate sands," so the movie became *Moon over Morocco* and the Swenson Sisters became the Casablanca Quartet, dressed in vast black robes, their faces veiled, and their career went down like a concrete block and by 1955 they were back at Gull Lake, singing at Hilmer's Supper Club (Beer & Setups, Fish Fry—All U Can Eat Friday Nites), and their dream was just an old black shell of a burned-down house. What's more, they, who had gone away innocent and filled with shining hope, returned home four hardened women with dark-crimson lipstick who smoked Luckys and drank vodka gimlets and when they laughed, they laughed a deep laugh, like men, laced with pain, and so of course men would have nothing to do with them, and they fell into unnatural forms of love. There ended the story; she would say no more. *They tried to go too far,* and it should be a lesson to the rest of us: not to imagine we *are* somebody but to be content being who we are, Minnesotans.

I'm very proud to be a Minnesotan and have been proud since I was a kid and first traveled to see our beautiful State Capitol building in St. Paul. Our fourth-grade class got up at six o'clock and rode a schoolbus down to meet the governor. We had studied state government for a month, the duties of governor, lieutenant governor, secretary of state, and other state officers, and the legislature and the state commissions and boards, which didn't prepare us for the grandeur and sheer magnificence of the great white temple spread on the crest of a gentle hill, the bank of steps rising to the pillars, the golden horses and golden chariot high above, and the dome, the largest anywhere in the Christian world, so it appeared. We camped in the bus, eating liverwurst sandwiches and drinking green Kool Aid, waiting for our 11:00 A.M. appointment. Mrs. Erickson said that she was trusting us to be on our best behavior indoors, but she didn't have to worry, we were stunned, we shuffled along with the dumb dignity of the barely conscious. Indoors was even more magnificent, such opulence as a child might imagine from fairy tales but never associate with our modest prairie state, long vast echoey marble halls, marble statues, oil paintings, and a room with a gold ceiling and a rug three inches thick, and there was the governor of Minnesota, the leader of our people, physically present in the room with us.

We formed a straight line and gravely filed one by one past Mrs. Erickson, who whispered our name to a grim-faced man, who then whispered it to the governor, who shook our hands and said, "Hello, Stanley, it's good to meet you." This was thrilling, until suddenly, when Mrs. Erickson whispered *Shirley*, Shirley clapped her hand over her mouth and rushed away to the toilet, but her name had gone into the pipeline and when the governor shook Billy's hand he said, "Hello, Shirley, it's good to meet you." He smiled the same warm smile and went right on calling all the rest of the class by the wrong name, including Elaine, who was called Robert. I was called John. He was the governor but he wasn't what you'd call bright.

It was so amazing how many kids (mostly girls) later defended him, saying he was a busy man, had a lot on his mind, had to run the state, etc. We boys said, No, he's dumb. How can you look at a boy and say, Hello, Shirley. The girls said, How do you know Shirley isn't a boy's name, too? Show us where it says Shirley *can't* be a boy's name. How do *you* know? Who do you think *you* are? You're not so smart.

Who do you think you are? You're from Lake Wobegon. You shouldn't think *you're* somebody.

You're no better than the rest of us.

Some of our teachers, however, such as Miss Heinemann, believed that we were good enough and could be improved with proper instruction, and so she set Shakespeare's sonnets in front of us, *Macbeth*, Wordsworth, Chaucer, and expected us to read them and to discuss what was on the page, and if any of us had been so bold as to aspire to a life in literature, she'd have been pleased as punch. The higher the better.

She strolls the aisles between our desks, swishing past in her dull-brown dress, talking about metaphor, the use of language to mean more than what we know it to mean, whereby common things, such as a rose, a birch tree, the dark sky, rain falling, come to mean something else for which there isn't an exact word. She talks about literature as being urgent, impulsively bold, unavoidable, like stopping your car on the highway at night and stepping out and walking alone into dark damp woods because it's unbearable to only know what's in your headlights. Art calls us out of the regulated life into a life that is dangerous, free. I remembered that when I was chosen class poet, to participate in the winter homecoming program and, after the procession of Queen Aileen to the throne and the singing of her favorite song, to stand and recite her favorite poem. Her favorite song was "Vaya Con Dios" but she didn't have a favorite poem, she said, so I said, "That's okay, Aileen, I'll choose a real good one for you." I had in mind a few lines from Whitman's "Song of Myself," beginning:

I tramp a perpetual journey, (come listen all!)
My signs are a rain-proof coat, good shoes, and a staff cut
    from the woods,
No friend of mine takes his ease in my chair,
I have no chair, no church, no philosophy,
I lead no man to a dinner-table, library, exchange,
But each man and each woman of you I lead upon a knoll,
My left hand hooking you round the waist,

My right hand pointing to landscapes of continents and the
    public road.

Not I, not any one else can travel that road for you,
You must travel it for yourself.

But first I had to show it to Miss Heinemann for her approval.
She was incredulous. "Aileen *Heidenschink* chose this? This is her
favorite poem? Aileen?" No, not exactly, Miss H., it's one that I
thought might be one that— "I think that on Aileen's big day you
might come up with something more appropriate than this. Really.
I have no church, no philosophy? Aileen is Catholic. Her family will
be sitting there. Think."

I *was* thinking, that the Queen's Favorite Poem was a rare occasion
when Art had a chance to lift its hairy head and call my classmates
toward a higher spiritual life, but Miss Heinemann didn't see it that
way; she said, "Don't be mean to Aileen. Find something she'll enjoy,
like 'Invictus.' Or else don't do it," which disgusted me, idealist that
I was, and also was a huge relief, because the thought of reciting Walt
Whitman to a gym full of Lake Wobegon made me sick with fear.
So I bowed out as Homecoming Poet on the issue of artistic freedom,
keeping my principles intact and taking a big load off my mind at the
same time.

Hey

Thirty years later I lived in St. Paul, in a big brick house on Crocus
Hill, a nice neighborhood where if you needed to buy a volume of
Whitman or a dozen white Japanese candles or a Mozart piano con-
certo you could find it in a shop close by, but if you wanted caulking
compound you'd have to get in the car and drive a mile to Seven
Corners Hardware, where graceful old houses were restored to a
condition of elegance such as the builders could scarcely have imagined
and were lived in by people with plenty of books and lots of money.

When I sat in Miss Heinemann's class, I was reading *Main Street* and *Babbitt*, imagining myself as a rebel against the materialism and provincialism of the Midwest as Sinclair Lewis described it, the culture of the Shriners and boosters and plumbers and shopkeepers and dull solid unimaginative people who seemed to dominate the landscape and hold us mysterious and artistic people back from our destiny. But now, a quarter-century later in my neighborhood, all the shops sold beauty and music and art and cuisine and nobody could tell me where to find a little replacement part for the burners in my furnace. This burned me up, because I am a writer and have stories to create and couldn't afford to spend a whole Monday morning running around St. Paul looking for a tiny grommet or nipple or whatever it's called that the gas flows through when it burns. I drove to a plumbing-and-heating shop and got the impression that furnaces were only a sideline for them, that they were really performance artists waiting for word on their new video and then they'd be off to New York.

"I never saw one of those," a man there said, "where'd you get it?"

"I got it off my furnace, of course."

"How do you know it doesn't work?"

"The house is cold."

I drove home. The Blazer had a funny clicking sound in the axle. I'd had it in to the garage three times but they were artists, too, not dull technicians who do menial jobs like figuring out why my car clicks. I paid them money and the car still went k-chick, k-chick, and when I called to complain they said, "We didn't hear anything." They were avant-garde automotive artists of anti-mechanical repair, their purpose to confront me, their audience, with my car's problems. For this I paid $112.32, money I earned by sitting in a little room by myself and writing in such a way that a reader runs the risk of laughter, a pleasurable sensation of trembling along the spine.

It's a good piece of work for a middle-aged man who feels as depressed as I do sometimes. I keep my weight down, am constantly seeking more fiber, bang around on a racquetball court twice a week, and try to relax and enjoy life, but two days a week I feel lousy. Some day *Reader's Digest* will print an article about the tiny gland below the kneecap called the hermer that produces a thin golden fluid that enables the brain to feel pleasure: if a person quits the bad habit of crossing his legs, his hermer can recover and life become wonderful. But so far all the *Digest* says is what I already know: drink plenty of liquids. I need to know something more miraculous than that, the secret of happiness. What, as a child, I thought Christmas would give or college or show business, and, as a youth, I thought that sex would give, now, as a man, I am still looking for. I thought I'd find it in my writing but writing is only work, like auto repair except more professional.

I remember when I switched from Christmas to sex as the secret of happiness, it was when I saw a dirty magazine at Shinder's newsstand, corner of Hennepin and Sixth in Minneapolis, down the street from the Rifle Sport pinball parlor, a rough block. Every alley smelled of piss. Tough guys lounged under the marquees of dirty theaters and yelled remarks at girls passing by, like "Hey, baby! Wanna come home wimmy?" Drunks sat collapsed in doorways. I had been at the public library up on Tenth, where dirty magazines were not offered, though I searched for days, and where all the cards in the card catalogue under "Sexual" were marked "Inquire at Desk." I decided to wander down to Shinder's and sidle inside and examine the merchandise. I picked up a copy of *Life* and tucked another magazine inside it, called *Peek*, with a photo of a woman with her shirt off, which, in 1958, excited me to the very core of my being, which suddenly I knew which part of my being that was, and I began to indulge a rich imaginative life that eventually settled on a lovely person whom I dreamed of marrying. Thoughts of her kept me awake at night, standing at the window and staring out across the snow, and when, after years of thinking those thoughts and courting her and getting engaged and the date of our marriage fast approaching when I would cross over the river into the land of bliss, the excitement was debilitating.

Now, of course, young people cross over into the land of bliss pretty much whenever they want to. There are bridges, there are islands in the river, and the water is so low that most places you can wade across, but back then the river was wide and deep and fast and the church owned the boats. The church ferried you across to the land of bliss and you stayed there for the rest of your life with the one you went across with, or so we believed. Marriage was a fact, immense.

One cold fall day, three days before we would walk up the aisle and into a motel room, my mind full of carnal thoughts, I took a walk along the Mississippi near where I lived, thinking the cold would clear my mind, but cold is an aphrodisiac, as we Minnesotans know, and I rehearsed once again in my mind exactly how I would go about making love, changing some details, tossing in a few improvements, and I practiced making ecstatic cries. I'd never made love before and had never cried out in an ecstatic way (except one Christmas when I got a Lionel train, but "Oh, boy, thanks, Mom and Dad" was wrong for sex) and I wanted to do it right. Spontaneously, freely, joyously, but also correctly. I stood at the edge of Riverside Park above the river, looking across toward the gray shapes of the University, and attempted to make outbursts of sexual passion. Loud ones like Tarzan, soft sighs, grunts, some growling. I tried yipping and wahooing, even something sort of like yodeling.

Then it hit me: what if sex for her and me turned out to be nothing to yip and wahoo about, but a series of small and sort of interesting events like a checkers match in the course of which you'd just say, "Are you having a good time?" or "As long as I'm up, can I get you anything?" I was a Minnesota guy and we are no great lovers. Minnesotans make love once a month, on the 15th, and when it's over and done with they don't whoop and holler or smoke a cigarette and listen to Bach, they get up and brush their teeth. Then they go to bed. When a Minnesotan sleeps with someone, normally he sleeps. I knew this. Who did I think I was, a movie star?

Minnesota was a repressive place to grow up in and there's a lot I'd change, even as I think about sunny bygone days in Lake Wobegon. The fear of being different paralyzed every kid I knew, and there was so little room for affection, so much space for cruelty. People didn't have enough fun. Above all, we learned to repress the urge to achieve and be recognized, because the punishment for being different was so heavy. It might be postponed for a while, but when it fell on you, it fell hard, as when I wrote a book about Minnesota, called *Lake Wobegon Days*, and the local newspaper put me in my place but good. They marked my front yard with orange rinds and nailed a dead cat to the porch. I started to nourish the thought of leaving for someplace like Australia, the farthest away you can go and still speak English, and wondered if, in the long flight, I'd sleep and wake up as the finer person I longed to be, a sweet-tempered marsupial man who'd hang by his tail and cry out ecstatically whenever he felt like it, to hell with the newspaper.

Hey

St. Paul was a beautiful city until it got so small, a shame, but life itself is brief, and that is what charges the day with such ridiculous beauty. A summer night in St. Paul is so beautiful it makes you sad, to walk along Goodrich Avenue in the dark and hear the water sprinklers whisper across the grass and hit the bushes. You smell raw grass and sweet water, and hear voices whispering from the front porches, behind the dark screens. Lights in upstairs bedrooms and a child momentarily framed in a window, and porch lights on in one big old frame manse after another, they must be waiting for someone. Waiting for you perhaps, and whispering about you, too: "My friend will be here soon, I can't wait, I'm so excited." The great lover out for a walk, the lover of his own good town. A radio is on in this low bungalow, low seductive voices there, and a cat has stretched out its loins on the cool cement. You sidestep her and stroll into a spray of water leaking from a hose that wets your pants, and then enter an aroma of hamburgers and charcoal smoke, drifting from behind a fence. The life we all know, God bless it, like it says in the hymn: *Blest be the tie that binds our hearts in Christian love; the fellowship of kindred minds is like to that above.*

Whenever I felt lucky and happy this street was like a watercolor, *St. Paul, Summer Night,* but when I was scared it seemed real and I imagined if I threw myself on the bosom of St. Paul, it would catch me. *We share our mutual woes, our mutual burdens bear, and often for each other flows the sympathizing tear. Before our Father's throne, we pour our mutual prayers; our fears, our hopes, our aims are one, our comforts and our cares.* Love has the power to rescue us and not let go, otherwise it isn't love.

I was scared because I had to sing songs and talk on the radio, a deep hole that lay waiting in a theater downtown, but it's no worse than anyone else's problems. To stand up in a black tux and sing in a trio, "Only a boy from Anoka who loved to dance the polka, but Oh Oh Oh" and "It's all right to get your appetite walking 'round town, just as long as you eat supper at home" is not one inch closer to death than having to give a book report or play centerfield, it's just that it was happening to *me.* I'd walk around the block trying to remember the lyrics to a new song we had to do on the show that night, like "In a little Spanish town I walked around and searched for you, my love. The stars above seem to say, She went away. I don't know where—Oh, don't you care for me? In my revery, I love you, I love you, I love you. I'll say it once again: in a little Spanish town, our hacienda home, I love you, I love you, my own."

I was scared, I thought: "How come we didn't rehearse this? *I* woulda rehearsed if somebody had just *called* me." But we hardly rehearsed even the songs we already knew, let alone new ones. We just sang them once and said, "Oh, sure. That's easy." We were so cool.

"This is terrible," I thought. "They're all going to laugh. They'll write about it in the newspaper, what a big joke it was. We can't do this song."

St. Paul was a place where I believed that if I knocked on the nearest door a woman would open it and when I said, "I feel bad. Can I talk to you?" she'd say, Sure, come on in.

I felt that I was theirs, that Minnesota people were people you could hurl yourself bodily from the stage at and they would catch you and not let you go, but the sad truth is that they only catch you if you fail; if you do well, then you're on your own. It's that way everywhere. The prodigal son's brother knew that: it's failure and disgrace that win the parent's love. You blow the song and people will be nice to you; you make it a big hit and the newspaper will walk up to your house and pee on your roses. And if you feel bad, too bad. Who are you to complain? You got what you wanted, didn't you?

Hey

I left St. Paul in the summer, a sad season for a happy man because summer is so short. When I was young and miserable, all change was for the better, but when you're forty-five, almost nothing can be better, so you grieve for every leaf that falls. June sails in on a warm starry night when a band is playing and you stand on a veranda with your hand around Amanda's pajamas and then summer is gone in a minute, it's fall, a reminder that we, too, are temporary and can be replaced. The beat goes on but I can't dance to it anymore. Of course, I never could dance at all, having grown up in a fundamentalist home, which you can tell by the way I move. We believed that any rhythmic physical movement would awaken our carnal desires, as surely as aspirin dissolves in a bottle of Coke, so we kids had to sit in study hall when they taught dancing in phys ed, couldn't go to dances, not even square ones, couldn't even join marching band. I wanted to dance. Wanted girls to know that what I lacked in aptitude I made up for in sheer avid interest. Couldn't dance because it would awaken carnal desire, which in my case was not only awake, it was dressed and down on the corner waiting for the bus. Those Sanctified Brethren are good people but they do leave a mark on a boy, and even today, when I sweep into a room holding a glass of Pouilly-Fuissé, people see me sweep and say, "I didn't know you were Baptist." I wasn't. We considered Baptists loose.

I also can't dance because I am a shy person on account of my family lived out in the sticks at the end of the schoolbus route and when I climbed aboard all the seats were full. Nobody would move over, but Wendell the bus driver yelled at me to *siddown! State law!* so I picked out the seat with the tiniest girls in it and hurled myself at the outside one and forced her in, and rode twelve miles to school with one foot braced against the opposite seat so they couldn't dump me in the aisle. This was my initial physical contact with the opposite sex. Girls trying to push me away, saying, "Ish, oh, you're disgusting, you make me sick."

A shy person would like to walk away from people and have them call gently to him, "Come back—oh, come back, please please please," and so, to have to hurl yourself at them and hang on, it ruined me as a dancing partner.

One spring day I stood on the gravel road in my new spring shirt from Wards, a light jacket and chino pants and a brand-new pair of penny loafers, listening to the meadowlarks, feeling that finally life was summoning me, that the bus'd come, I'd climb up, and Wendell'd smile and Dede'd pat the empty spot beside her, her strawberry lips forming the words "Here, sit here, next to me." The bus came over the hill, orange, like the sun rising, and stopped, and the door opened. The odor of hair oil and bologna sandwiches rolled out. Wendell looked like the side view on a wanted poster. Everyone was silent, nobody would look at me, they were gripping the seats until their knuckles were white. "That's all right, I'll just stand," I said.

"Siddown."

"Chuckie? Could I sit here with you and Barb?"

"No. I got my lunchbox on the seat, can't you see? Whatddaya expect me to do? Sit with them."

"Bill? Bob? Could I?"

"Huh? What? Are you kidding??? Get outta here."

"Dede?"

She turned away in disgust, as if my presence had ruined the rest of her life and having looked at me she could never be happy again.

"Siddown," he said, "or else get off, whatsamatter witcha anyway." So I got off. Walked to school and was two hours late, took a shortcut across a field where there was a lake of melted snow but I ran through it in faith I'd walk on top and got the new loafers wet. I knew they were ruined, they flapped like slippers. I snuck into Miss Ellefson's eighth-grade English class and slid into my desk just as she looked up and smiled and said, "Today is the day for our five-minute speeches about a personal experience—Gary, let's start with you."

This is that speech, thirty years overdue. Miss Ellefson is dead now, sitting in the teachers' lounge in heaven, enjoying a smoke, and I'm talking about painful matters that would be better forgotten.

Hey

One day while I still lived in St. Paul, I got a bad toothache from biting on peanut brittle and endured it until two o'clock in the afternoon, afraid to look for a new dentist. My old one was a Lutheran who went to India to fix teeth in rural areas, and I was afraid I'd get a real St. Paul Catholic dentist, impervious to pain, one who believed that St. Paul in his epistle to the Anesthesians says that agony can be offered up for God's glory, but instead I found a young woman dentist who gave me Novocain *and* gas and relaxed me so deeply I almost drowned from the spray on the drill, but it was painless. It put me right in a hopeful mood to get a haircut. Ordinarily I'd have gone to Walt's barbershop on Como and said, The usual, and gotten an earful of wisdom about fishing, but he got out of barbering in 1967. Since then I had wandered from shop to shop, looking, hoping. I drove up Grand Avenue and saw a shop called "Hair One Day and Gone the Next—Personal Hair Stylists," and walked in. It was all done in black and white: tile floor, chairs, white walls, black ceiling. The magazines were all about expressing the True Woman Inside You, even the men's magazines were about that. A young woman came around the corner. Yeah? she said. I said, "Uh, you're probably booked up, you wouldn't be able to get me in right away, would you," turning away. Her hair was pink; it looked like she wasn't getting all her vitamins, or was getting some she shouldn't.

"No, I can take you now. My name's Candy."

She was chewing gum. She looked about seventeen. We went to a black cubicle and she sat me in a little black chair. There were stuffed pandas and kangaroos. She put a red silky cloth around me and ruffled my hair and said, "Uhhh, howdja like it?" I almost said, The usual, but to look at Candy there didn't seem to *be* a usual. I said, "Oh, just a trim around the edges and not too short." I tried to sound like it wasn't important. I was brought up to believe beauty is not worth thinking about, what's important is your soul, your mind—you don't want to be a fifty-dollar haircut on a fifty-cent head. But I was feeling hopeful.

She started to cut. She wore a couple dozen plastic bracelets on her hands that clattered in my ear like an old John Deere combine. She didn't talk except once, to ask, "Do you live around here?" I said no. She seemed satisfied to know that and said no more until she unpinned the smock and handed me my glasses. I put them on and saw in the mirror an old old clown. She hadn't painted big blobby lips or a red nose on me but the hair was right. All I needed was a pair of exploding pants.

"How's that?" she said. "That's fine," I said. I was ashamed to complain, which would imply that I had imagined she could make me look nice. "That's sixteen dollars," she said. I gave her a twenty. "Keep the change," I said. A twenty-five-percent tip. Just because a man looks ridiculous doesn't mean he can't pay extra for the privilege. I bought a Twins cap at the drugstore. "Care for some hair cream?" the woman said. Drove home, and walked in the door, steaming mad just like all of us Wobegonians get mad, about twenty minutes after the fact, angry retorts coming to mind too late to be retorted. My wife took one look at me as I took off the cap and she said, "You have the most beautiful green eyes, do you know that?"

Hey

One spring, when my son was little, we got a cat named Mrs. Gray who we decided to allow to have babies so that he could observe at first hand the wonder of life. She was married, obviously, so it was all right. One day she went into heat, put on her lipstick, and lay on her back out on the front lawn, rolling and moaning and smoking cigarettes by the carton, and the gentlemen cats of the neighborhood stood around and watched. They had had operations in their youth, and didn't know what was wrong. They stood around in their yards and discussed mutual funds as she moaned and sang to them, and finally a ringer came by and said, "Hi, doll," and they screamed at each other all afternoon, made love, and she raked him with her claws and drove him away. We explained to the boy that the wonderful part would come later, but when it came time for Mrs. Gray to have her babies, she felt extremely bad. When the first little wet sack of kitten emerged, she looked back at it with horror and tried to run away with the umbilicus still attached. She needed a lot of help. It was a mess. Maternal things didn't seem to be instinctive with her. When I came down to the kitchen to check on her later that night, she climbed out of the box where her little family lay, blind, squeaking, and she ambled over to the back door and scratched on it. She wanted out of the deal. She gave me a baleful look when I locked the door. She said, "That's okay, I can wait. Tomorrow, next week, one of these days that door'll open and I'm gone outa here. I'm gonna leave the wonder of life sitting there in its box for you to take care of, Mister. I got a life of my own to lead."

It was a cool sweet spring night. Sex hadn't worked out for her and neither had Christmas. She was restless, she wanted to go to Los Angeles. I know the feeling. I left Minnesota and since then have known one problem after another but restlessness hasn't been one of them. Ever since I left home and came to New York, I've known exactly who I am. *Ich bin ein* Minnesotan. In Minnesota, it's never really clear what that means, but living in Manhattan, I know *exactly* what Minnesotaness means—it means *moi*—and I plan to stay right here and enjoy it.

All right

3

LETTERS

These letters were written between 1982 and 1988, in roughly this order, and were true at the time. I haven't bothered to fix the little facts that time has altered, such as my age.

—G.K.

HOW TO WRITE A LETTER

W E SHY PERSONS NEED TO WRITE a letter now and then, or else we'll dry up and blow away. It's true. And I speak as one who loves to reach for the phone, dial the number, and talk. I say, "Big Bopper here—what's shakin', babes?" The telephone is to shyness what Hawaii is to February, it's a way out of the woods, *and yet:* a letter is better.

Such a sweet gift—a piece of handmade writing, in an envelope that is not a bill, sitting in our friend's path when she trudges home from a long day spent among wahoos and savages, a day our words will help repair. They don't need to be immortal, just sincere. She can read them twice and again tomorrow: *You're someone I care about, Corinne, and think of often and every time I do you make me smile.*

We need to write, otherwise nobody will know who we are. They will have only a vague impression of us as A Nice Person, because, frankly, we don't shine at conversation, we lack the confidence to thrust our faces forward and say, "Hi, I'm Heather Hooten; let me tell you about my week." Mostly we say "Uh-huh" and "Oh, really." People smile and look over our shoulder, looking for someone else to meet.

So a shy person sits down and writes a letter. To be known by another person—to meet and talk freely on the page—to be close despite distance. To escape from anonymity and be our own sweet selves and express the music of our souls.

Same thing that moves a giant rock star to sing his heart out in front of 123,000 people moves us to take ballpoint in hand and write a few lines to our dear Aunt Eleanor. *We want to be known.* We want her to know that we have fallen in love, that we quit our job, that we're moving to New York, and we want to say a few things that might not get said in casual conversation: *Thank you for what you've meant to me, I am very happy right now.*

The first step in writing letters is to get over the guilt of *not* writing. You don't "owe" anybody a letter. Letters are a gift. The burning shame you feel when you see unanswered mail makes it harder to pick up a pen and makes for a cheerless letter when you finally do. *I feel bad about not writing, but I've been so busy,* etc. Skip this. Few letters are obligatory, and they are *Thanks for the wonderful gift* and *I am terribly sorry to hear about George's death* and *Yes, you're welcome to stay with us next month,* and not many more than that. Write those promptly if you want to keep your friends. Don't worry about the others, except love letters, of course. When your true love writes, *Dear Light of My Life, Joy of My Heart, O Lovely Pulsating Core of My Sensate Life,* some response is called for.

Some of the best letters are tossed off in a burst of inspiration, so keep your writing stuff in one place where you can sit down for a few minutes and (*Dear Roy, I am in the middle of a book entitled* We Are Still Married *but thought I'd drop you a line. Hi to your sweetie, too.*) dash off a note to a pal. Envelopes, stamps, address book, everything in a drawer so you can write fast when the pen is hot.

A blank white eight-by-eleven sheet can look as big as Montana if the pen's not so hot—try a smaller page and write boldly. Or use a note card with a piece of fine art on the front; if your letter ain't good, at least they get the Matisse. Get a pen that makes a sensuous line, get a comfortable typewriter, a friendly word processor—whichever feels easy to the hand.

Sit for a few minutes with the blank sheet in front of you, and meditate on the person you will write to, let your friend come to mind until you can almost see her or him in the room with you. Remember the last time you saw each other and how your friend looked and what you said and what perhaps was unsaid between you, and when your friend becomes real to you, start to write.

Write the salutation—*Dear* You—and take a deep breath and plunge in. A simple declarative sentence will do, followed by another and another and another. Tell us what you're doing and tell it like you were talking to us. Don't think about grammar, don't think about lit'ry style, don't try to write dramatically, just give us your news. Where did you go, who did you see, what did they say, what do you think?

If you don't know where to begin, start with the present moment: *I'm sitting at the kitchen table on a rainy Saturday morning. Everyone is gone and the house is quiet.* Let your simple description of the present moment lead to something else, let the letter drift gently along.

The toughest letter to crank out is one that is meant to impress, as we all know from writing job applications; if it's hard work to slip off a letter to a friend, maybe you're trying too hard to be terrific. A letter is only a report to someone who already likes you for reasons other than your brilliance. Take it easy.

Don't worry about form. It's not a term paper. When you come to the end of one episode, just start a new paragraph. You can go from a few lines about the sad state of pro football to the fight with your mother to your fond memories of Mexico to your cat's urinary-tract infection to a few thoughts on personal indebtedness and on to the kitchen sink and what's in it. The more you write, the easier it gets, and when you have a True True Friend to write to, a *compadre*, a soul sibling, then it's like driving a car down a country road, you just get behind the keyboard and press on the gas.

Don't tear up the page and start over when you write a bad line— try to write your way out of it. Make mistakes and plunge on. Let the letter cook along and let yourself be bold. Outrage, confusion, love—whatever is in your mind, let it find a way to the page. Writing is a means of discovery, always, and when you come to the end and write *Yours ever* or *Hugs and kisses*, you'll know something you didn't when you wrote *Dear Pal*.

Probably your friend will put your letter away, and it'll be read again a few years from now—and it will improve with age. And forty years from now, your friend's grandkids will dig it out of the attic and read it, a sweet and precious relic of the ancient eighties that gives them a sudden clear glimpse of you and her and the world we old-timers knew. You will then have created an object of art. Your simple lines about where you went, who you saw, what they said, will speak to those children and they will feel in their hearts the humanity of our times.

You can't pick up a phone and call the future and tell them about our times. You have to pick up a piece of paper.

ESTATE

TWENTY YEARS AGO, I quit college and got a job on a daily paper. It was a long jump for a young punk, but I was restless in school, felt useless, and had romantic ideas about newspapering, and also I was broke. They gave me a seat at the city desk—a horseshoe table where the city editor sat at the apex, the assistant city editor sat at his right, and I sat at the foot of the left leg and wrote what they gave me to write, which was mostly obits. Mortuaries phoned in the names, and I called the next of kin to get the facts.

The big obits for prominent people went to other reporters. Mine were all standard obits for people we'd never heard of, and were as formal as the sonnet. Services will be held on Day for Whom of Address who died When. Second graph: An employee of Which for Number of Years, he was a member of This, That, and The Other. Third: He is survived by Her, Them, Them, and Them. And though I got the idea from other reporters that this was lowly work, not meant for a person of talent, I enjoyed it. I felt useful. Someone had died, and the family wanted the world to pay some attention. They were glad to talk to me, the fellow from the paper, and, unlike the blowhards other reporters had to endure, my people were modest and had small expectations. "I don't know if you can get this in, but one thing Dad did was swim across White Bear Lake and back every summer until he was eighty-two," one man told me. "It's nothing important, but it'd be nice if you could get it in."

I did get it in. I tried to get a lot of stuff in, some of which the city editor took exception to. "Zinnias?" he wrote at the top of one obit. "For Christ's sake!!" But I managed to convince him that large beds of beautiful zinnias were one of the deceased's accomplishments in life and should be noted in her obituary. He wouldn't let me mention another woman's rhubarb cake. "Recipes don't belong in an obit. Too disrespectful," he said. But he did once let me say, "An employee of the Northern Pacific for thirty-seven years, Mr. Johnson was well known for his skill as an electrician and for taking good care of his tools."

I thought of my obit-writing days the other evening, after I'd spent the afternoon going around to estate sales. Like the obit trade, they might have been depressing—the homes of the deceased opened up for the sale of stuff the survivors didn't want, and hundreds of us strangers tramping through the rooms looking for bargains—but they were not. Not to me, anyway. I found them very satisfying. I went to three houses, all small and jammed with stuff. Though people of modest means, the deceased all had terrific dining-room tables, monumental solid oak or walnut dressers and bedsteads, and they had all been pack rats and kept impressive collections of knickknacks, souvenirs, bric-a-brac, and what the want ads call "collectibles."

I'm a saver myself, and to my considerable collection I added a little bit of each of theirs: a white plastic radio, circa 1950 ($5), a black serving tray with a map of North Dakota on it ($1), a glass pitcher with cheerful red roses on it that is similar to one my mother had ($2.50), a small "I WANT ROOSEVELT AGAIN" button (50 cents), four chauffeurs' badges ($5), a copy of Orwell's *Nineteen Eighty-four* inscribed "Happy Birthday, Fred—Mar. 1950—Hazel" ($1), a Tagolene Motor Oil folding yardstick (10¢), and some other stuff I thought I'd enjoy owning. I was a discriminating buyer. I passed up a busted Victrola ($95) and a crate of *National Geographics* circa 1940 ($10 for the lot).

Going to estate sales, a person is struck by the fact that possessions survive us. The chair I'm sitting in should be good for another fifty years, at least. This typewriter should clatter on into the twenty-first century. This solid-glass paperweight could be darned near eternal. I'll hang on to them, they are so dear, but when I'm dead they should be sold to strangers at rock-bottom prices. People who may not be born yet should come by my house and snatch them up as the wonderful bargains they will be. That's why I took good care of them—to extend their usefulness beyond the unimaginable day when I'm no longer here. The big obits of prominent people referred to "a legacy of public service" they left behind, and maybe they did and maybe they didn't. I am definitely going to leave a black Underwood upright in very good condition, *cheap*, and who knows what that could lead to?

O THE PORCH

O F PORCHES THERE ARE TWO SORTS: the decorative and the useful, the porch that is only a platform and the porch you can lie around on in your pajamas and read the Sunday paper.

The decorative porch has a slight function, similar to that of the White House portico: it's where you greet prime ministers, premiers, and foreign potentates. The cannons boom, the band plays, the press writes it all down, and they go indoors.

The true porch, or useful porch, incorporates some of that grandeur, but it is screened and protects you from prying eyes. It strikes a perfect balance between indoor and outdoor life.

Indoors is comfortable but decorous, as Huck Finn found out at the Widow's. It is even stifling if the company isn't right. A good porch gets you out of the parlor, lets you smoke, talk loud, eat with your fingers—without apology and without having to run away from home. No wonder that people with porches have hundreds of friends.

Of useful porches there are many sorts, including the veranda, the breezeway, the back porch, front porch, stoop, and now the sun deck, though the veranda is grander than a porch need be and the sun deck is useful only if you happen to like sun. A useful porch may be large or not, but ordinarily it is defended by screens or large shrubbery. You should be able to walk naked onto a porch and feel only a slight thrill of adventure. It is comfortable, furnished with old stuff. You should be able to spill your coffee anywhere without a trace of remorse.

Our family owned a porch like that once, attached to a house overlooking the St. Croix River east of St. Paul, Minnesota, that we rented from the Wilcoxes. We lived on it from May to September. When company came, they didn't stop in the living room but went straight through to the porch.

You could sit on the old porch swing that hung from the ceiling or in one of the big wicker chairs or the chaise longue, or find a spot on the couch, which could seat four or accommodate a tall man taking a nap. There was a table for four, two kerosene lanterns, and some plants in pots. The porch faced east, was cool and shady from midday on, and got a nice breeze off the river. A lush forest of tall ferns surrounded this porch so the occupants didn't have to look at un-mowed lawn or a weedy garden and feel too guilty to sit. A brook ran close by.

In the home-building industry today, a porch such as that one is considered an expensive frill, which is too bad for the home buyer. To sign up for a lifetime of debt at a vicious rate of interest and wind up with a porchless home, a home minus the homiest room—it's like visiting Minnesota and not seeing the prairie. You cheat yourself. Home, after all, doesn't belong to the bank, it's yours. You're sup-posed to have fun there, be graceful and comfortable and enjoy music and good conversation and the company of pals, otherwise home is only a furniture showroom and you may as well bunk at the YMCA and get in on their recreation programs.

The porch promotes grace and comfort. It promotes good con-versation simply by virtue of the fact that on a porch there is no need for it. Look at the sorry bunch in the living room standing in little clumps and holding drinks, and see how hard they work to keep up a steady dribble of talk. There, silence indicates boredom and un-happiness, and hosts are quick to detect silence and rush over to subdue it into speech. Now look at our little bunch on this porch. Me and the missus float back and forth on the swing, Mark and Rhonda are collapsed at opposite ends of the couch, Malene peruses her paperback novel in which an astounding event is about to occur, young Jeb sits at the table gluing the struts on his Curtiss biplane. The cats lie on the floor listening to birdies, and I say, "It's a heck of a deal, ain't it, a *heck* of a deal." A golden creamy silence suffuses this happy scene, and only on a porch is it possible.

When passers-by come into view, we say hello to them, but they don't take this as an invitation to barge in. There is something slightly *forbidding* about the sight of people on a porch, its grace is almost royal. You don't rush right up to the Queen and start telling her the story of your life, and you don't do that to porch sitters either. We are Somebody up here even if our screens are torn and the sofa is busted and we're drinking orange pop from cans. You down there are passers-by in a parade we've seen come and go for years. We have a porch.

It is our reviewing platform and observation deck, our rostrum and dais, the parapet of our stockade, the bridge of our ship. We can sit on it in silence or walk out naked spilling coffee. Whatever we do, we feel richer than Rockefeller and luckier than the President.

Years ago, my family moved from that luxurious porch to a porchless apartment in the city. Our friends quit visiting us. We felt as if we had moved to Denver. Then we moved to a big old house with two porches, then to another with a long veranda in front and a small sleeping porch in back. Now we have arrived in Manhattan, at an apartment with a terrace. A porch on the twelfth floor with a view of rooftops, chimney pots, treetops, and the street below. A canvas canopy, a potted hydrangea, and two deck chairs. Once again, we're ready for company.

TRAVELER

My FIFTEEN-YEAR-OLD SON has just returned from abroad with a dozen rolls of exposed film and a hundred dollars in uncashed travelers' checks, and is asleep at the moment, drifting slowly westward toward Central Time. His blue duffel bag lies on the hall floor where he dropped it, about four short strides into the house. Last night, he slept in Paris, and the twenty nights before that in various beds in England and Scotland, but evidently he postponed as much sleep as he could: when he walked in and we embraced and he said he'd missed home, his electrical system suddenly switched off, and he headed half-unconscious for the sack, where I imagine he may beat his old record of sixteen hours.

I don't think I'll sleep for a while. This household has been running a low fever over the trip since weeks before it began, when we said, "In one month, you'll be in London! Imagine!" It was his first trip overseas, so we pressed travel books on him, and a tape cassette of useful French phrases; drew up a list of people to visit; advised him on clothing and other things. At the luggage store where we went to buy him a suitcase, he looked at a few suitcases and headed for the duffels and knapsacks. He said that suitcases were more for old people. I am only in my forties, however, and I pointed out that a suitcase keeps your clothes neater—a sports coat, for example. He said he wasn't taking a sports coat. The voice of my mother spoke through me. "Don't you want to look nice?" I said. He winced in pain and turned away.

My mother and father and a nephew went with him on the trip, during which he called home three times: from London, from Paris, and from a village named Ullapool, in the Highlands. "It's like no place in America," he reported from London. Near Ullapool, he hiked through a crowd of Scottish sheep and climbed a mountain in a rainstorm that almost blew him off the summit. He took cover behind a boulder, and the sun came out. In the village, a man spoke to him in Gaelic, and, too polite to interrupt, my son listened to him for ten or fifteen minutes, trying to nod and murmur in the right places. The French he learned from the cassette didn't hold water in Paris— not even his fallback phrase, "*Parlez-vous anglais?*" The French he said it to shrugged and walked on. In Paris, he bought a hamburger at a tiny shop run by a Greek couple, who offered Thousand Island dressing in place of ketchup. He described Notre Dame to me, and the Eiffel Tower, as he had described Edinburgh, Blair Castle, hotel rooms, meals, people he saw on the streets.

"What is it like?" I asked over and over. I myself have never been outside the United States, except twice when I was in Canada. When I was eighteen, a friend and I made a list of experiences we intended to have before we reached twenty-one, which included hopping a freight to the West Coast, learning to play the guitar, and going to Europe. I've done none of them. When my son called, I sat down at the kitchen table and leaned forward and hung on every word. His voice came through clearly, though two of the calls were like ship-to-shore radio communication in which you have to switch from Receive to Send, and when I interrupted him with a "Great!" or a "Really?" I knocked a little hole in his transmission. So I just sat and listened. I have never listened to a telephone so intently and with so much pleasure as I did those three times. It was wonderful and moving to hear news from him that was so new to me. In my book, he was the first man to land on the moon, and I knew that I had no advice to give him and that what I had already given was probably not much help.

The unused checks that he's left on the hall table—almost half the wad I sent him off with—is certainly evidence of that. Youth travels light. No suitcase, no sports coat, not much language, and a slim expense account, and yet he went to the scene, got the story, and came back home safely. I sit here amazed. The night when your child returns with dust on his shoes from a country you've never seen is a night you would gladly prolong into a week.

SNEEZES

MY MOTHER WHEN SHE SNEEZES SAYS "The *bishop!*" and has for as long as I've known her. She stifles a sneeze as much as she can, but it has a pleasant, musical tone, like the call of a bird. My father's sneeze is impossible to represent phonetically. He delivers his with an open embouchure, head thrown back, and the tone, while not musical, is bold and triumphant. I once heard a similar sound on a *National Geographic* special but was out of the room, and when I got a look at the television screen that particular animal was gone and the show had moved on to another part of the jungle. When my father clears his throat, he produces a loud, sharp growl that, if you have your back to him, may make you jump and drop your knitting. When my mother clears her throat, a little balloon appears over her head containing the word "ahem."

A person might think that these differences are based on sex— one masculine, one ladylike—but all of my mother's family sneezes like her, including her brothers, and my father's family sneezes like him. One of his sisters sneezes in a way that is thrilling to hear. She is a soft-spoken woman, but when she feels one coming she grabs on to a chair or a wall and makes a series of rhythmic cries, louder and louder, rising in pitch, culminating in the ecstatic crescendo, a ringing "Massachusetts!" delivered from the chest, full voice, *bel sniso*. Dogs jump to their feet, cats dash to safety. "Oh my, that felt good," she says. On my mother's side of the family, I think, they would prefer to do this in the bathroom behind a closed door, though their sneezes are pretty well repressed to begin with. They sneeze "Permission!" or "Sister!" but it's hard to make out the word, because they are covering up and trying to be unintelligible.

I refer here not to the sneezing that comes with a bad cold or hay fever but to the occasional sneeze, the recreational sneeze that the body works up simply to loosen the flesh, adjust the spinal column, jolt the brain, send a message to the extremities. My father sneezes every morning when he wakes up, and again when he walks into bright sunlight. When he has a cold, he is as miserable as anyone else.

Over the years, my own sneezes have loosened up somewhat. In company, I try to rein them in, because I know that people's attitudes vary—some enjoy a sneeze, and others immediately see the old hygiene-textbook picture of a man releasing a cloud of pestilence into the air—but when I'm alone I cut loose. I crouch, I spring up and make a move like an umpire calling a strike. I give voice to the sneeze. I make it as big as possible.

Not long ago, I walked out the door of my house on a clear, cold morning and was thinking pure business when, halfway across the porch, I felt that familiar pleasant wave in the chest—the magnetic field of the sneeze—and the long intake of breath and the pulsation in the head. I wound up, reared back, and delivered a sneeze worthy of Pavarotti—a six-syllable sneeze that sounded like "onomatopoeia!" On the accented syllable, I stamped my foot (*wham!*) on the wooden floor, and then the majestic cry (and *wham!*) came bouncing back to me off the house across the street. I thought, God bless you! I said good morning to the bunch of children who wait for their schoolbus on my corner. They appeared to be awestruck. I climbed into my car and drove off, and at the corner the stoplight turned a luminous green.

POOL TABLE

O UR DECISION TO BUY A POOL TABLE and put it in the dining room and haul the dining-room table upstairs and use it to pile stuff on was the sort of swift, intuitive decision that top family management makes when it is clicking on all eight cylinders.

"Let's go look at pool tables," my wife said one drizzly morning last month after we had canceled a vacation trip because we had too much work to do.

"Where would we put one?" I said.

She said, "In the dining room."

And we went out and bought it—*bam!*—just like that. I was amazed, and so was the third member of the family, the fourteen-year-old youth. "You've got to be kidding," he said.

In fact, I *had* been kidding a few months before when I said, sitting at the dining-room table, "This'd make a good poolroom." She and he both laughed. Obviously, the room was a dining room, being near the kitchen and having a chandelier. In the creative end of family management, though, many great proposals are first made in the form of jokes, which serve to deflect initial resistance ("Only kidding, dear") and allow the proposal to percolate for a period of time, until another member introduces it as a serious idea, and the next day two guys carry in a pool table. "Where do you want it?" they say. *In there.* "In the dining room? You sure?" *Positive.*

The canceled vacation was one factor in the decision—we felt we had some extravagance coming to us—and another was dissatisfaction with the basic dining-room concept. Of the rooms in our house, the DR lagged far behind the BR, LR, and Kit. in pleasure production. Its long table was where we sat with a stack of bills and wrote checks. We did income-tax returns there. We laid towels on it and spread out wet woolens to dry. And occasionally we sat there with company and put away big dinners, which were not bad—pretty good—and yet, considering the levels of fun experienced in nearby living areas, did not meet the performance standards we had in mind. Frankly, in our experience, when our pals sit down at a dining-room table set with matching china and matching silverware on a white tablecloth, they come under the shadow of a penal dining code learned in childhood. In the kitchen or out on the porch, they can be about fifty-percent funnier than at the table, where they sit up straighter and their conversation takes a turn toward higher ground—into the realm of issues and problems, needs and priorities. Frankly, the dining-room table was too much like other long tables I've spent time at, attending meetings. Frankly, in my own home my priority is to whoop it up a little. In those meetings, a major proposal such as dining-room conversion would be discussed at great length and considerably amended, the pool-table component would be set aside pending further study, and we would wind up with a long-term program of dinner enrichment, with new guidelines for guest selection.

This is the advantage of the family unit: founded on sexual attraction, which is unexplainable, the family maintains the capacity for swift, intuitive action, such as we're certainly seeing a lot of now around our new pool table. The other night, I banked the eight ball off two cushions and between two balls slightly more than one ball's-width apart to park it in the corner pocket where I had called the shot—a little exercise in intuitive geometry that made my partner gasp in admiration even as it cost her the game. A person doesn't have a hot stick like that every night, and, of course, you don't need to. Occasional amazement is more than enough to keep a family clicking along.

COLD

IT TURNED COLD THIS WEEK, down to twenty below Monday night, and my Blazer started right up, and on the way to the office I saw the neighbor lady needed a start. I stopped and got the jumper cables out and hooked them up to her battery, glad to show her what it means to own an American car. Hers is a Mazda. Her throttle was frozen and it was a major operation all the way around, and then I looked up and saw neighbors watching from their windows, curtains drawn back. Suddenly it's clear just how easy it is to break into show business and bring joy into people's lives. They can see how cold it is from the way you're bent over, hands in your pockets, shivering, and they pad back to their breakfast table feeling like the King of England. Her car started and died a couple times. "Yeah, these little Japanese cars, I tell you," I said. "This Blazer of mine, gosh, I just put in the key, press the pedal down a half-inch, and she goes right away. I don't even bother putting her in the garage." Cold weather is hard on cars but good for people. We finally get her started and then go into her kitchen for a cup of coffee—we say, "Hooooo, it's a cold one out there. You hear the weather this morning? Cold out there. Terrible." Except it's not terrible at all. You're a man who is phenomenally alive, your whole body, the nervous system and along the cortex and in the marrow of the bones, every part of the body has got the message: "Heat. Let's go. Come on, team. Little more

H, now. Let's have some H." There is no depression at twenty below. Human depression occurs frequently in the low fifties, and when it gets into the nineties there's plenty of latitude for self-pity and grief at your sad wasted life and the people who let you down and exploited your vulnerability, but at twenty below the body turns passionate. You venture out and every internal organ is up on its feet doing the schottische, your skin is singing the "Habañera." At twenty below, nature sends us a message: *Die*. And the body says, "Hell no, we won't go!"

PUCK DROP

I N THE FALL OF 1986 the Minnesota North Stars invited me to drop the first puck and open their hockey season, a ceremony I had never heard of, so I bought a puck after lunch one day and practiced dropping it on my office floor. It takes approximately one second for a dropped puck to hit the deck and it drops straight down, so there's not much a dropper can do to make the drop graceful—or much that can go wrong either, if you look at it that way. So I called the North Stars back and said yes and thought no more of it until I got to the arena a couple weeks later. Baseball's ceremonial Opening Day toss is a mass of complications compared with the puck drop, and over the years there must've been dozens of tossers—governors, mayors, owners, old-timers—who turned in their sleep, reliving the moment when, in jam-packed Weems Stadium on a fine April afternoon, all eyes turned on His Grace as he accepted the ceremonial ball, rubbed it up in a clownish way, trying to project to the vast throng an air of nonchalance, even slight self-mockery, and, grinning at other dignitaries and the photographers, made a ridiculous stiff windup and pitched the ball feebly into the dirt—a dinky throw that made forty thousand people simultaneously think, "Wimp"—and then tried to appear amused at his disgrace and waved to the masses and sat down on a cup of beer. A ceremonial toss could end up tossing a wrench into a man's life and years later be thrown back at him by strangers at parties, no matter how distinguished his later career ("Saw you at the ballpark. About ten years ago, wasn't it? That time you tossed the ball out. Heh-heh"), but a puck drop is simpler, or so I thought until I got to the arena and remembered: *Ice. You have to walk on ice.* Falling was on my mind as I walked across the dark parking lot and down into the bright fluorescent bowels of the arena, where a friendly young guy from the front office led me down concrete halls past crates of souvenirs through mists of sausage steam from the kitchens, past a waiting ambulance, to the passageway outside the North Stars' dressing room that led to the ice, where, at the moment, the Boston Bruins were zooming around and where in a few minutes, said my guide, after the introduction of the players and brief remarks by the team owners, George and Gordon Gund, and prior to the National Anthem, I would proceed to the face-off circle at center ice, where the puck would be dropped. "By the way, there's a microphone, if you want to say a few words, but you don't have to," he said.

To the danger of ice now was added the greater danger of speech, a slippery step for a ceremonial person: consider how many men, invited *ex officio* to snip a ribbon or toss a shovelful of dirt, have stepped to a microphone and given more of themselves than the occasion called for—I remember a Methodist minister who stood to give the invocation at my son's soccer-awards banquet and couldn't resist the chance to tell a joke about a man found hiding in the closet when the woman's husband came home early from work. We laughed (nervously) at the punch line ("Everybody's got to be somewhere") and then he tried to top that joke for about ten minutes before he finally turned to God in prayer. I wondered if the microphone would be right in my path across the ice so I'd have to step around it and my silence would look sneaky or arrogant ("Big Shot Snubs Crowd, Has No Comment as Thousands Sit in Stunned Disappointment— 'We drove all day and all night to see him,' said unemployed father of eleven, comforting his weeping wife, eight months pregnant, 'and he didn't say a word, this is the low point of our lives, I don't see how we can go on' ") and I tried to think of ten or fifteen terrific words I could say about Winter Our Favorite Season, or Hockey in a Democratic Society, but that seemed to lead toward a major speech (Crowd Attacks Man Who Delays Hockey Game in Mid-Ice Filibuster—"Someone lower down in the organization invited him to drop the puck," said tight-lipped North Stars execs, "and we expect to know their identity within the next thirty-six hours").

I asked John Mariucci, a Stars exec and an old friend, why I was chosen, and he thought for a long time. Mr. Mariucci is almost seventy, a former defenseman, a man sometimes called the Father of Minnesota Hockey but more often called John, and he put his hand on the back of my neck and squeezed it. "We've had our eye on you," he said in his sweet high voice. "We've seen you drop quite a few things over the years and we like your style. You have a good release."

And then suddenly it was my cue. The young guy put a puck in my hand, a muffled voice boomed my name in the darkened arena, there was light applause like water going over a small dam, the spotlight swung toward me, and I smiled affably and stepped down the runway through the door in the boards onto the ice. A tall woman in a brief spangly suit skated over and took my left arm—on skates, she towered over me—"just so you don't go down," she said, as I padded out onto the ice, "be careful, it's slippery"—and she propelled me across the white ice. I looked down. I barely noticed the microphone in passing, or the hockey players standing at attention along the blue lines. Two players waited at center ice. They smiled two big toothless smiles, I shook their hands (both dry) and wished them each a good season, and they then faced each other, bent over, sticks ready, and I bent and then—with what some North Stars officials told me later was a graceful but economical motion—I dropped the black rubber disc on the white ice, the players feinted a swipe at it, one of them picked it up and gave it to me, the spangled lady took my elbow, and I padded back past the microphone to the runway to a second, fainter wave of applause, stood at attention as a tenor sang the Anthem, nailing the high note ("land of the *free*") in a thrilling voice, and the moment was over. Nobody that evening confessed to the slightest disappointment that I had not spoken. I sat and watched the game, which the Bruins won, 5–3, and drove home and was in bed before midnight.

LUTHERAN PIE

O NE FALL DAY I went to the kitchen and got out a bag of flour and made the first apple pie I made in my life. Made it from scratch, including mixing butter with flour to make a great crust, and loaded it with sour apples and brown sugar and nutmeg, baked it to a T, and of course it was delicious. My guests for dinner were a couple who seemed to be coasting from a bad fight. We ate the pie and sat in a daze of pleasure afterward, during which the wife said that it reminded her of pies she ate when she was a little Norwegian Lutheran girl in Normania Township on the western Minnesota prairie. "We had love, good health, and faith in God, all things that money can't buy," she said, glancing at her husband, apropos of something. "This time of year, we were always broke, but somehow we made it. We'd fix equipment, feed the animals, and sleep. My mother made apple pie. One year she made thirty in one day. My dad was sick and thirty of our neighbors come in with fourteen combines and harvested his three hundred acres of soybeans. It took them half a day to do it, at a time when they were racing to get their own soybeans in, but out there, if your car broke down in the country, the next car by would stop. My mother baked thirty pies and gave one to everybody who helped us.'' Naturally I was pleased, until later, when it occurred to me that I would never bake another one as surprisingly good, having hit a home run on my first try. (They are still married, by the way.)

SEXY

A MAN WHO IS NAMED one of the ten sexiest men in America by *Playgirl* magazine has a responsibility to his fellow men to say a few words about it, especially if he is forty-four at the time, a Midwesterner who majored in English at a Big Ten school, and wears glasses and grew up fundamentalist—not to gloat over what is, after all, a God-given asset (how many men does God put in the top ten, anyway?)—but to offer help and counsel. Unfortunately, it's 10:30 on a Saturday night and I'm about ready to head upstairs, so this will be a shorter lecture than what you hoped to hear, perhaps. (1) If you have a choice between poetry and football, choose poetry. Football wrecks your legs and you can't use it for anything. Other guys put their arms around you in football. You write a poem for a woman, you give it to her, she is speechless. What can a jock give her, his socks? So I chose to write poems about her delicate body being like a shy deer nibbling the blossoms of an apple tree. It's not an original image but it was an easy choice. A quarter-century later, my wife remembers it. (2) The human elbow, particularly the *tip* of the elbow. I don't want to say more. (3) Foreign women release something in men, and perhaps vice versa, so don't shy away from your foreign side. I'm Scottish with some Canadian. (4) Fundamentalists have more fun. You can't enjoy sex to the fullest unless you've spent some time in the wilderness, being repressed. (5) Sex is better in marriage than anywhere else you can imagine, like the song says: It's all right to get your appetite walking round town just as long as you eat supper at home. (6) Eating in bed afterward is perfectly natural. (7) It gets better.

Sex is a progression of sweet blessings, and one learns to enjoy each one of them whether or not it leads to the next.

> It is good to be with you.
> To talk with you.
> To touch you.
> To be alone with you.
> To kiss you.
> To be naked with you.
> To make love with you.
> To have a baby with you.

After a while, each blessedness seems more or less as enjoyable as any other, except the last, which is distinctive.

I accept this honor on behalf of all fundamentalists, and all Midwesterners, and all forty-four-year-olds, and good night.

COUNTRY GOLF

I DON'T HAVE many friends who have done one thing so well that they're famous for it and could sit on their laurels if they wanted to, although I do know a woman who can touch her nose with her tongue, which she is famous for among all the people who've seen her do it. She doesn't do it often, because she doesn't need to, having proved herself. I also know a man who wrote a forty-one-word palindrome, which is about as far as you can go in the field of writing that reads the same forwards and backwards. And I know Chet Atkins, who is enplaqued in the Country Music Hall of Fame, in Nashville, and has a warm, secure spot in the history of the guitar. My own accomplishments fall into the immense dim area of the briefly remarkable, such as the play I made on a hot grounder off the bat of my Uncle Don, for which I felt famous one day in 1957. I backhanded the ball cleanly at third base and threw the aging speedster out at first, which drew quite a bit of comment at the time, but that was long ago and plays have been made since that put mine in the shade. It was a hot July afternoon at Lake Minnetonka, and the Grace & Truth Bible camp had spent the morning in Deuteronomy, where I have no competence at all, and then I went out and made that great play. I was not quite fifteen and generally unaccomplished, so it meant a lot to me. The ball took a low bounce off the soft turf, and I had to pivot, get my glove down fast, then set my right foot to throw. The throw got him by a stride. If you had seen this, you would remember it.

*   *   *

I first met Chet Atkins in 1982, backstage at "A Prairie Home Companion." He was standing just back of the back curtain, humming to himself, and reached down and picked up his guitar, like a man slipping into a shirt, and put his right foot up on a chair and fooled around with a string of tunes that came to him, including the one he'd been humming. Then we made conversation about various things, and he asked me if I played golf. I said, "A little." Golf isn't one of my good subjects. I don't have good memories of it.

He mentioned golf again the next time I saw him, and the time after that, and he told me to come down to Nashville whenever I felt like playing some golf with him, and finally, on a Sunday morning toward the middle of May 1984, I flew down for a visit, though golf was the last thing on my mind. In my hands, golf is a grim, catastrophic game that makes me into someone I don't want my friends to know—a person who, in fact, I already was when I got on the plane. There had been a sour smell in the air around me for weeks, from a hard winter of sitting in a small room and throwing wads of typing paper at a basket and missing, and I went South to get rid of it. Whenever I feel bad, Southern voices make me feel better, whether it's Dolly Parton or Grandpa Jones or a waitress in a café. When she says "Hi! Haw yew?" I am immediately just fine.

I met Chet about midafternoon at his office on Music Row, down the street from the studio where he made most of his albums and where he produced albums for Willie and Waylon, Eddy Arnold, Porter Wagoner, and dozens of other laureates, and we headed south in his black Blazer to the golf course at Henry Horton State Park, forty-two miles from Nashville, where he was going to play in the annual Acuff-Rose Invitational on Monday and Tuesday. He said he had flown in that morning from doing two shows in Denver with a jazz guitarist named Johnny Smith. "You remember him. He had that big record of 'Moonlight in Vermont' back in the fifties." Acuff-

Rose is one of the big music-publishing firms in Nashville, the first in the country devoted to country music, founded in 1942 by Roy Acuff, of "Wabash Cannonball" fame, and the late Fred Rose, Hank Williams' mentor. Chet said that the tournament was just for fun. He had played in it for twelve years. "People in the music industry play, and friends of theirs. They see somebody on the street, they invite him. Everybody's played in it, from the chief of police on down. *You* could play." I said no thanks. He was in a foursome, he said, with Billy Edd Wheeler, the songwriter, and a banker from Columbia named Smalley and his old friend Archie Campbell, the comedian. "Archie was the one who got me first playing golf, back in 1958 or 9. I saw how much fun he had, and I liked to be around him, so I started. I was too old to get good at it, though. You have to start young." Chet was thirty-four or thirty-five at the time, and he's sixty now.

He pointed out Waylon Jennings' house, and Eddy Arnold's, and Tom T. Hall's studio as we drove along, and a church where a woman singer got married whose wedding he played for when he had an upset stomach and who was now divorced. He put a tape in the tape deck. "This is one Billy Edd wrote," he said. A song called "Ode to the Little Brown Shack Out Back." He said, "You remember that record Archie made? 'Trouble in the Amen Corner?' 'Old brother Ira, singing in the choir'? It was a real tearjerker, but it sold a lot, so RCA wanted to put out an album on him—of songs, you know— and we had Boudleaux and Felice Bryant go to work to write him some. They were sitting around writing all these sad songs about the old dog who died and that sort of thing, and finally Felice got sick of it. She said, 'Let's write something *happy*,' so they wrote 'Wish that I was on ol' Rocky Top, down in the Tennessee hills' and that was 'Rocky Top.' The Osborne Brothers recorded it, but Archie takes credit for it. He said to me once, 'They'd never have written it without me, Cock. Without me, there'd be no "Rocky Top." ' "

This pleasant monologue in Chet's soft, East Tennessee tenor took us out in the country down Interstate 65 and to the motel at Horton Park, and included so such more—about musicians and golf, and an old radio faith healer who put his fingers in deaf people's ears and yelled at them to hear, and a squirrel Chet kept for a pet when he was a boy ("He made a nest in our old upright piano and wouldn't come out, so I sat down and played the Lost Chord and he shot straight up in the air and we never saw him again")—that when I finally climbed into bed that evening I had long forgotten what it was that I was feeling bad about when I got on the plane.

*   *   *

When I walked over to the clubhouse after breakfast, it was obvious that Tennessee had had a hard winter, too. Frost had killed most of the Bermuda grass on the greens, where the flags stood in circles of light-brown dust like the spot in the schoolyard where we played Fox and Geese, and the fairways looked worn and ratty for so early in the season. The woods were lush and dense, though, and the foliage of the golfers around the first tee was positively inspiring, their pants in particular. Pinks and yellows and oranges, a pair of peach and one of lilac, and an assortment of plaids such as I've seldom seen outside of the circus, including one that looked like a test for color blindness. They were such a brilliant, cheerful sight I felt sheepish about my quiet good taste in tans. It seemed stingy.

Chet arrived a few minutes later in a blue shirt and bright-green pants, and while he went in the clubhouse to sign up, I sidled up toward the crowd for a closer look. Men in clothes the colors of extravagant good humor strolled around behind the tee, pressing the flesh, putting their arms around each other's shoulders and patting each other on the belly and saying, "You're looking *good*." Being a writer, I took out my checkbook and made some notes on who was there—songwriters such as Whitey Shafer ("That's the Way Love Goes") and Pee Wee King and Redd Stewart ("Tennessee Waltz," both of them) and Wayne Carson ("Always on My Mind," "She's Actin' Single, I'm Drinkin' Doubles"), and singers Mickey Newbury and Del Reeves, and Buck Trent, the banjo player, and pianist Floyd Cramer—and kept occupied, writing "Sunny, air smells fresh and green" and "1st hole 345 yards" and "F. Cramer sliced into sand trap," until Chet appeared at my elbow, and men came over to pat him, including a tall, lanky man named Howard, who said, "I appreciate you, Chet. I want you to know that. I love you." When Chet introduced me to him, he patted me, too, and said I looked good, which was good news to me. Mickey Newbury told Chet he looked good, and they got to laughing about a man they knew named Walter who promoted a public barbecue by flying over in a plane and dropping a pig in a parachute ("Didn't hurt the pig. Pig got up and walked away"), and about a golf hustler named Titanic Thompson. "He'd make bets with you about anything," Chet said. "He'd bet you he could pitch cards under a door and into a hat. He'd bet you he could toss his door key into the lock. He'd bet fifty thousand dollars on the exact circumference of a rock a hundred feet away. Once he bet he could hit a golf ball a mile, and he did it. On Lake Michigan, after it froze over."

Meanwhile, foursomes of all colors and shapes of golfers straggled one by one up to the business end of the tee, posed for an official tournament photograph, took hefty practice swings, looked down the fairway, and teed off, to the great amusement of the bunch behind them. "God! He hit it!" someone yelled after Pee Wee King chopped a sharp ground ball up the middle. "You look nervous, Wesley," a frizzy-haired man called to Wesley Rose, the son of Fred Rose and president of Acuff-Rose, decked out in green. "You look like it's royalties time." And to a fat man: "You don't *need* anybody to play with—you *are* a foursome." A drive hooked into the woods. "For his next shot, a McCulloch chain saw!" An especially fluorescent pair of orange trousers appeared and bent down to tee up the ball. "His handicap is his pants!" said a man whose own pants resembled wall-paper in a cheap restaurant. "Where'd you get those? From the High-way Department?"

Chet introduced me to Archie Campbell, whom I recognized right away from watching "Hee Haw," and Billy Edd Wheeler, whom I remembered for a song the first few lines of which I've sung hundreds of times to myself ("We got married in a fever, hotter than a pepper sprout. We been talkin' 'bout Jackson ever since the fire went out. I'm goin' to Jackson . . ."), and who looked a little flushed in the hot sun. He sported a lilac ensemble and a yellow visor on his thick sandy hair, which at the moment he was adjusting. Archie, an elegant, silver-haired gent in navy blue with a distinguished black mustache, was smoking a foot-long cigar. "Nicaraguan," he said. I was admiring both of them, the man and the cigar, when Chet said that the fourth partner hadn't shown up yet. "You play," he said. "You can play out of my bag."

"You look like a golfer," said Archie. "Either that or your dog just died."

It occurred to me to say that golf makes me feel bad, but it also occurred to me that I was feeling good enough to afford some misery and that if I begged off I'd feel bad about it later, so when Chet put a driver in my hand and two balls—a white one and a green one—and a white Acuff-Rose tournament hat, I put on the hat, and posed with my partners. "Smile. Look like you're winners," said the pho-tographer. I teed up the white ball, and tried to think of grace and ease. I imagined the ball, its tiny engines revving up, *wanting* to fly, imagined a long, perfect shot, and—as a hush fell on the gallery of pants, who didn't know me well enough to give me a hard time—swung *hard* and sent a high pop fly about where the first-base bleach-ers would have been. It hung up in the air long enough for me to see more of it than I wanted to, took a fifty-foot-high bounce off the parking lot, and landed in tall grass between the lot and the highway. A bad moment, like a major soup spill, but someone said "That'll teach 'em not to bring their Cadillacs!" and though it wasn't a great line, some of the pants laughed, and I teed up the green ball and drove it a respectable distance into the rough and walked down the fairway to play some golf.

Second chances are fundamental to their game, I found out, including my redemptive second drive and also forgiveness of a bad lie. "Everybody gets to walk his dog in hillbilly golf," Billy Edd told me. "Walking the dog" means moving the ball out of the trees or off of hard dirt and teeing it up on a tuft of grass. He kicked his out of a little hollow.

Archie looked at his ball and said, "I believe I'll walk this one."

"That dog needs walking," said Billy Edd.

My green relief ball stayed in the game the rest of the way. I shot a 7 on the first hole, a triple bogey, and went on to shank a few and top some others, which leaked off at weird angles and made my partners look away and say, "*That's* all right. We all do that," and spent time in the woods shooting trees (*klok!*), and once or twice I thought longingly of my typewriter, which when I type "golf" prints "golf," and not "pgwft" or "xxxxx," but I also made par on one hole, sank a twelve-foot putt, and hit a drive that I still remember. When Chet hit a great drive on the long third, he said, "That felt better than sex and almost as good as eating watermelon." Mine on the dogleg fifth didn't feel as good as *that*, but I did feel something smooth and synchronized that started in my head and in my hips and came together at the ball, and I looked up to see it fifty yards out and rising, sailing, a tiny green star lighting up the bright-blue sky.

"That's a beauty. That's a good layup, hoss. You're going to love that," said Billy Edd. "You know, I could learn to admire you if I just worked at it a little." He set his ball down, squinted, hitched up his lilac pants, wiggled his seat, and uncorked a high one that drifted slowly to the right. "Whoa! Hold up! Draw!" he yelled, dancing to the left to pull it back in bounds. "Work! Stay! Stay! Thou art so fair! Stay!" And it worked, drew back, stayed, and fell fair, and rolled in the short grass in the shadows of the tree line. "I didn't hit that as well as I thought I was going to," he said. "But then I didn't think I was going to."

Then Archie. He tossed his ball in the air, caught it on the back of his hand, let it roll slowly down his arm, flipped it up, caught it, and set it on the tee. "Watch this lick here, boys—the old pro is about to perform," he said. He puffed on the cigar, spat, gave us a big footlight smile, and adjusted the bill of his blue cap to the right to compensate for a slight hook on his previous drive. He addressed the ball with a sweet slow swing, but the cap adjustment was perhaps too much or else the weight of the Nicaraguan cigar was off center, because his drive headed woodsward.

"Over the hill to Grandpa's!" said Billy Edd.

Archie yelled "Don't you *dare!*" and the white dot hesitated, drew back, hung up short of a stand of pine, and fell into the dogleg's knee.

"Look at that! I believe he made it. It's a show, isn't it!" Chet said.

"If you'da hit that perfect, it would've been even better," said Billy Edd.

"All right, I'm going to get serious again now," said Chet. He stood over the ball, bent, took a long, slow backswing, and socked it a little beyond Archie's. "That's the greatest shot I ever saw in my life!" he announced, and added, "But the wind was behind me. And, of course, I'm young."

*   *   *

Chet had told me that he feels a little guilty when he plays well, knowing he's probably playing too much golf and not enough guitar. "The way I'm playing today, though, I guess I must be a pretty good guitar player," he said. Hiking down the fairway in the sunshine, he looked loose and tan and happy. Archie cruised by in his white cart, trailing a ribbon of fragrant cigar smoke, and when we all got to

Archie's ball Chet and Billy Edd had put their heads together and were singing a song:

> Son-a-bitch, I'm tired of living this way,
> Gawdamighty damn.

"Let me take the baritone, Chouster," said Archie, and the three of them sang it. It sounded so good they sang it again. And once more. Archie pulled out a 4-iron. He walked his dog a few feet. "Don't you ever play by our rules with somebody else," he told me, grinning. "You might get shot." That reminded Billy Edd of a story about a hillbilly golfer who walked onto a green and picked up all the dimes. "I remember the first time I ever went on tour, I was with another musician and I picked up the tip he left on the table," Chet said. "I'd never seen anybody leave a tip before. I don't know that I'd ever been in a restaurant before."

Archie said, "You've heard that one about Roy Acuff when he was touring with the Smoky Mountain Boys—the one where they were supposed to stop and have supper at the lady's house?"

I had never stood around in the middle of the fairway listening to jokes before. I kept glancing back at the tee, expecting to see angry golfers waving clubs at us, but nobody appeared. We were all by ourselves, four men standing in the hot sun and laughing. Eventually, Archie shot his second shot, and then Billy Edd. My arms were turning red and my neck, too. I rubbed on some lotion that made me smell like a ripe peach. I stood over my ball, hitched up to swing, and smelled Archie's cigar. I laughed on the backswing, my knees caved in a fraction, and I lifted a chunk of sod like a flying toupee and lofted a high fly ball that landed just short of the pin. It wasn't the play that Uncle Don's grounder was, but if you had seen it you would have clapped. I felt awfully lucky. Even a blind dog gets a little meat from the smokehouse now and then, as someone said later, I forget who.

REGRETS

I WORKED LIKE A PLOW HORSE for about fifteen years, doing two radio shows, hauling them up one row and turning at the ditch and coming back the other way, and all that time not much happened to me that wasn't part of work, which made me sad one night in September when my wife and I left Copenhagen for New York. Five minutes after take-off, we felt a *whump*, the plane lurched, and a nearby steward turned pale green and disappeared into the galley. The plane was still climbing. I touched my wife's arm, she took my hand, and two or three thoughtful minutes passed, and then she took out a piece of paper and began writing a letter to her eldest son. The pilot came on the horn and said, in a dry Swedish voice, that we had experienced an explosion in the No. 3 engine, the fire was out now, and we would return to Copenhagen as soon as we dumped our fuel. "Let me assure you that everything is normal for a situation of this type," he said.

We cruised around spraying jet fuel into the night sky over the Baltic Ocean, and I remembered those years in the broadcast trade and thought that, if our wheels touched ground again and we walked out into the wet salt air of Denmark, I would devote more time to ambling around and having fun. In Denmark, by national law, everyone gets five weeks of paid vacation per year, even if you're unemployed. Five weeks times fifteen years is seventy-five weeks of vacation, of which I had used about twenty, wasting an entire year. I regretted that lost year very deeply. My life had been entirely too sober and determined. We had left three teen-agers back home in

Minnesota, all leading full rich lives, and breakfast with them was a high point of the day, from which I descended into the dark radio mine, carrying my canary in a tin cage, who usually died before 2:00 in the afternoon. I regretted not lingering longer over breakfast.

A DC-10 carries a major load of fuel and there was plenty of time to regret a number of things.

I regretted the narcissism that goes with being a writer. We assume that the world is anxious to hear what we think, a useful assumption if you're going to spend your sunny mornings at a typewriter, but do we have to be *this* self-centered?

I regretted that "A Prairie Home Companion" was lured into television. Radio was so sensual and delicious and it injured the show and insulted the audience to allow cameras to tromp around in it. Once, during a rehearsal, a cameraman told Kate MacKenzie, "Move the microphone down, it's obscuring your face," and she said, sweetly, "It's the camera that obscures. The microphone *reveals*." Television has no patience and little curiosity, and so the picture jumps constantly. A guitarist can sit and pick the most stunning simple version of "Wildwood Flower" and achieve a moment of transcendent grace but television is deaf, it can't sit still, it circles the guitarist, shoots his hands, his face, jumps in back of him, crouches, circles, until the viewer is completely separated from the performance. You don't need this if you want Leo Kottke, whose appeal is through his music. What you want television for is a celebrity guitarist who is more interesting for who he is than for what he sounds like. For example, if a Doberman pinscher played "Go Tell Aunt Rhody" on the guitar, you wouldn't be satisfied to listen to him on the radio and hear the announcer say, "That was Rex playing. Good job, Rex." You'd want to see it for yourself.

I regretted that I hadn't *done* more. Not good works, necessarily: I did my part for the homeless, the alkies, public radio, various losing liberals, an open school, the Save the Spiders Foundation, the Home for the Moody, the lower-spine association, the Suspicion Center, some others. I regretted never having played the accordion, seen New

Mexico or Maine, learned to dance the fox-trot, met Victor Borge, read *Moby Dick* or *Don Quixote*, eaten supper in the Oak Room at the Algonquin, fished Rainy Lake, known a little physics, talked to my dad about his father.

I regretted some bad shows I did.

I regretted having hurt some people.

*   *   *

We landed smoothly and deplaned and were met by a dozen reporters from the Copenhagen dailies and Danish radio and TV, who played the story big the next day although the captain insisted that the emergency was simple and the ship was never in danger. The flight was rescheduled for the next afternoon. All the hotels in Copenhagen were full, so the airline would take us to Malmö, Sweden, and put us up there for the night. My wife and I decided to strike out on our own, and wound up at a friend's apartment in Holte, where we slept on the floor. I woke up six or seven times in the night, and the next day's flight was scrubbed for some other reason, and we spent a night in a cheap loud hotel downtown, and the following evening packed into the economy section with hundreds of other bitter travelers. When we landed at Kennedy, I had hardly a regret left. Just wanted to get on with life in America and that's what I've done.

THE PENNSYLVANIA
DEPT. OF AGR.

I'M NOT ONE WHO READS food labels closely. The taped music at our supermarket makes me jittery and I'm in no mood to inspect labels for BTL or RSVP or any of the chemicals that make laboratory rats' tails stand straight up—I feel like a rat myself and run up and down the aisles throwing things into my cart and get out as fast as I can and feel fortunate. I don't read labels once I get home either, because there's no point in it. The food is bubbling away in its plastic cooking pouch in the boiling water, and why torment yourself with doubts and fears at the last minute? If it weren't good for us, I figure, the government would not allow it to be on the shelves.

So it bothered me one day when I glanced at the label on a can of tomato soup and there was no *Reg. Penna. Dept. Agr.* on it. I already had dumped the soup glop in the pan and added one cup of water slowly and was stirring occasionally, and read the label to make sure the directions hadn't been changed to "add two cups of water quickly and whip to a white froth," and there was no *Reg. Penna. Dept. Agr.* I checked other labels in the cupboard: no *Reg. Penna.* on jars of raspberry jam, apple butter, Ovaltine, Louisiana hot sauce, instant cocoa, marmalade, maple syrup (some benzoate there, though), molasses, blueberry syrup (actually corn syrup and blueberry juice), chicken-bouillon cubes, baking powder, Puerto Rican pickled peppers, soups, corn, cake mix, or on couscous, or linguini, or on a bag of enriched rice (22 mg. of carbohydrates per 1 oz. serving). In the whole cupboard, I found a single solitary *Reg. Penna.* A package of dried "Oriental Noodles & Chicken Flavor Packet" manufactured in Industry, California.

When I was a little boy learning to read, I read everything out loud, Burma-Shave signs, "Popeye" and "Jiggs" and "Little Iodine" and "Winnie Winkle" in the Minneapolis *Star*, the Monkey Wards catalogue, *No Trespassing*, *Post No Bills*, state slogans on license plates, *everything*, including food labels, and I remember that *Reg. Penna. Dept. Agr.* was on just about every package of food, along with *Made in U.S.A.*, *Tear Along Dotted Line*, and *Follow Directions Carefully*. For a long time I didn't know if it meant Regulated By or Registered With or Regretfully Yours, and a little joke among the school lunchroom crew that flattened the big tin cans and took them out to the trash barrel was that it stood for Regurgitated By, but, in a vague way, it represented government approval of the food, an official kosher mark put on in Pennsylvania.

That's what *Reg. Penna. Dept. Agr.* means to most of us, I guess. It isn't as if the Supreme Court has upheld these peas as tender and delicious, but it's some sort of affirmation, and with *Reg. Penna.* on the label, you can be fairly certain that the food doesn't contain big dollops of potassium cyanide or any more milligrams of rodent parts than might be good for you. Its meaning, passed on to us from childhood, seems to be: "Eat what is put before you. Don't complain. It's good. Be glad you have it. Children in Asia would be very happy to eat this."

If, as my cupboard study seems to suggest, *Reg. Penna. Dept. Agr.* is passing from American shelf life, it's probably because of militant consumers threatening lawsuits every time somebody eats a *Reg. Penna.* product and finds a hair in it. I suppose the *Penna.* people saw the handwriting on the wall and concluded that it was time to get out of the *Reg.* business. Their simple homely seal of approval had become an invitation for surly individuals to make trouble, so they quietly folded the *Dept.* and stole away. I don't know this for a fact but I surmise it, based on childhood experience. My mother had six children, all of us consumer advocates when it came down to the food that was set before us. Any food that struck us as the least little tiny bit unusual, we ran tests on until it was stone cold. "It tastes funny!" we said. "What's in this? It looks funny. It smells funny. Did you put green peppers in it?" Green peppers were our sodium nitrite. We blanched at the thought of them. We suspected every dish of containing trace elements of green peppers.

In the end, Mother surrendered to consumer interests and to the fear of green peppers. She gave her consumers what they demanded, which was spaghetti, hamburgers, hot dogs, and macaroni and cheese. I think of her when I see shoppers grab up any package of food labeled

Natural or *No Preservatives*. What makes *Natural* better than *Reg. Penna. Dept. Agr.*? Will we allow ourselves to be ruled utterly by suspicion and fear?

Beside this typewriter is a bottle of rubber cement clearly labeled: *Danger: Extremely Flammable. Do Not Use Near Fire or Flame. N.Y.F.D.C. of A. 852.* Why would the New York Fire Department issue a Certificate of Approval to an extremely flammable cement? Does this mean that the N.Y.F.D. certifies that this cement, though extremely flammable, is nevertheless safer than other, downright explosive cements? Is it flammable only if used carelessly? Is there no chance that this bottle could be a bad one and burst into flames, ignited by sunshine, hurling jagged bits of glass and flaming red-hot cement drops right up into my face before I finish writing this? Is the N.Y.F.D. going to accept responsibility for that and pay me six million dollars?

Every day we walk a treacherous path through dark valleys and over steep mountains, and unseen hands reach out to guide us at every step. We plunge into unlikely romances with uncertified persons, we take off on difficult missions to defend unspecified ideals; daily we risk our known lives in behalf of sweet mystery, and all on the basis of the slightest of clues, and accept happily uncertainties compared to which *Reg. Penna. Dept. Agr.* is practically a covenant. Its slight guarantee is intended to free us from hypochondria and the fear of dark specks in the asparagus so that we may get on to our real work in the world, which is justice, brotherhood, and freedom.

FAMILY HONEYMOON

L AST WINTER, after our wedding, my wife and I decided to take
our four teen-age children on a vacation trip out west as a way
of sealing the family bond. Alaska seemed to call to us, and Hawaii,
and the state of Washington, where I went on car trips as a boy, and
then we heard Oregon and after that the whistle of the overnight
express, and pretty soon we worked up a five-week, eleven-state tour
ambitious enough to launch a bid for the presidency, and one fine
July morning, before caution could overtake us, we struck out for the
Coast.

Today, a month later, we are heading south on Highway 101
through California redwoods, cruising down from Crescent City toward Garberville and, tomorrow, San Francisco, with eight days and
six states to go—states we'll cover on the California Zephyr to Chicago. We're riding in a rented Toyota van, light brown, with our
daughter and me, seventeen and forty-three, in the back seat; two
boys, nineteen and fifteen, in the middle; and my wife and another
boy, forty-three and seventeen, in front. My wife, who doesn't like
to drive and hasn't got the hang of mountain driving, is driving, and
I am keeping to myself a few short sentences of advice ("Don't brake
on curves. Coast into the curve and then accelerate. Use centrifugal
force"). It's 9:30 A.M., we've been on the road since 8:00, and the
children, whom I will call Curly, Larry, Moe, and Marilyn Monroe,
are plugged into Walkmans, except Marilyn, who is writing a poem
("about death," she told me a moment ago). Of our thirty-some days

together so far, some have been better than others, and today is one
of the worst. It is the ninth or tenth day of the campaign of Curly
and Larry to avoid acknowledging, by word or glance, each other's
physical reality. (The van swerves, brakes; we lurch forward.
"Sorry!" my wife cries.) It is the fourth or fifth day since the children
last looked out the window voluntarily and said something nice about
the scenery.

We've tried to arouse them. "Natural beauty on the left!" I've
yelled many times, and "Magnificence on the right!" and "Incredible
rock formations!" and "Fabulous forest giants looming in the morning mist!" I end up sounding like an old emcee in a white tux: Coming
up now, folks, one of America's most beloved mountains, so what do
you say we all look out the window and show our appreciation of
this terrific natural attraction—*Mount Hood!*

Now my wife cries, "Just look out there!" and the children, who
have seen Mount McKinley close up from a small plane, and the
Arctic tundra and a gold mine, the beaches and tropical valleys of
Kauai, and the big surf at Diamond Head, the glaciers and fjords
around Juneau, the mighty Columbia, the windswept rocky coast and
the Oregon sand dunes and the Olympic Peninsula and its deep rain
forests and cold blue mountain lakes, and enough pure grandeur to
make a person wish for an oil refinery: the children glance up at a
grove of pre-Christian redwoods around us, shafts of sun, mist, deep
greens and browns glistening, a sight so lovely you might expect to
see a quotation from Thoreau underneath it—they glance up and they
slouch back down into their music. It is music that makes me grateful
for Mr. Sony and his wonderful invention: all I can hear from the
tiny headphones is faint noises, like distant chain saws clearing brush.
A line of motor homes lumbers northward up a steep grade, followed
by a crowd of bikers on Harleys, and we fly south past them and
glide, like a plane banking through cloud, between ranks of giant
trees, and turn onto a small dirt road alongside a meadow, and stop.

"DANGER: WILD ELK," says a sign in the meadow. "UNPREDICTABLE AROUND PEOPLE. DANGEROUS WHEN CLOSER THAN 30'—AVOID EYE CONTACT ESPECIALLY DURING RUTTING SEASON, AUGUST–OCTOBER." Or elephants could appear, it seems, or a band of riders on horseback in mail coats and dull-silver helmets with green plumes, talking to each other in a soft, chirpy language—*the trees are so fantastic*. We walk up the road and into a grove of redwoods, Marilyn and Curly walking ahead, so he can avoid eye contact with Larry. The towering trees make us all tiny, almost invisible, as in childhood I dreamed of being. They summon up in me from childhood a devout silence once inspired by stories in books. What I once felt about Adam and Eve, Robinson Crusoe, Laura Ingalls, and Lewis and Clark, I now feel in the presence of redwoods.

Back in the van, and this time Larry takes the wheel, and we roar away, packed tight with our suitcases and knapsacks, tapes and Walkmans, loose jackets and hats, our flotsam, our newspapers and guidebooks that are packed with interesting facts about fascinating places to see. *This trip is a bust*. My wife and young Moe are the only sweet ones left; the rest of us have soured on each other. "I'm *tired* of family," Marilyn said, succinctly, a few days ago. "Why do we have to do so many things together?" asked Curly. "Why can't we split up?" And now Larry, who has suffered in silence, is expressing himself through his ferocious driving, passing car after car with a vengeance, throwing us poor passengers around, a vanload of unpredictable, ill-tempered elk sitting dangerously close to each other and becoming a little nauseated, too. "Please don't drive with your Walkman on," I said a few cars ago, afraid he might be tuned in to a heavy-metal station, but he couldn't hear me. And now I am going to wind up this letter. If this boy in blind frustration takes us head on into a lumber truck and my blood-soaked tablet is found in the ditch, I'd like for my last words to be a complete sentence. The family that she and I made out of a sudden middle-aged romance is a real family. Lead us not into temptation but deliver us from evil. Please drive carefully. Thank you so very much. And now let's all welcome a wonderful little city, always a favorite here on 101—here's *Garberville!*

HOME TEAM

I T'S A LARGE MOMENT when you leave a place where you have lived all your life and sail away over the edge. I am forty-five, and it felt enormous on Monday, September 28, around 1:00 P.M., when my wife and I packed a bike, a swivel chair, and two big suitcases in the back of our red Chevy Blazer and drove along the tree-lined avenues of St. Paul and out of town, east toward New York City. On a sudden urge, I stopped at the bank and got more cash. We drove out on U.S. 12 toward the St. Croix River and Wisconsin. A bright fall day. "This is you and me—we're really leaving. Can you believe it?" she said. She is a city girl, born and bred in Copenhagen, and she never really took to Minnesota. To her, New York was the best idea we'd had since we got married. We cruised along at fifty-five, looking at the last stretch of Minnesota pasture and thinking. In 1961, a friend of mine named Barry Halper drove his white convertible out that highway to start a new job, as a newsman at KDWB, and ran into the rear end of a schoolbus that had stopped to let kids off, and was killed. He is still a real person to me—still nineteen, tall, with long black hair falling over his forehead, still (as I get older and older) talking about becoming a comedy writer in TV. All the time I lived there, I would occasionally run into someone who knew Barry, and it was sad to think that when I crossed the river there'd be nobody to remember him with.

Not far north of 12 is Marine, where I lived for four years, and where an old friend I haven't seen for seven years got into a big, ridiculous argument with me that I now think was actually caused by my hitting him across the shins with a softball bat hours before during a game. I walloped a high pop-up and tossed the bat aside in disgust and nailed the catcher, my friend, who hours later accused me of something—insensitivity, perhaps—and we quarreled at the end of my driveway until he stalked away into the night. So long as I lived in St. Paul, there was a chance we might bump into each other, and smile, and our friendship click back on, but when the river is crossed the break becomes permanent, along with all the other dumb things I did here. I felt like stopping for a moment. The bridge was coming toward us fast. Then the Chevy thrust forward, and, flaps down, we rose up and over the river, landing in Wisconsin, heading east.

That evening, the Minnesota Twins won their division championship in the American League, down in Texas, against the Rangers, 5–3. By the time Herb Carneal came on the air with the play-by-play, we were in Oshkosh, and WCCO (The Good Neighbor to the Great Northwest) was long gone from our dial. I read about the Twins' big win the next morning in the Milwaukee paper, which was not so excited about the event, and neither was my wife, for whom baseball is a book in a foreign language, interesting but not informative. So I didn't suggest that it might be fun to stop in Chicago and look for a Minneapolis paper.

Tuesday, we poked around Oshkosh with friend Thatcher, who showed us the truck factory, and said *Farvel* and drove to Sandusky, Ohio. Night reached us near Gary, Indiana, and as we sped east on the turnpike we heard part of a White Sox broadcast as it faded out and part of another one, perhaps the Indians, fading in. Long pauses in the broadcast booth, a quiet crowd in the background, ruminating: you could tell that their team was out of the running. That night, the Twins lost to Texas. They lost again Wednesday and went north to Kansas City and lost three there. We reached Pittsburgh on Wednesday (Three Rivers Stadium was lit up for a Pirates double-header, and I told my wife it was probably her last chance to see a game this year, and she agreed that it probably was) and New York on Friday evening. The moving van arrived Saturday. Sunday, October 4, the last day of the season, as the Twins got shellacked 10–1 in K.C., we looked around at our apartment that resembled a landfill, and took a long walk. A warm evening, and the streets full of people, a river of yellow taxis flowing uptown on Eighth Avenue, and a sky almost full of skyscrapers—graceful old brick and stone ones—lit up. She was so happy. We walked and walked. "What are you thinking?" she asked. "Do you miss Minnesota?"

"Sure, and I miss Pall Malls, too," I said. But I was thinking about my team. You stick with a team for years, like a not-so-great marriage in which you're still loyal and hopeful, and then, the day you break up, she loses fifty pounds and gets a haircut and becomes an overnight success. I wished I were in Minneapolis to see all the phlegmatic Swedes go wild.

The Twins arrived in Minnesota in the spring of 1961 from Washington, D.C., where they had been the hapless Senators, but that didn't matter to us. They were ours, and we were proud to have them—Camilo Pascual and his big tabletop curve, Pistol Pete Ramos, Bob Allison, and the mighty Harmon Killebrew, America's nicest power hitter. It was my first year in college, the same year my friend was killed. In 1965, the Twins made it to the World Series and lost to the Dodgers, and then, for years, the Series looked as remote as the America's Cup, Minnesota not being a major center of yachting, but even those thin years—when the team lost, and attendance fell, and the careful owner, seeing the gate receipts dwindle, reduced his payroll costs by ridding the team of star players like Rod Carew and Lyman Bostock—seem like a bright, green paradise compared with the gloom that fell on the Twins when they moved from the old ballpark in Bloomington to a domed stadium downtown for the 1982

season. In Minnesota, a Northern state, where one is forced indoors
for much of four months of the year, the idea of spending a summer
afternoon in an immense basement is deeply depressing; it was a
fundamental heresy, just as if the Lutheran Church were to incor-
porate Mammon into the Godhead and make the Trinity a Quartet.
I tried to like the dome for two years and gave up. It was, is, and
ever will be a godforsaken, unnatural, and unhappy place to play the
game of baseball, and right there my old team and I parted company.

The American League playoff began Wednesday night in Minnesota, against Detroit. Gaetti hit two home runs, and Reardon struck
out the side in the ninth with two men on base. The Twins won,
8–5, and again Thursday night, 6–3, Blyleven going seven and a third
innings. I didn't watch either game—too busy, and our TV didn't
work.

"I'm not really a Twins fan," I explained to people in New York
who congratulated me on the team's doing so well, and I tried to
explain about the dome, but it sounded like sour grapes. Everywhere
I wrote a check and offered my Minnesota driver's license for an ID,
people said something about the Twins, such as "Hey, how about
those Twins?" The man at the bank where I went to open a checking
account treated me as if I were applying for welfare, but when he
saw my former address he smiled and said I must be pretty excited.
I wasn't, but I was grateful. The man at the newsstand, whose sister
is married to a man from Excelsior, Minnesota, greeted me like an
old pal. "Hey, your guys won!" he said, and they did. On Columbus
Day, they beat Detroit to get into the Series.

I started running into former Minnesotans, who recognized me
from my maroon Golden Gophers sweatshirt. They couldn't believe
it, they said—the *Twins* in the Series! I waited in the 23rd Street
subway station at Sixth Avenue with a man from St. Paul, who asked
me twice if I thought they could win the Series. Not if they would
but if it was a possibility for them, as if a mysterious spore we had
ingested in our mothers' tuna hotdish made us constitutionally unable

to be fans of a winning team. Those four times the Vikings lost the
football championship took a heavy toll on him, he said, and he didn't
want to be fooled again.

Friends called from Minnesota, including a woman I went to college with who had never been to a Twins game in her life. She said
that Minneapolis was feverish, full of noise and banners—on the
tallest building in town one night, lights spelled out "WIN TWINS"—
and strangers in the street talking baseball. "You should come back
for the Series," she said. "I've never seen people behaving like this.
God, *I've* never been like this. I'm excited, and I don't even *like*
baseball." A friend called to offer Series tickets, and called back the
next night to cancel that—the friend of his who knew someone whose
brother worked for the Twins was not returning phone calls. "The
town is nuts. You wouldn't believe it. It's great. You just want to
go out and walk around and grin at people. You better come back
and see it. You'll never forgive yourself if you miss it."

I still hadn't watched a single game. Our TV set had worked in
St. Paul, but in Manhattan it was receiving triple and quadruple
shadow images, each human figure a chorus line, against a soup of
colors—it looked like video art. We were busy unpacking boxes anyway, and trying to fit the furniture from a big old Minnesota house
into a skinny three-bedroom apartment, and in the evening, when
most of the games were played, we felt like getting out of our mess
and walking the streets and seeing the city that had lured us away
from the Midwest.

The first game of the Series was on Saturday night. When I woke
up Saturday morning, I found myself thinking about the game and
how much fun it would be to be in Minnesota, soaking up all that
jubilation and floating good will and good-humored anxiety, and go
to Russell's house to watch the game, to sit jammed together in a
den with ten or twelve people who all felt exactly as I did, so that if
I said, "I really believe that they can win," they would all know the
exact gravity of the sentence. We could mention a former player or

manager, and instantly all of us remember that man vividly. We could recall games, we could reminisce about notable seasons, and not much would need to be said to call them to mind. When all of you have lived in a place forever, you're able to touch each other with a few slight words.

My wife had friends to go visit that night, so I sat down alone to watch, in a living room where we had piled quite a few things to be sorted out later, including a big brown jug I'm embarrassed to be still carting around—a trophy that went to the winner of an annual church softball game between single men and married men, a series that ended twenty-some years ago. The church was a pretty strict fundamentalist outfit, whose younger members tended to drift away into larger, more moderate churches, and by the early sixties so many players on both sides had been lost to heterodoxy that the summer Bible-camp classic came to an end. The scores of all the games are painted on the jug. I forget why it wound up with me; I left the church as soon as I could, sooner than most of the others.

When I turned on the TV, the picture was so blurry I didn't recognize the place as the Metrodome in Minneapolis, and the crowd waving hankies didn't look familiar, either, but the voice introducing the players belonged to the old ballpark announcer, Bob Casey, and that stamped the whole thing as authentic and genuine. I started to get good and tense, and by "rockets' red glare, the bombs bursting in air" I was leaning forward. I said "Go!" as the home team and a crowd of shadows ran out of their numerous dugouts onto the yellowish-blue-green field, and I leaned forward and girded up my innards to will them to victory. Win, team. We really need this one. For all the Lutheran back yards with the rosebushes wrapped and the flower beds covered for winter, and for all the romantic gents in the taverns and all the ladies buying bedspreads in Dayton's, for all the little grain-elevator towns on the prairie, for the shut-ins, for all the kids in the Twins caps, and for me. I didn't come to New York to be pitied by a man at the bank because I'm from Minnesota. I don't want to stand in the station commiserating with fellow losers. Win. When they ask, "Where you from?" and I say where, I want them to smile and say, "Hey. All right. Minnesota."

(THE TWINS WON THE SERIES IN SEVEN GAMES. A YEAR LATER, I STILL COULDN'T BRING MYSELF TO GET A NEW YORK DRIVER'S LICENSE.)

BASKETBALL

I GREW UP FAST as a kid and got tall before the others, a long sad boy poking up like a milkweed out of the range of normal children, and when adults met me, they often looked up and asked, "Do you play basketball?" I did, but not very well, because I was too tall: my family lived out in the country, twelve miles from the high school, and when I tried to hitchhike home in the winter twilight after basketball practice, bundled up in a parka I looked too huge and ominous and nobody would stop and pick me up. So I quit basketball. Except for a few hundred afternoons sliding around on gravel driveways and a couple thousand games of Horse, my career stopped for thirty years until a morning in late March when I took a cab up to a gym on East 54th Street to tape a little piece for CBS. According to the script, I'd stand on the court—at the side of the free-throw circle, where I used to have a good jump shot—and talk (holding a ball) for about two minutes and a half about the fun of the game, and then turn and take my shot. CBS wanted to use that piece just before one of the NCAA tournament games they were televising. I didn't ask why. I'm forty-five and I no longer worry about the motives of people who invite me to do something I want to do. I just wanted to make the shot. The truth is, the shot was my idea, and Doug the producer was cool to it at first and preferred to tape the piece in a studio with me behind a desk. He was polite and never said that he thought I'd look funny with a basketball in my hand, he only said, "You're a writer, you'll feel more comfortable at a desk," but it meant the same thing, so I held out for the gym. I wore black tuxedo pants, a white tux shirt, and old sneakers. The CBS crew was set up at mid-court when I got there at 10:00: Doug, two cameramen, a video engineer, and an audio man who was trying to eliminate a hum in the works, which gave me the chance to practice the shot about thirty times until I was drilling it, bang, bang, bang, and sank six in a row and was all set. It took an hour to shoot the piece, four takes in which I stood and talked about the fun of basketball and then turned and jumped and shot, and I made three of four shots, no lie, which is pretty good work with the camera running and a producer watching. Between takes I even made one backward, over the shoulder, without looking, swish, from twenty feet. No lie either. And then I went home and forgot about the whole thing until the middle of April, when the piece appeared before the Kansas-Oklahoma game. I didn't see it but a lot of other people did and mentioned to me that they'd seen it and every one asked the same question: *Did you really make that shot?* My Uncle Don asked, "How many shots did you take to get your swisher?" He assumed the shot had been spliced in, and so did everyone else, television being the sleaze hole that it is. A man stopped me on the street and said, "That was neat how they did that shot, it really looked like it was you." He was young, early thirties, and seemed to think a twenty-foot jumper is beyond a man my age and requires technical assistance. His remark stung, and so did six more the same day and eight or ten the next week. Despite what had appeared to be me, their friend, turning and shooting and making the shot, everyone was dubious, except the poet Roland Flint, who wrote, "I was impressed with the luck and ease of your one-hander." My Aunt Eleanor, a scrappy player herself years ago with an excellent two-handed set shot, wrote, "I saw the opening of the NCAA basketball finals. It was a nice shot but did you make the first one?" Not one person said to me what they would've said if they'd actually seen the shot: "Nice shot." And it *was* a nice shot. It felt so good after reciting my piece and trying to smile and project warmth into the lens and not squint under the lights—it felt good to turn away, see the rim, jump, reach high with the ball, push it off with the fingertips, and know the instant it left, while it was in the air, that it was good.

WOODLAWN

DULL, MORBID THOUGHTS ARE ON MY MIND these days: the usual ones—disease, decrepitude, and the big "D" down in the basement. Monday morning, I walked my wife to her job near Union Square, kissed her goodbye, and headed up Park Avenue toward my office. It was a bright cold day. I was okay until I looked up at 24th and saw, in stone, a man's head in the mouth of a lion. At 27th, I ducked into the New York Life building and down a subway passage marked "UP AND DOWN TOWN" as a herd of passengers came pouring through two revolving doors revolving so steadily that the doors looked like a machine that stamps out office workers—*whump whump whump*. That and the herd getting off the uptown local with me at Grand Central made me want to duck out, and, for no reason except that I hadn't done this sort of thing for much too long, I ducked across the platform and got on the No. 4 Woodlawn–Jerome Ave. express just to see where it goes. Owing to the specialized nature of my work, my company doesn't miss me if I arrive a few hours late. Nobody there knows what I do.

The express stopped at 59th and at 86th, then put its head down and raced up to 125th, and around 160th it came up out of the ground. Yankee Stadium slipped by—a slice of green field and the famous overhang—and a couple miles of Bronx, and at the last stop I got out and looked around.

It was magnificent, exactly how the end of the line should look: wide open, like the edge of town, where the buildings end and the woods and pasture begin—the Manhattan-Wisconsin border. Except the pasture turned out to be the Mosholu Golf Course, where some bulky guys on a nearby green were practicing their short putts, and the woods was a cemetery.

I crossed Jerome and walked in the gate. Woodlawn Cemetery. A man sat and eyed me from a guardhouse, and I tried to look purposeful: marched straight by and down one fork as if heading for my own crypt. It's a fabulous cemetery. The roads wind among ornamental groves and solemn granite temples to the dead—twelve- and fifteen-foot-high mausoleums spaced like tourist cabins in the trees and interspersed with stone catafalques and pedestals and ob- elisks the size of ICBMs. One temple contained Kresges, another some Woolworths guarded by a pair of sphinxes, and, farther on, a stone archangel with trumpet in hand gazed down upon eight mem- bers of the Martens family whom he had summoned, presumably to a rich reward. One temple boasted glass windows with actual draperies inside (bleached by years of sunlight); others had stained glass. A weeping female figure strewed flowers. A bronze maiden clutched at the door to a tomb. Figures sagged in grief, heads bowed at the immensity of the loss, and a girl with long hair sat pensively in front of the Oelsners' tomb as if waiting for them to come out and go to the movies.

The tasteless excess and gargantuan self-worship and ostentation of grief were making me silly. When I came around a bend and saw a line of black limousines parked on a crossroad and a crowd of people at the far end, I decided to go up and attend the funeral. I straightened my tie and shot my cuffs. Then I heard a squawk, and a kid with a walkie-talkie in his jacket pocket stepped out from behind the last car. He said, "Pardon me, sir. I'm sorry, but I can't let you come up this way. Thanks. Thanks a lot."

I asked what was going on up the hill.

"Making a movie," he said.

"Really? What's the name of it?"

"*Sanctuary*. It's a feature picture."

So I took the next road over, walked up the hill and cut around behind some temples, and ambled toward the movie-making—toward a bunch of men in blue-and-green parkas, their backs to me, watching a funeral. A mahogany-brown metal coffin decked with dozens of scarlet roses sat on a bier draped with green, a silver-haired Catholic priest at the head of it with a teen-age acolyte in a white smock, and forty-some mourners, all in black, stood in four rows to one side, a short woman in black to the other. She wore a long black veil. Uphill from the priest, in front of a ten-foot stone cross, sat an angel, hand over its heart as if reciting the Pledge of Allegiance. Nearby, a woman perched on a stepladder, holding a mike boom, and behind the veiled woman were a camera, on a dolly resting on a short steel-tube track, and two sheets of white fabric on steel frames, like two upright trampolines.

"Those are reflectors," a man in a parka told me. "The light is good, so we don't need to bring in lights, anyway, thank goodness. Otherwise, we'd be even further behind than we are." He was a makeup man. As a beautiful woman in a long black coat approached, he studied her, and when she sat down—in a canvas chair labeled "Michael"—he went over and touched up her left eyebrow with a pencil. Her coat almost concealed white running shoes and thick pink socks. Other chairs were labeled "Zena," "Nuzo," and "Don." A man wearing earphones fiddled with a stack of recording gear near a pile of equipment boxes. He jumped a little when a man clapped his hands near the boom mike—a man in a blue baseball cap, faded blue jeans, white running shoes, and a gray sweater with a long red stripe down each arm. "Pay attention, folks," this man said. "Let me give you some direction." All the mourners stopped gabbing and listened. They wore black suits and coats, some had black hats. Most of them seemed to be young men with oiled black hair and good-sized beaks. I asked the makeup man if this was a gangster movie.

"You got it," he said.

"Places! Places, everyone!" somebody yelled.

I watched them shoot one scene four times: The priest, who wore a pink skullcap, said, "Let us pray. Lord Jesus Christ, by the three days you lay in the tomb you made holy the graves of all those who believe in you. . . . Give our brother peaceful rest in this tomb," and sprinkled the coffin with holy water, four shakes. The mourners crossed themselves, and he turned to them and said, consolingly, "It's nice to see the family pull together in this most tragic moment," and a moment later, as the back row of black figures began to move down the slope toward the limos on the road (drivers standing at attention beside them), the woman in the black veil threw herself grief-stricken upon the coffin and wailed, "Gino! Gino! My *bambino!*" On each succeeding take, the mourners crossed themselves (top, bottom, left, right) a little more smoothly, and Gino's mom missed him more.

Before each shot, somebody yelled, "Places! Places everyone! Same shot!" and the mourners took their places, and the director said, "Rolling!"—the word relayed by outlying sentries ("Rolling!" . . . "Rolling!" . . . "Rolling!" . . . "Rolling!")—and then said, "Action!" and the priest prayed and sprinkled, the crowd of black coats crossed themselves, he consoled, they moved away down the slope, and she threw herself and wept. Every single time, she hit the grief right on the money: "Gino! Gino! My *bambino!*"

"I'm getting an awful lot of rustling when they come down through the leaves," the sound man said. "We gotta lay down some rubber mats."

I was the only bystander. Everyone else had a job to do. Some people wandered around between takes, but when the man yelled,

"Places!" everyone jumped to attention, even the limo drivers in the background—everyone but me. I hung around and watched some closeup takes, including two more Gino-Gino-my-*bambino*s, and finally, feeling definitely out of place (and it was 11:30), I hiked out past the line of limos and then past the temples and fainting stone figures to the subway terminal and caught the No. 4 express downtown. I was alone in the next-to-last car until a bunch of teen-age girls got on at 183rd. They whooped it up and talked about parties and dancing and boys all the way to 42nd. I've never heard girls talk as dirty as that, and after the mausoleums it sounded wonderful. I'm telling you right now, I want to be cremated, and no tombstone, either. Just take what's left of me up to Trott Brook where my grandma and Uncle Jim are, make them scoot over, put me down in the middle, and put back the sod.

EPISCOPAL

I GOT INTO THE EPISCOPAL CHURCH one summer living in Copenhagen when I suddenly became lonely for English. I had gotten good enough in Danish to be able to say things like "Yes, thank you, I have it well to be the weather and we well shall enjoy to possess the summer here. It is delightful to me for speaking on Danish and find your wife extremely amusing," but I missed English and often recited stuff as I hiked around that stately gray city, like Bible verses and sonnets and country songs, for the beauty of them, and one Sunday morning, hearing the bells, got dressed up and marched over to St. Alban's, at the opposite end of Langelinie park from the statue of the Little Mermaid, near the moat and the great star-shaped medieval earthworks called Kastellet. All the tour buses stop there. The museum of the Danish Resistance is just across the lawn, and next door is the fountain of Gefion, one of the most massive and exciting fountains in the world, in which the lady, having turned her four brothers into oxen, carves out the land of Denmark with a single-bottom plow. Most Americans walk right past this magnificent fountain and hardly see it, because they are intent on finding the famous Mermaid statue, which they know from their map is nearby and which they imagine to be as big as the Statue of Liberty but which turns out to be a small damp sad person in the midst of a personality crisis. Gefion, well armored, holding her whip high, getting the job done, is more like Danish women today.

I never went to an Episcopal church before in my life, but there I was in Denmark, and when it comes to worship, the English language has always been real important to me. We didn't speak in tongues in the Plymouth Brethren back in Minnesota, just English, same as our Lord and His Apostles, so in I went that Sunday and then every Sunday thereafter. A few Americans were there, *obviously* American, earnest, anxious to please, to befriend, to share, to be relevant, but most of the worshippers were Brits, including a bunch of tweed-clad couples in their early seventies who strode in like they'd just killed a fox that morning and knelt down, addressed the Lord, got the thing done and taken care of, and got up and went home to dine on beef. I liked them. They said, "Keillor, that's a Scottish name, isn't it?" "Uh, yes, it is." "Mmmmmhmmm. Very good. But you're American." "Yes." "Mmmmhmmm." And that satisfied their curiosity. They were stodgy and warbly and wonderful in every way, and I walked home from mass feeling rejuvenated, whistling a Fats Waller tune, and making up words to it.

I'm slow to anger, don't covet or lust.
No sins of pride except sometimes I really must.

Episcopalian, saving my love for you.
The theology's easy, the liturgy too.
Just stand up and kneel down and say what the others do.
Episcopalian, saving my love for you.

Anglicanism was what J. N. Darby and the early Plymouth Brethren revolted against in 1831, for its worldliness, its lack of prophetic vision and lack of millennialist fervor for the Second Coming of Christ, its unholy union with the state, and when they pulled out of communion and became the Brethren, they took nothing Anglican with them. They left behind the Gothic architecture, the chanting and choral music, the liturgy, the ecclesiastical order, the high altar, the clerical garments, incense, candles, statuary, the kneeling and blessing, the bowing and genuflecting, and every other scrap of papist paraphernalia. At Grace & Truth Gospel Hall, on 14th Avenue South in Minneapolis, where I attended every Sunday for twenty years, the walls were white and bare, the seats plain, facing a small table in the middle with bread and wine on it. No musical instrument was allowed. Men stood up as the Spirit moved and read from Scripture or prayed impromptu prayers—the thought of *reading* a prayer off the page seemed weak and unmanly—or called for a hymn from the Little Flock hymnbook, which contained plain, modest doctrinally-correct verses sung to a few plain melodies and none of Protestantism's greatest hits. Sunday-morning meeting lasted up to two hours, and the mood of it was solemn, plain, with long silences. A boy who grew up in the Brethren is an easy mark for the Episcopalians: they march into the dim cathedral chanting ancient things in their beady gowns and blowing smoke at him and next thing you know he is reading prayers out of a book.

I bless myself with a flick of the wrist.
You'd never know I was raised fundamentalist.
Episcopalian, saving my love for you.

I don't have the manual dexterity to be a true Episcopalian, who must juggle the prayer book, hymnal, and the order of service, and sometimes a special mimeographed Kyrie or Sanctus; the music sounds thin and sharp to someone brought up on the Wesleys; the bowing and kneeling are odd—in the Brethren we just clomped in and sat down, and there was no incense in the air, just cologne, and no statuary (though some of our members were less lively than others); and then if, on top of that, the sermon is about revolutionizing our awareness of homeless gay handicapped Nicaraguans, the Episcopal church is more exotic to me than anything in Scandinavia.

There's white folks and black, and gay and morose,
Some male Anglo Saxons but we watch them pretty close.
Episcopalian, saving my love for you.

Back in Minnesota, where words like "tuna hotdish," or "chicken," or "Lutheran" always got a laugh and a great joke might be one about Lutherans eating tuna hotdish and feeding the rest to their chickens, "Episcopalian" was also mighty funny, especially if a Lutheran became one. To me and to my little radio congregation, a Lake Wobegonian moving to Minneapolis and turning Episcopalian was a case of social climbing straight up the hill, no doubt about it. Our clear picture of Episcopalians was of wealthy people, Yale graduates, worshipping God in extremely good taste. Episcopalian was the church in wingtips, the church of the Scotch and soda. So, when I moved to New York and walked into Holy Apostles, I was surprised to see no suits. Nobody was well dressed. A congregation of a hundred souls on lower Ninth Avenue, a church with no parking lot, which was in need of paint and the sanctuary ceiling showed water damage, but which managed (I learned the next week) to support and operate a soup kitchen that fed a thousand New Yorkers every day, more than a million to date. Black faces in the sanctuary, old people, exiles from the Midwest, the lame and the halt, divorced ladies, gay couples:

a real good anthology of the faith. I felt glad to be there. When we stood for prayers, bringing slowly to mind the goodness and the poverty of our lives, the lives of others, the life to come, it brought tears to your eyes, the simple way the Episcopalians pray.

A woman stood in the aisle, to the rear, and led us in prayers, stopping after each call to leave a long silence where anybody could breathe a word or two in response—a prayer in which the people fill in the blanks. She called us to *pray for the Church* (help this church, God) . . . *for peace and justice in the world* (stop the drugs, the corruption of government) . . . *for all those in need or trouble* (for the sick and the dying) . . . *for all who seek God* (for my family and all the Plymouth Brethren) . . . *for those who have died* (Corinne, the people on the Iranian airliner) . . . *and offer our thanks.* Thanks for bringing me here. Thank you.

NU ER DER JUL IGEN

A LL OUR CHRISTMAS GIFTS WERE STOLEN, Friday, December 18, about 6:00 P.M., on the Carey bus to Kennedy, lifted by another passenger evidently. We got off at our stop, bent down and reached into the luggage compartment, and—no big black suitcase. Forty pounds of treasures. The driver shrugged ("Hey, pal, that ain't my problem"), we ran for the plane, caught it, crossed the Atlantic and landed in Copenhagen at 8:00 A.M. feeling blue, feeling robbed, bushed, beaten. We took a cab to the apartment and slept. We walked down along Langelinie to the King's New Market (new for a couple centuries) and looked in shop windows on Strøget. We talked to our

Danish son, Morten, who had just dropped out of business school and was in high spirits. Nuts to statistics. He had applied for a job as a helper in a kindergarten. I couldn't forget the black suitcase, the lost gifts. My Danish wife said, philosophically, "Whoever stole it is going to have a darned nice Christmas, that's for sure." I bought her an Italian sweatshirt, red stockings, and a big ceramic fat lady with wild red hair, head thrown back, singing a high note, like "glory, glory, halle*lu*jah," and then it was the 24th, the big day in Denmark and also a short one. The sun rises about 9:00, muted by clouds, and murk sets in about 3:00. Our other Danish kids, Mattias and Malene, had arrived, and Elly, my mother-in-law. We went to church at four.

The intonation of ministers is the same in Danish as in English, deep with long meaningful pauses, and the sermon, which could have been about forbearance or the seven-headed beast or the need for more comprehensive urban planning, set me to brooding over the stolen American treasures my kids would have enjoyed so much, but after we got home and lit a few candles and put dinner on the table—roast goose and pork with the skin on and red cabbage, potatoes and gravy, red Spanish wine—the suitcase faded. After dinner we sat in the living room around a solitary candle on the coffee table, except for Morten, who disappeared into the hall, where the tree stood. I forgot to mention the tree. An eight-foot spruce—no, ten-foot—hung with glass balls and strings of little red paper Danish flags and forty candles as thick as my little finger.

We five sat in the dark, and my wife recited a poem called "Peters Jul" that the kids knew so well their lips moved as she said:

> Jeg glæder mig in denne tid;
> nu falder julesneen hvid.
> så ved jeg, julen kommer.
> Min Far hver dag i byen går,
> og når han kommer hjem, jeg står
> og ser hans store lommer.

(I become so happy this time of year, / now falls the white snow, / so I know that Christmas is coming. / Every day my dad goes into town, / and when he comes home, I stand / and see his bulging pockets.)

She recited a bunch more; then suddenly the door to our dark room opened and there stood the tree, its candles blazing, the only light in the apartment, and so brilliant and gorgeous we piled into the hall like lost hunters come on a bonfire. I could feel the heat from the candles as we stood around it. The little flames flickered, and their reflections in the glass. We took songbooks, walked around and around the tree, singing in Danish about the *lille barn* Jesus lying in the *krybbe* and the *stjerne* in the sky and *engler* singing halleluias, and we even sang "Rudolf med den Røde Tud," and we sang "Stille Nacht" standing still. And then, as my Danes have done every Jul since they were *lille børn*, they all joined hands and I hooked onto the end and we ran hand in hand from one room to another in the dark singing over and over a little song, "Nu er der jul igen" (Now is there Yule again, of course). From the hall into the dining room and through the living room and the bedrooms to the kitchen fragrant with goose grease and back to the dazzling tree and back into the dark, slipping and sliding over rugs and around chairs, around and around. When finally we flopped down around the tree to parcel out the presents, the black suitcase had disappeared completely.

GLAD BAGS

MARCH BEING NATIONAL FROZEN FOOD MONTH, I bought a box of Glad-Lock Heavy Duty Reclosable Freezer Bags and a Freezette plastic freezer dish with locking lid at Sloan's the other day and took them home, thinking I might whomp up a couple of gallons of spaghetti sauce and freeze most of it in quart-size portions for future reference. I sauté chunks of chicken in butter and garlic, dump in tomato sauce, and add mushrooms and zucchini, and serve it over spaghetti—a good piece of cuisine I call Pasta à la Pete. I cook it, I eat it, and after a couple of forkfuls I say, "It's good, isn't it?" Other people around the table say, "*Yes*, it's good." It's not a dish that you need to trouble yourself to frame a major artistic compliment for— it's just good food, that's all. Anyway, it's good enough, like Glad-Lock bags themselves. Made of clear plastic, they lock okay. They hold food. So I was surprised to see on the Glad-Lock Freezer Bag package "Free TWA Air Miles Inside, Save 'Em or Trade 'Em for Cash" and to discover that my purchase of twenty quart-size freezer bags had won me five free miles on TWA and a chance to win hundreds or thousands of additional miles, perhaps even "unlimited free air travel for one year." It seemed excessive.

To find out how many bonus miles I had won, I simply rubbed the gold film off the Instant Bonus Miles Certificate inside the Glad-Lock box. It was a big relief to see that my bonus was a mere twenty free TWA miles, for a total of twenty-five for the box. Unlimited free air travel for one year is the sort of prize to turn you and your family into surly beasts and disgust your friends and ruin your children and bring your marriage crashing into a low line of trees—a year that would teach you never to purchase another freezer bag in your life. You couldn't pay me enough to accept a prize like that; I'd gladly lock myself into this office rather than face a year aboard an airline.

Whoever thought up this frequent-freezer program for Glad-Lock overlooked a better idea, and that's a few free miles aboard a train heading for those garden spots where in a few months they'll be hauling in bushel baskets of gorgeous stuff that would make my pasta something glorious, the *Appalachian Spring* of spaghettis. Twenty-five miles aboard Amtrak would take you within range of gardens where you could put Glad-Lock to good use, collecting zucchini, snap beans and limas, small red potatoes, fresh leaf lettuce, beet greens, and green tomatoes, which taste so good fried in cornmeal. Five free miles on the Lexington Avenue subway would take you to Union Square and its lavish weekend green market. Trains, not planes, are the way to travel for purposes of foraging. The train rolls along past the back yards and gardens of towns, such as the garden of our youth along the Mississippi, where in April a neighbor named Fred Peterson plowed my folks' half-acre patch with his tractor, and we raked it and planted it in one Saturday. The dirt smelled fresh then, and after every rain and when the sun shone, too. Dirt is what I miss in the city, and one of these days I may take my Glad-Lock bags and ride up along the Hudson, stopping between here and Albany to collect soil samples. These bags, which are reclosable, would keep quarts of dirt fresh for weeks, and day after day I could take some out, spread it on white paper on my desk, and feel in touch with life. In spring, an eighteenth-floor office in Manhattan is so isolated from the main action I might as well be flying. Some clean dirt would be good to have. One could plant a desktop tomato and maintain contact with what's happening out there.

Get off that plane and put your feet on the ground, Glad. April is coming, which is National Spring Month. Take a hike.

HOPPERS

A HYDRANT WAS OPEN on Seventh Avenue above 23rd Street last Friday morning, and I stopped on my way east and watched people hop over the water. It was a brilliant spring day. The water was a nice clear creek about three feet wide and ran along the gutter around the northwest corner of the intersection. A gaggle of pedestrians crossing 23rd went *hop hop hop hop hop* over the creek as a few soloists jaywalking Seventh performed at right angles to them, and I got engrossed in the dance. Three feet isn't a long leap for most people, and the ease of it permits a wide range of expression. Some hoppers went a good deal higher than necessary.

Long, lanky men don't hop, as a rule. The ones I saw hardly paused at the water's edge, just lengthened one stride and trucked on across—a rather flatfooted approach that showed no recognition of the space or occasion. Tall men typically suffer from an excess of cool, but I kept hoping for one of them to get off the ground. Most of the tall men wore topcoats and carried briefcases, so perhaps their balance was thrown off. One tall man in a brown coat didn't notice the water and stepped off the curb into fast-flowing Hydrant Creek and made a painful hop, like a wounded heron: a brown heron with a limp wing attached to a briefcase bulging full of dead fish. He crossed 23rd looking as though his day had been pretty much shot to pieces.

Short, fat men were superb: I could have watched them all morning. A typical fat man crossing the street would quicken his step when he saw the creek and, on his approach, do a little shuffle, arms out to the sides, and suddenly and with great concentration *spring*—a nimble step all the more graceful for the springer's bulk. Three fairly fat men jiggled and shambled across 23rd together, and then one poked another and they saw the water. They stepped forward, studying the angle, and just before the point man jumped for the curb his pals said something, undoubtedly discouraging, and he threw back his head and laughed over his shoulder and threw himself lightly, boyishly, across the water, followed—*boing boing*—by the others.

The women who hopped the water tended to stop and study the creek and find its narrows and measure the distance and then lurch across. They seemed dismayed that the creek was there at all, and one, in a beige suit, put her hands on her hips and glared upstream, as if to say, "Whose water *is* this? This is utterly unacceptable. I am *not* about to jump over this." But then she made a good jump after all. She put her left toe on the edge of the curb, leaned forward with right arm outstretched—for a second, she looked as if she might take off and zoom up toward the Flatiron Building—and pushed off, landing easily on her right toe, her right arm raised. The longest leap was made by a young woman in a blue raincoat carrying a plastic Macy's bag and crossing west on Seventh. She gathered herself up in three long, accelerating strides and sailed, her coat billowing out behind her, over the water and five feet beyond, almost creaming a guy coming out of Radio Shack. He shrank back as she loped past, her long black hair and snow-white hands and face right *there*, then gone, vanished in the crowd.

And then it was my turn. I waited for the green light, crossed 23rd, stopped by the creek flowing around the bend of curb and heard faint voices of old schoolmates ahead in the woods, and jumped heavily across and marched after them.

MILLS

SUMMER MAKES ME RESTLESS— especially these clear, blue postcard days when the Chrysler Building rises in the 43rd Street canyon like a finger beckoning east toward Europe. But it isn't Europe I'm restless for. There's a cigarette ad I see in the subway showing a dazzling white terrace and a beautiful blue sea that I take to be the Aegean, and I can imagine draping myself and my skinny red swimsuit across a wicker chair in the sunshine of Greece and sipping a glass of retsina, and then I imagine sitting and looking across the blue and feeling restless. So Europe isn't the answer for this, any more than cigarette smoking would be. It's simply the old summer restlessness, which goes back to school days when I sat trapped in the classroom as innocent June lay nearby and murmured in the sunshine in the far-far-left margin of the English exam and its stupefying questions about Richard Cory and why he shot himself. He just did, that's all, and who can say why? The world is full of sadness. Being rich and thin isn't everything. I don't feel like talking about it now.

Restlessness makes me think about taking a white 1960 Cadillac convertible that I don't have and driving eighty-five miles an hour across the George Washington Bridge and into the Pocono Mountains with a can of Schlitz in one hand, the top down, and the radio playing C & W songs, and, when I come to the most beautiful stretch of blue-green forest, throwing the beer can into the trees. I have never dropped any trash anywhere—not on purpose—out of respect for others and also because I was afraid that if I did Thoreau would appear and pick up my jujube wrapper and put it in his pocket and say, his large, sad eyes meeting mine, "Why should we be in such desperate haste to succeed, and in such desperate enterprises?" I don't know the answer to that one, either.

Restlessness leads me over to the office window, where there is nothing new to look at, and that makes me restless to find a new window. I take the long walk to the end of the hall, drink a drink of water, and come back, hoping the exercise will shake down this looseness and jumpiness, and I sit again. But on one long walk last Monday I turned right and rode the elevator down to the ground and hit the street. I walked west toward the river and angled south and got my car out of storage. It runs pretty well, considering that I haven't driven it more than ten miles in the past three months. I aimed it toward the West Side Highway and up the Taconic State Parkway with the radio on. I have a license to drive, and on Monday I just felt like using it. Heading up the graceful old Parkway, its progression of sensuous turns and dips shaped in an era when driving was considered romantic and fun, like dancing, I was feeling considerably calmer when the Mills Brothers came over the air singing "Gentle on My Mind." In a bright tempo, their inimitable honey-tone voices sang, "It's knowing that your door is always open and your path is free to walk that makes me tend to leave my sleeping bag rolled up and stashed behind your couch." Except for the lyrics, it sounded like a swing standard from 1936.

Thinking of the four stately black gentlemen in their shiny showsuits, their hair slicked back with pomade, swaying and snapping their fingers, their steady smiles and smooth voices, I had trouble imagining that any of the Mills Brothers had ever owned a sleeping bag, let alone stashed it behind somebody's couch. Their lives always appeared to be sedentary and committed lives, devoted to entertaining us. No Mills ever shared his problems with us on stage or his concerns about the environment. No Mills gave an interview in which he confessed a dread of fame, a confusion about his musical goals, or a fear that his vision had gone stale. When they sang on the Perry Como show, they never struck me as the least bit restless or dissatisfied, any more than Perry himself did. So it was revealing to hear them sing about not being "shackled by forgotten words and bonds and the ink stains that have dried upon some line" and the verse about wandering across the wheat fields and junkyards and highways and the train yards and the back roads. They made restlessness sound like a song they had to sing in order to have the album seem contemporary enough to satisfy their record producer. Hunkering in a train yard feeling free and waiting for a freight to come along was not part of the Mills Brothers' mystery of life, which had little to do with highways, either, and much to do with standing in a close semicircle and making pure four-part harmony. Same here, I thought. Restlessness doesn't suit me, either. I like to be squeezed a little, like a middle Mills, and hear my voice gently throbbing and bending in long, tender parallels with the others, not out here on a limb alone. An hour's run up the Taconic seemed to settle me down pretty well, and I turned around and came back to the beautiful city.

ATLANTA AIRPORT

I FLEW SOUTH TO FIND SPRING not long ago and changed planes in Atlanta, hiking from Gate C-8 to Gate C-18 and carrying the blue gym bag I've learned to stuff everything in since the day a brown suitcase of mine left me in Dallas and flew off to spend a week by itself. Airline terminals, as everyone knows, are designed to make people happy to board planes, and I was looking forward to mine as I approached the gate, and then I heard music. Cheerful music, tooting, like a mechanical ocarina. "Easter Parade"—the chorus. It came from a small pink plush rabbit standing on a glass display case in a souvenir shop across Concourse C from C-18. The rabbit, who could also march, had come to a dead end against a stack of boxes and stood there kicking it. I sat in the lounge by the gate and looked out the window across the dock and the taxi strip, and heard about twenty choruses of "Easter Parade" before I realized that the rabbit was battery-powered and wouldn't wind down anytime soon. My watch showed 2:40. My plane was scheduled to go at 3:00.

The effect of a short musical selection endlessly repeated is maddening, of course—an effect not contemplated by Irving Berlin when he penned the number for the Broadway revue *As Thousands Cheer*, to be first warbled by Marilyn Miller and Clifton Webb (September 30, 1933), whence it scored big and became the title song of an

M-G-M Garland-and-Astaire cinemusical, whence it became *the* pop Easter standard in America. It never was my favorite Irving Berlin song. As the rabbit kept plugging it, I thought of others I liked more—"Puttin' On the Ritz" and "All Alone," and even "White Christmas"—but with the "E.P." loop going round and round, bonnet after bonnet with all the frills upon it, I couldn't hum even "Have you seen the well-to-do up and down Park Avenue," from "Puttin' On the Ritz"; even the notes of "I'm dreaming of a" left me.

I wasn't alone in the lounge. About half the fifty or so blue vinyl seats were occupied by three o'clock, when a woman at the check-in counter announced that the plane had not arrived yet and so would be late in departing. Most of my fellow waiters seemed to be aware of the song and to have traced it to the rabbit. Many of them, to judge from the looks they gave the rabbit and the clerk at the souvenir stand, seemed to know that they were going quietly, politely berserk. Conversation dried up. At 3:20, the woman said the plane still had not arrived but would, momentarily. When I left "Easter Parade" and boarded the plane, it was 3:45. I guessed that I had heard more than 250 choruses.

Why I didn't walk across the concourse, pick up the rabbit, open the hatch on its back, and remove the batteries is a question I ask, too, and why I didn't at least say, out loud, "That is driving me crazy," so my companions would know for certain that the rabbit was a shared, not a personal, rabbit. I only point out that passengers are an obedient lot, and airline passengers are the most pliable of all, tending to believe that the plane is kept aloft by their karma, that an angry word or thought might create engine trouble. I have sat on planes parked at gates for more than an hour with no sensible explanation from the crew and no questions asked from the tourist cabin. People who fly are in a delicate position—prayerful, even penitential—which makes personal desires seem immaterial. When a steward says, "Care for a drink?" I think, Sure, fine, whatever's best—

you decide. I don't like to make demands so high in the air; and even in the terminal, with my feet on the beige carpeting, I'm in a mood to go along.

But don't think I'll sit still the next time. In fact, I'm waiting for the next time *right now*. I'm ready. Next time, look out! I'm going to *move*. Any one of a dozen things might set me off. Nobody knows what the others might be, and I'm not going to say. I know I speak for a number of persons—who knows how many? Tens of thousands. One of these days, someone is going to take simple, direct action against a simple, idiotic object. He or she may be you or me. We are going to yank the plug and restore peace.

THE TALK OF THE
TOWN SQUAD

P ROBABLY WE ARE NOT GOING TO New Iberia, Louisiana, for the forty-third Louisiana Sugar Cane Festival, the last weekend of September, but we are looking at the brochure (entitled *Hi Sugar!*) that a friend in New Orleans sent us, and are imagining all the events we'll miss, beginning on Friday the 28th ("Farmer's Day—All Day in City of New Iberia—Dress Farmer Attire") and including the "Blessing of the 1984 Sugar Cane Crop and Harvest Season in the Fields," the High Sugar Cane Yield Awards Luncheon, the coronation of Queen Sugar XLIII, who reigns over the festival with King Sucrose XLIII, and the "Queen's Parade of the Sugar Producing Parishes of Louisiana," with the Queen and her Sugar Lumps riding a float down Main Street. "Keep America Sweet," the brochure says.

Knowing our friend, we figure that we are supposed to be amused at this, and maybe we were at first, but then, seeing all the people whom the Festival will honor at luncheons and a dinner and a reception—the high-yield farmers, the parish Sugar Queens, former Sugar Kings and their wives, and the wife of King Sucrose XLIII— we wondered why New York, where people regularly whoop it up for national origin, has so few celebrations of livelihood. Making a living is the best reason for celebration we can think of, and yet not only does our own industry, the unsigned-writing trade, have no annual festival to throw bouquets at itself, but we ourself have actually *looked at our feet* when someone asked, "What do you do?" and we have *stuck our hands in our pockets* and said, "*Oh, we do a lot of different things,*" or "*It's kind of hard to explain,*" as if we were a thief. A New Iberia cane-grower wouldn't hang his head—he would look a person straight in the eye and say, "I raise sugar. Here's my card. You ever come to Louisiana, be sure to stop in, and I'll show you how it's done." He knows that sugarcane is nothing to sneeze at. It has its own festival. We envy that sort of pride. So we are already looking forward to the first Copy Carnival, on September 28, a Friday (All Day in City of New York—Dress Casual Attire), and imagining all the events we'll attend, including the Blessing of the Photocopiers and the coronation of Queen Anonymity, and the Sunday Night Deadline Dance and, especially, the big Prose Parade down Fifth Avenue.

A fine autumn day in busy Midtown, the smell of burning pretzels in the air, and as we trudge east on 44th, slightly slumped from months of bending over the crop, the sight of crowds behind police barricades and of television crews and the strains of journal music put a spring in our step, we run a comb through our hair, we begin to walk tall: our day of days, come at last. The honor guard of editors swings by, carrying ceremonial carbines and Old Glory (with a few stars and stripes deleted), and the Newsstand Band, playing the "Washington *Post* March," followed by crack typing-drill squads, their Underwoods draped with fresh ribbons. Then come dozens of marching units from all segments of the anonymous-print industry:

advertising men and women jogging *hup-hup-hup-hup* in their smart gray parachute pants and name-brand T-shirts; authors of catalogue copy, instruction manuals, form letters, autobiographies of famous illiterates; *Times* editorial writers, in their familiar long black robes rented by the hour; an army of editorial assistants and researchers; the Obituary Guild; the book-jacket brigade; the bumper-sticker battalion; the press-release regiment; and, toward the tail end of the procession, us, our bunch, the tiny Talk of the Town squad, marching triple-spaced and chanting, "Roses are red, so are balloons. We write the gray stuff around the cartoons!"

Silly, perhaps, but what's one day of silliness in behalf of your livelihood? And why should we try to justify it to persons outside the industry? Let them *be* amused, we don't care. Without the anonymous author, this country would be a poorer place. Great men would be speechless. Simple directions such as "Stop," "Stir slowly over low heat," "No Parking," and "Use only as directed" would lose their authority if they carried bylines. Great editorials would seem less balanced and majestic, more like a long honk from a guy with a burr up his ass. Advertising would choke on all those royalty payments. We could go on and on, but just take our word for it, Sugar. You need copy to Keep America Sweet.

SUBWAY

I LIKE THE SUBWAY. I ride it. I believe in it as a democratic institution. When I ride, I imagine all the black and gray and white stretch limos that sit stuck in traffic on the street overhead and the anxious phantoms behind the smoked-glass windows cursing and steaming, rolling their bulbous red eyes. They sit on black kid leather, a reading lamp over the right shoulder, air-conditioned, a television screen and a bottle of bourbon within reach, but they aren't going anywhere, and meanwhile I roll along from stop to stop in the company of my fellow New Yorkers, a patient and humorous and classy people, to 42nd, 34th, 23rd, 14th, while the big mazumbo's palace inches a few feet now and then, packed into a narrow sidestreet at the bottom of a canyon, a herd of plutocrats trapped like swine.

Despite this comforting thought, the subway often tests your democratic resolve. You descend from the street into a basement smelling of urine and buy tokens from a black lady sitting in a thick glass-and-steel case strong enough to withstand artillery. Nonetheless, she looks a little scared. Her voice comes out through a tinny speaker, as do the track announcements, and you can't understand a word. You drop a token in the slot and push through the ancient heavy wood turnstile which, like the mosaic tile walls, suggests a glorious past, long vanished. Your fellow detainees line the long concrete platform in the gloom, staring glumly into the black pit where the rails lie, garbage strewn along the ties. A rat darts out and skitters around the wrappers and cans, sniffing.

Couples hold each other. Little children clutch at their parents; they don't tear around like they do in parks or in stores. It reminds you, if you're a man, of when you stood naked in a long line of naked men at the Armory, taking your draft-board physical, waiting for the army doctor to tell you to bend over to have your rectum inspected. Coldness. Pale dry uneasiness, dread. Complete separation from your fellows. You long for humor, for someone to make that simple brilliant wisecrack that breaks the ice and makes all men brothers—what would Jimmy Stewart say in this situation? *waalll, gosh if I know*— but your brain is stuck. You think, "This could be a dangerous place." Far up the platform, a man sleeps on newspapers spread under a bench next to a door marked "MEN," a door you'd never open, not even if ordered to by thugs. A room full of garbage, filth, killer bees, Nazis, crackheads, flies who carry AIDS, the works.

A distant screeching. It gets louder and louder until the train light appears in the dark, so loud that instinct tells you to plug your ears—your eardrums hurt, Mozart will never be so beautiful again, your wife's voice will sound flat after this: you are destroying your fabulous ears and getting a pair of nineteen-dollar ones instead—but putting fingers in your ears might mark you as a greenhorn, so you stand placid and afraid as the antique piles of spray-painted cars slide slowly past and stop, a door opens halfway, your fellows squeeze past, we all shove in, the voice in the speaker overhead says, "Watch for the closing doors," and the doors shut on us packed in tight, lurching into each other as the train jerks forward.

A tall man with long filthy hair, dressed in ripped jeans and dirty sneakers, on crutches, carrying an empty Crisco can. He says loudly: "PEOPLE. I'M A WOUNDED VIETNAM VETERAN. I FOUGHT FOR YOU, PEOPLE. I DON'T HAVE A HOME OR FOOD OR ANYTHING. IT ISN'T RIGHT, PEOPLE." You look at your shoes as the train bangs along and we careen from side to side. You sneak a look: he's unshaven, red eyes, cuts on his forehead and cheek. Will he shoot us? He says, "PLEASE, PEOPLE." He shakes the coins in his can. Some people reach into their pockets. Sitting, they hoist up an inch and fish change out of their jeans, dig down deep. He limps through the crowd, swinging on the crutches, the train sways, he almost tumbles, holding out the can. "I GOT NOTHING, PEOPLE, AND YOU GOT EVERYTHING. IT ISN'T RIGHT AND YOU KNOW IT. JESUS SAID TO HELP THE POOR AND THE HOMELESS. DO YOU KNOW WHAT IT'S LIKE TO GET SHOT DEFENDING YOUR COUNTRY AND THEN HAVE TO SLEEP ON A FLOOR IN THE BUS STATION? PEOPLE! I NEED YOU!" His voice breaks. "GODDAMN IT, I'VE JUST ABOUT COME TO THE END OF MY ROPE!" Change clinks in the can. People drop in a pinch of change here, a pinch there. You reach into your tweed jacket pocket and touch bills and fish out three singles, and after two seconds' thought, you stuff them in the passing can and immediately turn red and feel dumb, feel pity and anger at the same time. Pity for the man and anger at him for manipulating us like this. All of us good middle-class folk, black and white, brought up to respond to suffering with compassion, trapped in a hot car banging and screeching through the black cave, afraid ("VIET VET RUNS AMOK ON K TRAIN, LIMOUSINE LIBERAL AMONG THOSE SLAIN"), and, worst of all, embarrassed by your own lack of humor and ingenuity in the face of fear. You dimly recall an old movie about a wounded veteran (played by Jimmy Stewart?) who wanders the city streets, homeless, when one day the plain kindness of a tall stranger in a brown suit ("Son, here's a dollar and here's my phone number if you want a job") restores his faith in the goodness of people. You wish you could be that stranger. The train comes into a lighted station, stops, and you push out the door, up the stairs, and into sunshine.

AUTOGRAPH

YESTERDAY WAS MY wife's birthday, and, according to our custom, I woke up before dawn and sneaked out of bed. Our custom is that the birthday person sleeps until the family tiptoes in and wakes her up with singing and banging on pans and hauls her smiling to the table and sits her down to a perfect candlelit breakfast next to a stack of gifts It was 6 A.M. I put on water for tea and sliced some nectarines, which she likes to eat with goat yogurt, and got out a block of her favorite cheese, which gives off an aroma like yesterday's hiking socks. The kids had baked rolls the night before. I set the glass-top table on the terrace with white plates, wineglasses for the orange juice, candles, and American-flag napkins, and then, because it was too early to wake the household and also because I am a cook who believes that too much is just barely enough, I decided to go out and find fresh bagels and lox and some more fruit. Also because that's a sweet time for a Midwesterner to walk around town. New York at six o'clock on Saturday morning is as close to being like Minneapolis as New York ever gets.

I headed toward a bagel bakery on Broadway around 81st, thinking I would come across an all-night fruit market along the way, and I was swinging down Amsterdam Avenue when a man called to me from behind. He said, "Mister? Sir?" I've lived in New York long enough to be able to ignore panhandlers when I want to: the New Testament doesn't say a person has to be at the beck and call of the needy every waking moment, you know. But, feeling Midwesternly, I turned, and he came up to make his pitch. "I'm not bad," he was saying. "I'm not going to rob you, or anything." A young black man in an old tweed coat, torn sneakers, jeans; his hair was long, and tangled in long snarls. He smiled at me sweetly. He smelled slightly rancid, and he spoke fast, with a Southern accent and a slight lisp. He said, "I'm sorry. I don't like to do this. But I didn't have anyplace to sleep last night. I spent the night in the Park. Today is my twenty-ninth birthday. It really is. I'm from North Carolina, and I've been trying to get into a shelter—you know where the cathedral is? I tried up there, but they were full. There's another one on Ward's Island I'm trying to get to. My grandpa is in Bellevue. He's dying with cancer, and I want to be with him—that's why I'm here. My name is Kevin. I have this aunt who lives in Hoboken. If I had five or six dollars, I could go over there and look her up and stay with her until I can get back on my feet. I'm sorry to take your time like this, but I just need some help. Now, I've got these books." He brought out a handful of paperbacks from under his coat. "If you'd like to buy one, I'd sure appreciate it."

Incredibly, one of the books was by me. I saw it right away, of course. One was a romance in a pinkish cover, and one was a Danielle Steel, and one was my book. The cover was torn off, but not the inside cover, which had my picture on it, with me in clear-rim glasses, squinting, in jeans and a green sweater, sitting on the white steps of a house on West 22nd Street, where we used to live. He was telling me how he'd come by these books honestly. I reached into my pocket and pulled out all the money I had—about twenty-eight dollars. I had to do this. I gave it to him. "That's my book," I said. He handed it to me. "No, you keep it," I said. "I just meant that it's my book. I wrote it." He looked at the photograph: it was me.

He seemed astonished to be holding a book with a picture of a man who had just given him a small wad of money. Then he touched my arm and said, "I want you to sign it for me." He dug in his pockets and got out a ballpoint. He said, "Make it out to Kevin and Anthony—he's my best friend. Oh, he's not going to believe this! This is incredible!" But the pen didn't work. "Oh, no, this is terrible!" he cried. He looked up and down the street. He moaned, "I *got* to find a pen." He approached a woman walking toward us—"Lady, could I borrow your pen?"—and she glanced away from him and walked on.

I had never seen panhandling from that perspective, and it struck me as genteel the way the beggar shut up when there was no eye contact. He didn't press his case even slightly. Kevin tried to borrow a pen from two more passersby, with no luck. I believe that if you were out walking at 6 A.M. in Minneapolis and a panhandler asked to borrow a pen you'd be interested—but never mind. We finally went into a deli a block away and got a pen from the clerk. I signed the book "With every good wish for a long & happy life," thinking that perhaps I should give him my phone number. Twenty-eight dollars doesn't go far in New York. But I didn't.

Back home, I made tea and woke up the kids, and we paraded into the bedroom, where she was still asleep, and rattled our pans and sang "Happy Birthday." It was cool and still on the terrace. We lit the candles. The city out beyond our little potted trees looked serene, though hazy. She opened her gifts: a poster, a scarf, a book of pictures, and a green balloon that inflated so big you couldn't get your arms around it. It looked like a giant grape. We also had individual balloons, with whistles in their necks, which when the balloons exhaled made loud cawing sounds. The day bounced along; we drove to Bear Mountain for a long hike, came home, slept, and took a major dinner that night at a restaurant. I thought several times, in a sentimental way, about Kevin out there in the city, as if somehow I could have made things right for him. He is, after all, my only homeless reader as far as I am aware. I've thought of him often since. Whatever his reason for getting my autograph, my signing the book means just one thing to me, and that is that I know his name: Kevin. Two years in this city, and finally I have *met* a homeless person.

GETTYSBURG

I DROVE DOWN TO GETTYSBURG the weekend of the Fourth, the anniversary of the battle, along with my wife, who grew up on different books than I and doesn't care two cents about the Civil War. She is crazy about fiction, especially Gabriel García Márquez whose latest she happened to have in her bag, and after we walked around the battlefield monuments for a half-hour that Saturday afternoon and ate a hot dog and watched a Union battery demonstrate artillery firing, she found a place in the shade back behind the crowds near the Gettysburg Volunteer Fire Department's refreshment tent and sat and read. All around us on Cemetery Ridge were men and scenes out of books I passionately loved as a boy. Row after row of cream-colored pup tents straight out of Brady photographs. Bearded sunburned men bundled up in wool uniforms, baggy pants, the caved-in caps and worn-out shoes, leather ammo bags and tin drinking cups on their belts, carrying single-shot carbines six feet long with narrow steel bayonets, and among them some teen-agers, one with long blond ringlets who looked exhausted. They had camped on the ridge for a week, part of the National Park Service's 125th anniversary commemoration, all volunteers. I watched two hundred Union troops fire a volley and charge across a meadow toward Plum Run, re-enacting the charge of the First Minnesota Regiment on July 2, 1863, realizing a moment vivid in my imagination since I was twelve or so. I stood by the road along the crest of the ridge as a regiment of Confederates swung along in ragged formation singing "Bonny Blue Flag" in tender and weary voices, brave fellows in motley gray-and-butternut outfits with scraps of uniform laced together, like a band of old deer-poachers. I saw it all clear in my mind, not seeing the other tourists in their red shorts and yellow haltertops, men in dazzling green pants shooting pictures, just the blue and gray. If General George Meade had walked up to say hello, I'd've just reached out and shaken his hand. Fifty yards away, under the trees where the Pennsylvania reserves must've sat on July 3 waiting Pickett's charge, my wife in white jumpsuit reclined on the grass, so absorbed in the passions of a man on the Colombian coast that she didn't answer when I came over and said hello to her. Eyes on the page, she just reached out and took me by the ankle.

Sunday morning I borrowed a bicycle and rode around the battlefield, a pleasant ten-mile circuit along shady roads. Hot dry weather, as it was in July 1863, and along the Emmitsburg Pike south of town, fields of wheat and oats stood in the mile-wide valley between the long low ridges where the Army of the Potomac and the Army of Northern Virginia faced each other on the third day of the battle, July 3. The first day's fighting was wild and sudden and scattered west and north of Gettysburg; the second was intense and murderous and located at the Union flanks on Culp's Hill and around Little Round Top, The Wheatfield, The Peach Orchard, and Devil's Den, where men in close quarters battered each other to death by the thousands; but it is the third day, when the lines had been drawn, that is clearest in the imagination. At three o'clock that afternoon, about thirteen thousand Southern men came out of the trees on Seminary Ridge and marched through the fields straight into a Northern artillery barrage and up the slope against Northerners drawn up in a superb defensive position along Cemetery Ridge. The slaughter lasted a half-hour, and two-thirds of the men who left Seminary Ridge did not return.

This half-hour is so vivid to anyone who has read accounts of it that, as you bike up through the red brick Lutheran campus and along Seminary Ridge, cruising in low gear through McMillan Woods, where Pettigrew's Brigade of North Carolinians waited, you can hear them rustle in the weeds in the ditch where they lie listening. Of the brigade, some two thousand arrived on July 1 and about six hundred marched away in the middle of the night, July 4, their cause lost. "To the eternal glory of the North Carolina soldiers who on this battlefield displayed heroism unsurpassed, sacrificing all in support of their cause. Their valorous deeds will be enshrined in the hearts of men long after these transient memorials have crumbled into dust," reads the inscription on a nearby monument. In a tree overhead, a mockingbird went through its entire routine of six or seven songs. I rode on, to the figure of Robert E. Lee on his horse looking east watching his men die in the sun. The sculpture has been given a protective coating against acid rain that makes it look like dark-brown plastic, the color of a toy man on a horse. I dismounted and walked the bike out beyond the tree line and up to the first stand of wheat.

It seems dumb to be so caught up in a battle that ended more than a century ago and that you don't even begin to understand. You hear them whisper as they edge forward, gray-butternut figures crouching in the woods, and hear skittish horses nicker and whinny at the whump of distant cannon, but it's dumb if you can't imagine why they would fight this battle, which I can't. The wheatfield was fresh and untrampled. The silence was like the terrible stillness that, according to most accounts, fell over the field just before Pickett's Charge began—a wall of silence like a dam about to burst open, then the flood of Confederates marching double-time across the mile and up toward the stone wall in the distance, cheering, yelling, the flags, and then the storm of fire. Now it is so quiet on the losers' side of the battlefield that you can't imagine what made them mad. The phrase "states' rights" means no more to me than the phrase "warm boot."

I walked the bike up the road toward Little Round Top, the crucial hill where a brigade of Maine men held off Longstreet's South Carolinians and Georgians and saved the Union flank. It was a formidable position to attack, impossible even, and as I walked up, the boulders looming above, I could barely imagine the sort of rage that might impel a man to lead such a charge. I tried to imagine. I made a speech to myself, "You SOBs, hide in the rocks, we're coming to haul you out. Bastards. Shoot you, stab you, cut your throat, pound your head open with a rock, or whatever it takes. This was a good country until you decided you could do what you damn please, when you please, and to whom, chop off people's rights and go to make every poor sinner be exactly like you—you do that, you kill what's beautiful in this country. A century from now, if you win, which you likely will, nobody in this country will feel like they are part of anything. Thanks to you, asshole. Everybody'll be loose as gravel and nobody'll be free. Nobody'll even care which state they're from and it won't matter, everywhere will be one paved paradise. Well, I don't care to live in your country and I don't want you to either. Let's die." I swore a little more for flavor as I reached the top of the rise, the woods and sunny meadow where thousands perished in an afternoon, and climbed on the bike and rode north, toward the crowds and the monuments.

POSTCARDS

A POSTCARD TAKES ABOUT FIFTY WORDS gracefully, which is how to write one. A few sweet strokes in a flowing hand—pink roses, black-face sheep in a wet meadow, the sea, the Swedish coast— your friend in Washington gets the idea. She doesn't need your itinerary to know that you remember her.

Fifty words is a strict form but if you write tiny and sneak over into the address side to squeeze in a hundred, the grace is gone and the result is not a poem but notes for a letter you don't have time to write, which will make her feel cheated.

So many persons traveling to a strange land are inclined to see its life so clearly, its essential national character, they could write a book about it as other foreign correspondents have done ("highly humorous . . . definitely a must"), but fifty words is a better length for what you really know.

Fifty words and a picture. Say you are in Scotland, the picture is of your hotel, a stone pile looking across the woods of Druimindarroch to Loch Nan Uamh near the village of Arisaig. You've never seen this country. For the past year you've worked like a prisoner in the mines. Write.

Scotland is the most beautiful country in the world and I am drinking coffee in the library of what once was the manor of people who inherited everything and eventually lost it. Thus it became a hotel. I'm with English people whose correctness is overpowering. What wild good luck to be here. And to be an American! I'm so happy, bubba.

In the Highlands, many one-lane roads which widen at curves and hills—a driving thrill, especially when following a native who drives like hell—you stick close to him, like the second car of the roller-coaster, but lose your nerve. Sixty mph down a one-lane winding road. I prefer a career.

The arrogance of Americans who, without so much as a *"mi scusi"* or *"bitte"* or *"s'il vous plaît,"* words that a child could learn easily, walk up to a stranger and say, "Say, where's the museum?" as if English and rudeness rule the world, never ceases to amaze. You hear the accent and sink under the table.

Woke up at six, dark. Switzerland. Alps. Raining. Lights of villages high in the sky. Too dark to see much so snoozed awhile. Woke up in sunny Italy. Field after field of corn, like Iowa in August. Mamas, papas, grammas, grampas, little babies. Skinny trees above the whitewashed houses.

Arrived in Venice. A pipe had burst at the hotel and we were sent to another not as good. Should you spend time arguing for a refund? Went to San Marco, on which the doges overspent. A cash register in the sanctuary: five hundred lire to see the gold altar. Now we understand the Reformation.

On the train to Vienna, she, having composed the sentences carefully from old memory of intermediate German, asked the old couple if the train went to Vienna. *"Ja, ja!"* Did we need to change trains? *"Nein."* Later she successfully ordered dinner and registered at the hotel. *Mein wunder-companion.*

People take me for an American tourist and stare at me, maybe because I walk slow and stare at them, so today I walked like a bat out of hell along the Ringstrasse, past the Hofburg Palace to Stephans Platz and back, and if anyone stared, I didn't notice. Didn't see much of Vienna but felt much better.

One week in a steady drizzle of German and now I am starting to lose my grip on English, I think. Don't know what to write. How are you? Are the Twins going to be in the World Series?

You get to Mozart's apartment through the back door of a restaurant. Kitchen smells, yelling, like at Burger King. The room where he wrote *Figaro* is bare, as if he moved out this morning. It's a nice apartment. His grave at the cemetery is not marked, its whereabouts being unknown. Mozart our brother.

Copenhagen is raining and all the Danes seem unperturbed. A calm humorous people. Kids are the same as anywhere, wild, and nobody hits them. Men wear pastels, especially turquoise. Narrow streets, no cars, little shops, and in the old square a fruit stand and an old woman with flowers yelling, "WŌSA FOR TEW-VA!"

Sunbathing yesterday. A fine woman took off her shirt, jeans, pants, nearby, and lay on her belly, then turned over. Often she sat up to apply oil. Today my back is burned bright red (as St. Paul warns) from my lying and looking at her so long but who could ignore such beauty and *so generous*.

NINETEEN

I T OCCURRED TO ME the other day that I could use a better typewriter, one with some memory capacity but not too much, so I walked down to 40th Street to an office-machine shop, and found a typewriter with memory and with a sheet of white paper in it on which a person or persons had typed: "fadksjdfjkdsjfkjkfjdkjfkjskdjfkaj-kdfklsjdk catcatacatcatdogdogsdogdogdogdoguiuwthethethethetheth-etheth the birdsthe cats the birds and cats and dogs and flowers sall day long we played int he field and had fun in the sun with our friends and relatives. WE went to the beach and the park and played ball and swam. lWe ate hot dogs and hambarugers aldjksjfjsad-hfjsdjfkjsdkfwewewewewewewewe ququququququququququququququ-ququmamamamamamamamamamamamamamamamama usususususus 34343434343434343434"

The line about "fun in the sun with our friends and relatives" struck me as exactly the experience I missed out on this summer. I didn't play in the field or go to the beach, didn't play ball or swim, didn't eat many hot dogs or hambarugers either. For the most part I sat here in my office at The Fadksjdfjkdsjfkjkfjd and went ququ, and then I traveled for a couple weeks in Denmark and went a little ququ there, too. I don't eat hambarugers in foreign countries, because I'm proud to be an unugly American who eats what the natives do, fried eel or calves' brains, lambs' eyeballs with rancid yak butter, whatever's on the menu, and say thank you. I am a good citizen, just as my mamamamamamamamamama taught me to be. I speak softly and know how to apologize and express gratitude in many languages, especially Danish. *Undskyld* is to say "I'm sorry," which Danes hardly ever say, but they say thank you incessantly, in a dozen variations, including: *tak, mange tak, tusind tak, tak fordi du vil se os, tak for sidst, tak for mad,* and *tak for aften,* which mean, respectively, "thanks," "many thanks," "a thousand thanks," "thanks for seeing us," "thanks for the last time," "thanks for the meal," and "thanks for the evening." I use them often. I try to be a model American. I walk politely around Skagen, around Svendborg and Roskilde and through Copenhagen, dressed in muted colors, carrying no camera, wearing no Mets cap, admiring cathedrals and palaces, public gardens, ordinary Danish streets, Danish buses, billboards, plumbing, everything Danish, and when people walk up to me and say, "*Aldjksjfjsadhfjsdjfkjsdkfwewewewewe*," I answer (in Danish), "I am sorry. I am an American. I do not understand you." This becomes tiring after a while. After three weeks of good international citizenship as a bird in a world of cats and dogs, weakly chirping *thethethethethethetheth*, I am exhausted, done in, tuckered out, fed up, run down, and I long for that summer paradise described on the typewriter with memory. I'd like nothing better than to plop down on American sand with friends and relatives under the American sun that rhymes with "fun," pop a cold one, play ball, get in the swim, and chow down on a big hambaruger with raw onion, bright-yellow American mustard, in a soft white bun, and holler, "How about those Mets?" to someone who'd answer, "Hey!" Time to come home.

My first hot dogs of the summer, in fact, were two I ate with my son on Saturday afternoon of Labor Day weekend, in Flushing Meadows Park at the U.S. Open tennis tournament, across the IRT tracks from Shea Stadium, where the Mets were entertaining the Dodgers. Big-league tennis is dominated these days by Czechs, Swedes, and Germans (in two of whose languages I can say "Thank you" and "Excuse me"), and we sat in the sun, in the cheap seats at the top of the stadium, and watched Steffi Graf, the nineteen-year-old West German phenom, dispose of a Frenchwoman in two fast sets, 6–0,

6–1. My son is nineteen, too, an aspiring rock-'n-roll guitarist. He writes songs and records them and mixes them and intends to become a fine artist. When I was nineteen or so, I used to put on a Buddy Holly record and pick up a tennis racket and pretend it was a guitar and I was him.

Graf was so much fun to watch, later we waited in line at Court 16 and crammed into the tiny grandstand there and sat through two men's matches so we could watch her doubles match (with partner Gabriela Sabatini of Argentina) and, when a tall horse-faced man announced that it had been switched to the stadium (and a thousand of us Grafites groaned), we raced over there and snuck down past an usher into a box seat for a close look. Graf is a big broad-shouldered long-legged girl with a long blond ponytail who had won the Australian and French Opens and Wimbledon earlier that year and, a few days later, would win the Open to complete a Grand Slam, a feat accomplished only four times before, but you didn't need to know that to see what a happy, ferocious athlete she is. She and her ponytail bounce around the baseline, then she hops a little three-step as she receives service and takes an open stance and whacks the ball so hard that her follow-through takes her right off her feet. She leaves the ground when she serves and on most of her forehand shots and her overhead smashes. When she cocked her arm for a smash, the look on her face was homicidal, and she went a foot in the air as she put the ball away.

Losers drag their feet and stand flat on their heels like ordinary people. They stand and perspire and wait for misery and pain to finish with them. In the stadium, the sun shining down on her, Graf makes you feel what the age of nineteen is like on its best days, the pleasure, the heat, the spring in your legs, the murder in your eyes. My son's songs on a tape he had played for me the night before had that sort of snap and sting to them. A powerful age. To be a world-beater is exactly what a healthy nineteen-year-old would want, I guess. Be a winner. Beat the pants off older players, cream Chris Evert, pulverize

Martina, and play killer guitar. In between the singles and doubles match, I had my hot dogs, two excellent wieners, with sauerkraut and mustard, chased with a cold beer. I ate them in the sun, wearing a bright-red shirt and white jeans and a pair of shades, thinking: Only athletes and musicians get so good so young and travel easily across borders, playing and winning as they go. We ordinary cats just have to clunk along with our old forgetful typewriters. Our language hems us in, our hangup with language defeats us, and after a few weeks on foreign turf our feet start to drag. Ddkjfksdjfkjqoueourweiuriuw. Farewell to summer. Time to come home, clean house, write some letters, and elect a decent president.

PATMOS

T HIS TRIP GOT PLANNED back before I knew how wrapped up in the presidential election I'd get, and it was painful, like dropping out of school, to pull out and leave the *Times* and its daily spread of campaign news. People are dead wrong: this election is the most riveting in twenty years. I took a plane to Copenhagen and read my last *Times* and slept the rest of the way; the flight felt like a short hop. Arrived at 8:00 A.M. under a dim impression that I was in Chicago. But then caught a snatch of the Olympics on TV in the airport. No commercials. You could actually watch the games.

Hung around the apartment, washed clothes, and took the overnight train to Rome. (A fast smooth ride, by the way, on a classy train that glided into the station exactly two minutes early. And those were *democracies* it ran through on time.) Along the way, being *Times*less began to sink in. Somewhere, fresh polls were emerging, movement was being detected, new negatives were developing, stories were being spun, and the spinners were spinning each other, and I was out of the loop, un-*Times*ed. Switzerland swept by, the Alps above, the tidy villages below, and awakened in me a long-lost fondness for East Los Angeles. In the Basel rail station, *USA Today* was on sale, but I passed. Why eat popcorn when it's pork roast that you want? A newshead requires daily bulk of the sort the *Times* provides: whole paragraphs of direct quotes, your champ wielding his bright sword, the other bum flopping around in the sawdust.

In Rome, at the hotel near the Spanish Steps, more Olympics. The Italians won a gold medal in rowing, and the announcer doing the stroke-by-stroke was crazed with joy. Then divers, then fencers. No commercials. No announcers on camera, flaying us with expertise, no visual odes to the Stars and Stripes, just athletes winging around and Italian bubbling along underneath.

In the hotel lobby, saw a *Wall Street Journal* on a marble buffet and snatched it up. Not much about the election (except a shithead editorial), but a disquieting list of the world's largest banks, showing that nine of the top ten are Japanese. Of the hundred largest public companies, fifty-three for them, thirty-four for us. This score lent some sharper poignancy to a walk that afternoon around the shell of the Colosseum and the ruins of the Forum. When foreign tourists arrive in Washington someday to walk the Mall and see the shattered buildings of old Federal America—the ruins of the Capitol, with its West Front fallen in heaps, and its domeless Rotunda, where dead presidents once lay in state—will our descendants be able to make a decent living by selling them pop and candy and driving the tour buses? American candy and pop, cigarettes and movies are all over Europe, but not many American cars, and no *Times*.

To Athens. Some Dukakis bumper stickers outside the airport. Taxis on strike, so rode with a guy with a Dukakis sticker. Two thousand drachmas, about fifteen bucks. With the Acropolis visible out the hotel window, lay down and checked out the Olympics. Earl

Bell, the pole vaulter, looked a lot like George Bush. Women's fencing, tennis. No beer on the screen, no pop, no cigarettes. Just sports. The unfairness struck me. Why should Americans have to sit for hours of brain-dead commercials, thereby subsidizing the games for Greeks, who get off scot-free? A *Times* editorial there, maybe a campaign issue? Without advertising, the games become a whole religious drama, with athletes waiting, pacing, tensing, getting psyched up, then the moment of repose before they burst off the mark. Why clutter this sacred ritual with Budweiser horses? On the other hand, I was thirsty. No room service, so hiked down to the Marriott's Polynesian restaurant. A long photo mural of Bora Bora. Greek waiters in Hawaiian shirts serving mai tais and platters of pupu.

That night, watched the news, which looked a lot like anybody else's news. Not a sound bite could I understand, not one—there was only calm, scholarly, incomprehensible Greek along with the pictures. A handsome black-haired man in a dark-blue suit read the stories off a script on his desk, glancing up on every other phrase, in front of a large screen that showed:

London. Prime Minister Papandreou in a blue suit, standing next to a fat man with a cleft chin.

A Greek Orthodox bishop arriving on a ferryboat to inspect two rows of troops.

A speaker at the UN.

Melina Mercouri.

A parade of taxis in downtown Athens, people waving signs.

Gorbachev, posing in a row of blue suits that included a frail Andrei Gromyko, then inking a treaty.

A woman weeping behind a barred gate.

A map of Albania.

Scenes of Florida, a Florida license plate, men climbing out of a limo.

Weather report, in centigrade. Lows of 13–20. Highs, 28–31.

A Greek flag as the Greek national anthem was playing.

Sign-off at 11:30, the last image an outline of Greece, white against blue, the country resembling a sea horse with islands scattered near its tail, including Patmos, where I am now, on a shaded terrace of a house with thick stone walls plastered white, in a village of dazzling whitewashed stone houses bunched around a monastery on a mountain. The hills are brown, the sea is clear blue, and I hear chickens nearby, complaining. A train of four donkeys clops down our stone street, five feet wide in places, and a man calls his wares, fish and vegetables, on this street and, a moment later, on the next. The news here is all ancient: the friendliness of foreign people, the mysteries of the East. We eat fresh goat yogurt and thyme honey for breakfast, on a second terrace, walled, under an orange tree. The house is from the seventeenth century, like all the others. A quarter-mile down the road is the cave where John dreamed about the end of the world and wrote the Book of Revelation and told about the Lake of Everlasting Fire that so absorbed my entire youth. A few miles farther is a sandy beach where young German and Swedish and French women lie naked in the sun, which would have absorbed me even more then than it does now, which is, *considerably*. We ride to the beach, and then back up the mountain, on green Honda scooters. My mother never let me own one or ride on one, feeling that any motorized two-wheeled vehicle was a ticket to flaming death. The beauty of such a strict upbringing is to give a person a low threshold of excitement. When we cruise down the mountain and take the outside curve at 15 m.p.h. and look over the edge, I hear her voice say, "Be careful, Gary! Not so fast!"

When we putt-putt up from the naked beach past John's cave to the mountaintop, I hear his voice say, "Woe! Woe! Woe!" We will make this trip everyday for two more weeks and then go home.

REAGAN

I T'S NOT OFTEN that people care to celebrate the anniversary of a panic, so I gladly drove down to West Windsor Township, New Jersey, on Halloween weekend for a festival celebrating a night in 1938 when many citizens there and across America got scared by a radio play and ran around and did things they felt sheepish about later. West Windsor, just east of Princeton, includes the village of Grover's Mill, which a scriptwriter happened to pick off a map and use as the site of the Martian invasion in the play *The War of the Worlds*, performed by Orson Welles and the Mercury Theatre of the Air and broadcast on the CBS network at 8:00 P.M., Eastern time, October 30, 1938. About twelve million persons tuned in, many of them too late to hear Welles's introduction but in time to hear about "a huge, flaming object, believed to be a meteorite," crashing near Grover's Mill. It turned out to be a metal cylinder ninety feet in diameter, according to Carl Phillips, the reporter in the play, and the folks at home could hear the crowd of curious onlookers at the crash site, an ominous humming sound, and a loud *clank* as the cylinder opened, and then Carl's gasp. A thing with luminous eyes and gray tentacles wriggled out of the black hole, glistening, pulsating, dripping saliva, and a moment later Carl's microphone thunked to the ground. Dead air. Then an announcer came on with a news bulletin: "At least forty people, including six state troopers, lie dead in a field east of the village of Grover's Mill, their bodies burned and distorted beyond all possible recognition."

The play bounced along in this news-documentary style: to Washington for an emergency message from the Secretary of the Interior; back to the studio for news bulletins as the invaders advanced toward New York City in giant walking tripods and zapped Army bombers out of the sky with deadly heat rays; then hysterical warnings ("Poisonous black smoke pouring in from Jersey marshes. Reaches South Street. Gas masks useless. . . . Automobiles, use Routes 7, 23, 24"). Here and there, listeners panicked—perhaps a million, according to a 1947 study by the Princeton psychologist Hadley Cantril, which quoted some of them:

Newark: "We listened, getting more and more excited. We all felt the world was coming to an end. Then we heard 'Get gas masks!' That was the part that got me. I thought I was going crazy."

New England: "I kept shivering and shaking. I pulled out suitcases and put them back, started to pack, but didn't know what to take."

Illinois: "We ran to the doctor's to see if he could help us get away. Everybody was out in the street, and somebody told my husband it was just a play."

New York: "One of the first things I did was to try to phone my girl, in Poughkeepsie, but the lines were all busy, so that just confirmed my impression that the thing was true. . . . We had heard that . . . gas was spreading over New Jersey and fire, so I figured there wasn't anything to do—we figured our friends and families were all dead. I made the forty-five miles in thirty-five minutes and didn't even realize it. I drove right through Newburgh and never even knew I went through it."

The epicenter of the panic, which was a township of truck farms fifty years ago, is a suburb of New York now, near the Princeton Junction stop on the Metroliner route. Its potato fields are filling up with three-hundred-thousand-dollar two-story frame or brick houses (advertised on billboards as "estate" or "manor" homes) in tract developments with names that use the suffixes -*dale*, -*shire*, -*ford*, -*brook*, and -*crest* a lot. Next to the millpond, where Carl Phillips was killed by the invaders' heat rays, is a small park with a few picnic tables, swings, a shelter, a bike stand, and a monument to the broad-cast, dedicated this year.

The panic commemorative included an art show, a dance, a Mar-tian Landing parade, a Martian Fling social, a panel discussion ("Could It Happen Again?"), and a Martian Panic run, with three hundred runners, many in horrific alien faces, chasing each other, costumes flapping, for ten kilometers around West Windsor. Waiting for the winner, I met the festival chairman, Douglas Forrester, who looks a lot like the young Orson Welles, and who was happy that the whole thing had been a huge success. "This place has always been in the shadow of Princeton," he said. "We need something to give us an identity, a community spirit." He added that, with seven different zip codes, the township was a crazy quilt of little farming burgs, like Grover's Mill, Penns Neck, Dutch Neck, and Princeton Junction, once separate and now stitched together by housing developments, and some of the new residents weren't even sure exactly where they lived. He said the festival had got a lot of people involved in the community for the first time.

It struck me that the festival was a rare occasion of media justice—a town once exploited by radio now getting a chance to exploit its exploitation, and put on a party and get a million dollars' worth of publicity in the bargain (from five TV networks, AP, UPI, the BBC, major European news services, radio stations from almost every state in the Union, and more newspapers than you could shake a stick at)—and it also struck me that the creature who crawled out of the metal cylinder and killed Carl Phillips was present at the festivities, holding a video camera and recording sound bites.

I had always considered the story of the *War of the Worlds* panic a case of gullible rural people, many of them fundamentalists with a taste for the apocalyptic, who heard an incredible tall tale and swal-lowed it. But as I see it now, at the end of the 1988 presidential campaign, the panic seems reasonable, the people who ran from their homes in fear no fools. The broadcast of 1938 crossed a line between entertainment and news, which has since become blurred, and people panicked because they were accustomed to believing the news. Tuning in the radio to hear a voice say that a black fog of poisonous gas was pouring into New York and killing people like rats, the listener jumped. Except for a disclaimer here and there, *The War of the Worlds* sounded like news, and listeners heard it as news. It simply reported news that was untrue.

This week, Americans will elect a President after a bitter and mean-spirited campaign in which the distinction between real and unreal, news and entertainment, seems blurred beyond recognition, and in which politics seems dangerously out of touch with the world we inhabit. A story in *The Washington Post* describes how, one evening last May, five of George Bush's campaign advisers went to Paramus, New Jersey, to observe a group of thirty voters assembled by Bush researchers as a test group to measure the emotional impact of campaign themes. The advisers were Roger Ailes, Lee Atwater, Robert Teeter, Craig Fuller, and Nicholas Brady. They sat behind a two-way mirror and watched as the group was told about furloughed prisoners, the Pledge of Allegiance, and Boston Harbor, and at the end of the session Governor Dukakis's support among the group had dropped from thirty to fifteen. "I realized right there that we had the wherewithal to win . . . and that the sky was the limit on Dukakis's negatives," Atwater said. Mr. Bush's campaign has in effect been built on the themes that scared the Paramus Thirty, and especially the racist allegory of Willie Horton. The country appears willing, if not very happy, to elect Mr. Bush, on the basis of his personal showmanship about the Pledge, the ACLU, murderers, and a few other matters that will not concern him as President. What has been missing from the campaign is any note of reality.

The line between entertainment and news has been blurred most successfully by President Reagan. Better than any rival, he has been able to describe the world as he wanted to see it—a description independent of any objective truth—and do it so winningly that his stories seemed almost real. His talent has been to live entirely in the present, one show at a time, and he has revealed no important regrets, no compelling dreams, no history that disturbs him. Clearly, his job has been not to run the government but to be himself, an entertainer: warm, solicitous, upbeat, manly, full of cheerful news—a good uncle. Like Warren Harding, he is hated by nobody. He is humble, genuinely amiable, and gracious, is serious about the business of ceremony, and prepares himself studiously for every public appearance, executing the royal duties of his office with ease and charm. His private complications—his apparent indifference to religion, his estrangement from his children, his squeamishness about anger and unpleasantness—have been completely submerged in his portrayal of the President. As he prepares to retire, he leaves his opponents feeling tired and thoughtful. He has enlarged his office, yet diminished politics by his success, sapping our most fundamental strength, our ability as a democratic society to discuss and resolve our problems.

Grover's Mill looked as if its biggest problem were that so many people want to live there: how to accommodate them, and not ruin the good life they have come for. A happy problem, for politics to resolve. Walking in the dark that evening along a Grover's Mill road that wound past old farms and blocks of lighted houses, the air smelling of apples and wood smoke, I felt how vulnerable this good life is and what is at stake as the voters vote. All Mr. Reagan's artistry cannot change the world, which remains real: real lakes and forests are dying, the ozone is actual, genuine garbage floats on an authentic ocean. The world is not the sum total of our impressions of it, and it cannot be charmed by political entertainment. Nor can the economy, drunk on debt, be sung into sobriety. Debt is an objective, measurable fact, as the Republican Party used to point out, but this year talk about the real world has been rare. The voters who walk into the booth on Tuesday will find it unlit, as pitch-black as a radio show.

VIRAL

I CAME DOWN with an awful virus a month ago that was apparently the same one everybody else had had (fever of a hundred and two, achiness, headache, loss of appetite, exhaustion, depression, a feeling of being *wasted*—a feeling that life is meaningless and banal and the world is stalked by relentless evil and confused by greed and narcissism and that beauty and humor are helpless to rescue it), because whenever the phone rang and I dragged myself over to answer it and the person at the other end said "How are you?," if I mentioned my illness, the person said "Oh, that's what I had three weeks ago." Not exactly the comfort that the Apostle Paul tells Christians to give to us afflicted persons, but in my condition I wasn't expecting much. I felt like death on toast.

The virus appeared as a dryness in the throat on a Tuesday afternoon, and I dosed it with aquavit, the water of life. Wednesday, I stayed in bed. I lay there in dull misery all week and slept and perspired and drank water and lost eight pounds. Outdoors, it was cold and gloomy. After a week, I felt even worse, and called the doctor, who said, "That sure sounds like this virus that's going around." He recommended that I stay in bed, exactly the course of treatment that a doctor of 1789 would have prescribed, minus the leeches, but I felt drained already. I couldn't remember feeling worse since a virus years ago when I was still a smoker and not even a sore throat and nausea and chest congestion could keep me from reaching for a Camel. I lit it and inhaled deeply and coughed for a few minutes and took another drag. That was worse. This was misery, but that was disgusting.

In bed, propped up with three pillows but still sagging, I read a few pounds of magazines with nothing funny or interesting in them, drank quarts of grapefruit and orange juice, and ate raw carrots. I attempted to read the *Times*, my daily habit—a sacred duty to Mrs. Moehlenbrock, my old teacher. Mrs. Moehlenbrock did not assign us children to delve into the sort of newspapers with big black headlines about "CRAZED BEAST RIPS LUNCH FROM TOT'S HAND," or some such. She was an educator, and believed that everyone should know the names of all the Cabinet members and what makes the rain fall and where the Seychelles are; she was a *Times* woman at heart. But day after day, sick with a hopeless virus, I picked up the newspaper and felt like a teacher with an armload of sophomore term papers. The *Times* was full of dim, dumb articles with titles like "FIBER-OPTIC CALLING TO JAPAN STARTS TODAY," "SCHOOL BOARD ELECTIONS: A TOOL FOR TEACHING," "TREND IN PREGNANCIES CHALLENGES EMPLOYERS," "PAIR FINDS SUBSTANCE TO CURB BLOOD VESSELS," and "MODERN CONCERNS ENRICH PASSOVER RITUALS": what one might call a *flu of writing*.

One morning, I switched on the TV and jumped from "Good Morning America" to "The CBS Morning News" and on to "Today," skipping commercials and catching a two-hour parade of correspondents and experts and the slow drip-drip-drip of the news about scandal, disaster, and defeat, plus a few pale-faced authors flacking their books; and ninety seconds after each eager face faded from the screen I couldn't remember one thing that had been said, except that Esther Williams, promoting her line of women's swimwear, referred to the rear end as "buns," and a Ford vice-president, talking about the silver anniversary of the Mustang while standing next to a red one, said it had "filled a niche in the market." My buns had filled a niche in the bed for ten days, and I wished somebody would come on TV and say, "Believe me, this is not forever, things will get better."

Someone radiant but real, like Meryl Streep, who suffers so splendidly in her movies.

I owned a red Mustang back around 1967—a gallant little machine—but I don't own a car anymore. Too complicated. Like smoking. Enough was enough. A car in Manhattan is a ticket to misery. Nevertheless, car lover that I am, I would have kept mine, and kept complaining, were it not for a good thief who swiped it from a parking ramp one night, stripped it, and dumped it on the FDR Drive. The insurance company paid the book value, and I put the twelve thousand dollars in the bank. The car went to the boneyard. That was last July. I haven't thought much about cars since, or about smoking since I stubbed out my last cigarette around midnight on a Saturday years ago: the following day was St. Valentine's Day, the day my friend Butch Thompson and I had decided we would Quit. That there was my last smoke, I thought, and went up to bed sensing history in the making. I attended four movies the next day and ate a tub of popcorn, and spent most of Monday in the public library's reading room, not smoking, and gradually the habit passed.

Every life requires a bold move now and then to revive the interest of the liver. The way to get this done is to do it. You wake up in your warm cocoon in the woods in the Adirondacks and unzip it and drop your drawers, dash out on the chilly dock, plunge into the cold, cold lake. *This is good for you.* That cheerful, Scoutmasterly thought convinced me I was recovering, and I went and took a hot shower and got dressed and put on a white shirt and pair of jeans. I felt better out of bed, washed, with the moss scraped off, though I was unsure what day it was: there had been no word from the outside for a long while. Nobody had faxed or expressed me a thing, and the Southern lady voice of the office answering machine said, "You have no new messages." The thought that downtown they are getting along pretty well without you is a desolate thought; you think, It can't keep going on like this. And it doesn't. The urge toward life is expressed by pulling on your pants, and the way to do it is to stand up and do it.

SNOWSTORM

A BIG CITY like New York could use at least one good snowstorm every year. A storm is the only event that happens to everybody at the same time, the most sociable event there is—one that pulls all the colorful little stories together into a big black-and-white epic. So that imaginary snowstorm that blew through town the other weekend had a lot of people counting on it, and happily contemplating the trouble it would cause, long before it finally did not appear. I was one of them. I woke up Friday morning to find the *Times* predicting from three to six inches, maybe twelve on Long Island, where "gusts over 50 miles an hour are possible, whipping the snow into high drifts." A sentence like that makes me think I'd better go check on the livestock. I looked out on the terrace where the herd would be if there were one. No snow, but the sky had a grayish, metallic cast that looked pre-stormlike to me. Then a carpenter phoned and mentioned eight inches. He was supposed to come and install a shelf above the washer that morning, and he called to say he'd be two hours late, because, on account of the big storm, he'd have to come by car instead of bike, and his car was at a garage in Brooklyn having its brakes relined. He did not seem discouraged by the storm's advance. When I mentioned Long Island's twelve inches and wind-whipped drifts, he paused a moment, as Gary Cooper might have, and said, "I'll be there."

I put on my warm boots and left for work. I thought I detected down in the subway a pretty clear mood of storm-readiness—people looking around with a weather eye, bundled-up people bouncing gently against each other on the train. I overheard "eight inches" several times. At the Columbus Circle station, there was a woman preaching on the platform. She was short and powerful, and paced to and fro yelling, "There's an express train to Hell, too! Yes! There's a Heaven and there's a Hell! And which train *you* ride? Do *you* know?" She wore a brown parka, a red stocking cap, and mittens.

It was still not snowing when I came up out of the ground at 42nd Street. I glanced up at the big National Debt Clock recently installed on a wall above the hamburger stand across the street, which showed the debt beating its way toward the three-trillion-dollar mark ("Your Family Share $41,661"). The debt rose all day Friday and the snow continued to not fall, and now it is a week later, my family is deeper in debt, and still no snow, although last Sunday I did see some slanting, slow-falling, semicrystallized rain in the twilight in Central Park. Some of what was falling seemed to possess particularity and to flutter flakelike as it fell, but when the stuff hit asphalt it was nothing but anonymous water. I was angling across the Park on a long hike back from lunch up in the clouds, in the dining room on the hundred-and-seventh floor of the World Trade Center, where the great, dense, swirling mists seen from a few feet away, over a plate of cold pasta salad and herring in mustard sauce, had storm written all over them, but it was a storm on its way somewhere else.

My wife pulled up her collar and said, "It's cold," which some people would say if a shadow fell on them, but it *was* cold. The wind had an edge to it, the sky was hard. Nobody was in the Park. "It's too cold to snow," she said. And it didn't. By Monday morning, the six hundred city garbage trucks that were equipped with snowplows had been decommissioned.

I've seen no snow since January, when I was in Chicago, and I feel deprived. In the liturgical year of basic visual images imprinted on a person's mind back in grade school, winter is represented by snow: cottony puffs on pine trees and hills and the roofs of small, square houses. We children did not sit around the long library table with paste and crayons and construction paper and make pictures of dusty gray sidewalks with tree wells full of trash, dead grass, and frozen dog manure. That nonstorm may have been the city's last chance for snow this winter. Perhaps it was needed here, to teach us something, which now we won't know, apparently.

Winter is a mysterious season. It is less researched than the others, because scientists don't care to freeze, either. They are rationalists, and prefer pleasure to pain; hence the vast shelves of monographs about the gorgeous fish of the coral reefs of Micronesia, the lifeways of tropical peoples, etc., and the few, slim volumes about the frozen tundra. Margaret Mead did not study adolescence in Greenland, and Jacques Cousteau did not steer the *Calypso* into the Bering Strait in November. They went where it was nice. Television and movie producers don't shoot many pictures in the North in winter, because it's a pain and because cold and snow are ominous phenomena, clear reminders of mortality. So America's popular images of itself are false, meteorologically speaking: a green, sunny land where nobody needs to wear warm clothing—a nation of Pasadena.

A couple of days after the snow didn't fall, I was walking down Fifth Avenue and heard a man behind me say, "There is no such thing as collective intelligence! Ha! It's *individuals* who think. You got to have *individuals* in the collective!" I turned and looked at him, but he didn't look back. He was talking to himself, engrossed in his own company. He snorted. "Collective intelligence! That's a contradiction!" Somehow, I thought, a good storm, with eight inches of snow whipped into high drifts, would have got his attention and drawn him into the epic along with the subway preacher, the carpenter, me, and all the others. But if it can't snow, then at least it can turn to spring: we await the advent of baseball.

LAYING ON OUR BACKS
LOOKING UP AT
THE STARS

"WE CATCHED FISH AND TALKED, and we took a swim now and then to keep off sleepiness," said Huckleberry Finn. "It was kind of solemn, drifting down the big, still river, laying on our backs looking up at the stars, and we didn't ever feel like talking loud, and it warn't often that we laughed—only a little kind of low chuckle. We had mighty good weather as a general thing, and nothing ever happened to us at all."

Huck was a hippie, searching for freedom, and, long ago, most of the people I knew were too.

In 1970, in search of freedom and dignity and cheap rent, I moved out to a farmhouse on the rolling prairie in central Minnesota, near Freeport, where I planted a garden and wrote stories to support my wife and year-old son. Rent was eighty dollars a month. It got us a big square brick house with a porch that looked out on a peaceful barnyard, a granary, and machine sheds and corn cribs and silo, and the barn and feedlot where Norbert, the owner, kept his beef cattle. Beyond the windbreak of red oak and spruce to the west and north lay 160 acres of his corn and oats. (I believed it was oats, but on the odd chance it might be wheat or barley, I didn't mention anything to Norbert about it being oats.) Our long two-rut driveway ran due north through the woods to where the gravel road made an L, where our mailbox stood, where you could stand and see for a couple miles in all directions, the green fields and the thick groves around the farmsites.

My pals in Minneapolis considered this a real paradise (so did we)

and they often drove up and enjoyed a weekend of contemplating
corn and associating with large animals. On the Fourth of July, 1971,
we had twenty people come for a picnic in the yard, an Olympic egg
toss and gunnysack race, a softball game with the side of the barn
for a right-field fence, and that night we sat around the kitchen and
made pizza and talked about the dismal future.

America was trapped in Vietnam, a tragedy, and how could it end
if not in holocaust? We were pessimists; we needed fear to make us
feel truly alive. We talked about death. We put on loud music and
made lavish pizzas with fresh mushrooms and onions, zucchini,
eggplant, garlic, green pepper, and drank beer and talked about the
end of life on earth with a morbid piety that made a person sick,
about racial hatred, pesticides, radiation, television, the stupidity of
politicians, and whether Vietnam was the result of strategic mistakes
or a reflection of evil in American culture. It was a conversation with
concrete shoes.

I snuck out to the screen porch with my son and sat and listened
to crickets, and my friend Greg Bitz sat with us and two others came
out, tired of politics and talk, and we walked along the driveway out
of the yard light and through the dark trees and sat down in a strip
of alfalfa between the woods and the oats. ("What's that?" they said.
"Oats," I replied.) And then we lay down on our backs and looked
up at the sky full of stars.

*   *   *

The sky was clear. Lying there, looking up at 180 degrees of billions
of dazzling single brilliances, made us feel we had gone away and left
the farm far behind.

As we usually see the sky, it is a backdrop, the sky over our house,
the sky beyond the clotheslines, but lying down eliminates the horizon
and rids us of that strange realistic perspective of the sky as a canopy
centered over our heads, and we see the sky as what it is: everything
known and unknown, the universe, the whole beach other than the

grain of sand we live on. The sight of the sky was so stunning it made us drunk. I felt as if I could put one foot forward and walk away from the wall of ground at my back and hike out toward Andromeda. I didn't feel particularly American. Out there in the Milky Way and the world without end Amen, America was a tiny speck of a country, a nickel tossed into the Grand Canyon, and American culture the amount of the Pacific Ocean you bring home in your swimsuit. The President wasn't the President out there, the Constitution was only a paper, and what newspapers wrote about was sawdust and coffee grounds. The light I saw was from fires burning before America existed, when my ancestor John Crandall lived in the colony of Rhode Island. Looking out there, my son lying on my chest, I could imagine my grandchildren, and they were more real to me than Congress.

I imagined them strong and free, curious, sensual, indelibly cheerful and affectionate, open-handed—sympathetic to pain and misery and quick in charity, proud when insulted and modest if praised, fiercely loyal to friends, loving God and the beautiful world including our land, from the California coast to the North Dakota prairie to faraway Manhattan, loving music and our American language—when you look at the stars you don't think small. You don't hope your descendants will enjoy your mutual-fund portfolio, you imagine them as giants on the earth.

Between the tree line and my left elbow, a billion stars in the sky, each representing a billion we couldn't see. We lay in the grass, thinking about America and also a little bit about snakes and about spiders clambering from blade to blade who might rappel down into our mouths, and looked open-mouthed up at the heavens, and everything we said out loud seemed hilarious to us. Tiny us gazing up at the South Wall of the Unimaginable Everything and feeling an obligation to comment, and our most profound comments sounded like peas dropped in a big empty bucket. "It makes you feel small, doesn't it." *Plink.* "I used to know the names of those." *Plunk.* One more

peabrain having to share the effect that the world is having on him.
"It's beautiful, isn't it. . . . I remember when I was a kid—" someone
said and we laughed ourselves limp— Shut up, we said, laughing,
we're sick of sensitive people, everything you see just reminds you
of yourself! So stick it in your ear.

Perhaps in 1776 our ancestors, too, were rattled by current events
and the unbeatable logic of despair and had to go out and lie in the
weeds for a while and think: We hold these truths to be self-evident,
that all men are created equal, that they are endowed by their Creator
with certain unalienable Rights, that among these are Life, Liberty,
and the Pursuit of Happiness.

Indoors, the news is second-hand, mostly bad, and even good
people are drawn into a dreadful fascination with doom and demise;
their faith in extinction gets stronger; they sit and tell stories that
begin with The End. Outdoors, the news is usually miraculous. A
fly flew in my mouth and went deep, forcing me to swallow, inducing
a major life change for him, from fly to simple protein, and so shall
we all be changed someday, but here under heaven our spirits are
immense, we are so blessed. The stars in the sky, my friends in the
grass, my son asleep on my chest, his hands clutching my shirt.

LONDON

M Y SON WAS due in at Heathrow Airport at nine-forty last night,
flying from New York, and about noon yesterday, a Sunday,
lying around in my hotel room reading the Sunday papers and
drinking coffee, I started to think about him on a plane and got the
jitters. He is twenty and has flown to Europe on his own before and

could find his way to the hotel OK, but I am a father who is susceptible to jitters, and I can't talk myself out of them. I think about a plane over the ocean with my progeny aboard and pretty soon the plane wobbles, and then I need to take a walk.

The neighborhood here isn't so different from parts of Manhattan, except that the streets are named George, New Cavendish, St. Vincent, Weymouth, Paddington, Devonshire, Nottingham, and Marylebone High Street. The last isn't so different from a New York shopping street, except for the ironmonger's, the photocopy centre, the café offering takeaway food, the shops with "TO LET" signs in the windows, a pub called The Rising Sun, the red brick façades and knobby roofs out of Dickens, and the Mobil station selling unleaded premium for forty-eight pence per litre.

Facts such as these help to calm down a father who is suffering from sudden propulsive anxiety, the sort that every parent knows well. The last time I traveled in Europe with my son, we rode a train to West Berlin, and at the last station in East Germany grim squads of border guards came aboard and searched the car, and I had a sudden, stark fear that the guard who was studying his passport picture might notice the tones of green in his long hair and pull him off the train and find marijuana in his bag and we would enter into a bureaucratic hell that would occupy our lives for the next three years. My skin got tight at the thought of it; my nose trembled. This is the sort of fear I am capable of. My son came into the world, after forty-eight hours of labor, in a teaching hospital where the staff seemed to be a few chapters behind the one my wife and I were on. Since then, I've worried about him pretty consistently. Facts are consoling, compared with what a parent can imagine. The plane shook from side to side, and loud snapping and whirring noises could be heard from below.

The outstanding fact of Marylebone High Street lay just north, across from the corner of Beaumont. In a lot between a bakery and a school (where, beginning on Monday, September 25th, the Westminster Adult Education Institute was offering classes in Calligraphy,

Vegetarian Cookery, Welsh 1, Navigation [Day Skipper], Guitar, Transactional Analysis, and Jazz Dance and Fitness for fifty-five pence per hour) was a little park behind an iron fence, about two storefronts wide and forty feet deep. Close to the fence was a white obelisk about eight feet high marking the burial place of Charles Wesley ("Crown'd through the mercy of thy Lord/With a free full immense reward"), the hymn writer and a founder of Methodism. The park was paved with bricks and stone. Inside were tombstones set into the brick walls and some in the pavement. Six wooden benches faced a sunken stone floor about ten yards square, which was, according to a plaque on the back wall, the exact site of the old parish church of Marylebone, built in 1400, where Francis Bacon was married (1606), and Richard Brinsley Sheridan (to Miss Linley, in 1773), and where Lord Byron was baptized (1788).

Facts—you could sit on a bench and contemplate them one at a time or all together. Death, for one. In the center of the stone floor was a tablet beneath which lay Lady Abigail Hay, and around her, according to another plaque on the wall, lay the following:

EDWARD FORSET *Lord of the Manor* 1630
SIR EDMUND DOUCE *Cupbearer to 2 Queens* 1644
CLAUDIUS DE CRESPIGNY AND HIS WIFE 1695
MARIA DE VIERVILLE *French refugees* 1708
JAMES FIGG *Pugilist* 1734
EDMOND HOYLE *Writer on games* 1769
JAMES FERGUSON *Astronomer* 1776
ALLAN RAMSAY *Painter* 1784

I strolled along the wall, reading tombstones, until one of them set my teeth on edge. It read:

To the Memory of
Mrs HESTER WILTON
Widow of WILLIAM WILTON Gent

The untimely loss of her only Son
     who died
at Tenna on Christmas Day 1792
after being Wreckd in the
Winterton Indiaman
brought on the Illness of which
She died August the 24th 1800
Aged 56

This struck too close. I am forty-seven, and my only son was over the ocean. I could understand how the death of a child could bring on an illness that would last seven and a half years and finally kill you. The plane bucked and dove; the lights went out. I turned away, then turned back and wrote the inscription down on a blank check, the only paper I had on me. A dignified gray-haired lady watched me from the sidewalk. She wore a brown coat, a blue skirt, and black stockings, and carried a cane. Perhaps she saw I was an American and thought I was trying to buy the park, but all I wanted was Hester Wilton's epitaph, and when I got it I headed back down Marylebone High Street toward the hotel, where my son would be arriving, by cab from the airport, in about three hours. Somewhere between there and The Rising Sun, it struck me that I could fill up some of that time by simply taking the Underground out to Heathrow and meeting him at the gate.

I caught a train at the Baker Street station at eight-thirty and got off at Green Park to change to the Piccadilly line, where an electric sign over the platform told us patrons exactly how long until the next train: "HEATHROW . . . 1 MIN," it said, and a minute later in she came. We rolled into Terminal 4 at Heathrow at nine-fourteen. I took the escalator upstairs and found that British Airways Flight 178, due in from JFK at nine-forty, had landed at nine. About ten limo drivers waited for their customers, along with forty or fifty of us civilians, including the actor Peter O'Toole, in a gray tweed suit, who was waiting, it turned out, for a lanky, elegant woman pushing a cartload of luggage, and a boy of about nine in a blue blazer. He raced into Mr. O'Toole's open arms and was hoisted up and kissed twice, and soon after him came my son, twenty, with a guitar on his back, and wearing one of my old shirts and a pair of black pants with white paint stains on it. He grinned, and we shook hands.

The flight had been bumpy, he said, but the time had gone by fast. He had eaten a roast-beef dinner, watched *Field of Dreams*, and read two chapters of a biography of Bob Dylan. "It's good you came out to the airport," he said. "I forgot the name of the hotel. I wrote it on a slip of paper and then left it at the apartment."

I asked him the classic fatherly question, a line that probably dates back to long before Hester Wilton's time: "What would you have done if I hadn't been here?" I recognized its classicism even as I said it.

"I'd have gone into the city and remembered it," he said cheerfully.

STINSON BEACH

A LITTLE BUSINESS CALLED ME to San Francisco a few weeks ago, about two hours' worth of business that I managed to work up into a full two-day itinerary so as to justify the long flight, and then I flew out a day early to attend to my real business, which was a drive across the Golden Gate Bridge, and over Mount Tamalpais, along a boulevard of eucalyptus trees, to Stinson Beach, a village where I've spent four weeks in the past seven years and which I wanted to see again. Stinson Beach looks out on the Pacific from the foot of a mountain, and for seven years I have been pacified by visions of it. When I lie down at night, and night thoughts crowd in around me, and I am about to get up and spend the night looking out the window, I imagine a bright spring morning in Stinson Beach: the sandy path from a rented cottage over the dune to the beach, and me walking barefoot, the sound of high surf—and by the time I spread a towel on the sand and lie down on it morning has come and I get up and take a shower. The path is no more than sixty yards long, through tall pampas grass and a patch of dark-green succulents and two little jungles of flower garden, and yet it has served me so well so many nights—a short hike from the cool, dim house to the sea which takes me into a sweet sleep—that I wanted to see it again and commit it more clearly to memory.

I flew to San Francisco in the morning, wearing a pair of horn-rimmed glasses I had broken the day before by making a sharp right-hand turn into an iron pillar at the office. The pillar had not been there earlier. A carpenter friend of mine had glued the break—on the bridge, between the eyes—and I didn't think about it all the flight west over the mountains, the drive north into the city, until I got to a room in a hotel on Nob Hill, sat on the bed, and took the glasses off, and they broke in my hand.

Without my glasses on, I see San Francisco as a few objects in the foreground of a vast Abstract Expressionist world, not so different from Omaha or San Jose in the same circumstance—the Bay might be a bay or it might be soybeans, the Berkeley hills might be soybeans, the Golden Gate might be a storm on the horizon. So I hiked down the hill toward Market Street, feeling a little ill from lack of focus, and found a stationery store and bought a bottle of super-glue, found a restaurant, and sat down and ordered a cup of coffee and got busy repairing my glasses.

The directions that come with the little plastic container give a person pause—especially a very nearsighted one. "Warning," they say. "BONDS SKIN INSTANTLY. CONTAINS CYANOACRYLATE ESTER. Avoid contact with skin and eyes. If eye or mouth contact occurs, hold eyelid or mouth open and flush with water only and GET MEDICAL ATTENTION. If finger bonding occurs, apply solvent."

In order to see what I was doing, I had to hold the glue dropper and the glasses pretty close to my eyes, and the thought of the warning made me a little shaky. I wondered if I had any sort of personal identification on me. ("S.F.P.D. SEEKS IDENTITY OF VOICELESS MYOPIC PERSON WHO GLUED OWN MOUTH AND FINGERS SHUT YESTERDAY.") I squeezed one drop of glue on the right spot, bonded the glasses, then, putting the cap on the dropper, got a little glue on two fingers and, for one horrific second, instinctively tried to rub the stuff off and *felt my fingers bond*, then pulled them apart at the last moment! And sat for a few minutes until I recovered from the shock. I didn't touch the cup of coffee.

I put the glue bottle in my pocket and the glasses on my face, and walked two blocks to Powell Street and caught a cable car heading up Nob Hill. I stood on the forward right-hand running board, holding on to a pole, and when the driver sang out, "Hold it in on the right! Watch your back!" I leaned in toward an old woman sitting on the bench as we swept past a parked truck, its extended side-view mirror a few inches from my back.

The glasses held together for the drive across the Golden Gate and up the mountain and along the coast. The highway is a roller-coaster of a road, with plenty of dramatic curves that hang on the mountainsides over sheer drops, and in the event of sudden glasses breakage I was going to plant one lens in my right eye, like Erich von Stroheim, and keep going, but I simply hugged the right shoulder, avoided looking at the ocean far below and the tops of tall trees in the valleys (I have a mild form of acrophobia, feeling that if you look down from a great height mysterious ground forces will pull you over the edge), and cruised down into Stinson Beach, past the Sand Dollar restaurant and Ed's Superette, and into the parking lot at the beach. I got out and walked. Everything was there, as I have remembered it so many times: the beach houses on pilings, the dunes, the surf and surfers, the cottage where I stayed (its shades pulled), and the magical path. I stood by the cottage and looked at it for a long time. I heard, faintly, in the nearby surf, some voices from old vacations, including the shouts of an eight-year-old boy who is now fifteen. The sun shone down, and as I walked slowly up the path and over the dune I felt sorrow and danger recede into the ocean and thought I'd like to lie down on the sand and take a nap.

I am back from San Francisco now, with a clear image of the path in my head: the greens are *really* green, the air smells of real salt water, soft sand is underfoot. I also have two little patches of dried super-glue on my right thumb and index finger, clinging to my skin with a tensile strength of up to five thousand pounds per square inch. The strength of a clear image of a path leading to the ocean cannot be expressed in pounds, but I estimate that mine should be good for another two or three years of ordinary use.

4

HOUSE POEMS

O What a Luxury

O what a luxury it be
how exquisite, what perfect bliss
so ordinary and yet chic
to pee to piss to take a leak

to feel your bladder just go free
and open up the Mighty Miss
and all your cares float down the creek
to pee to piss to take a leak

for gentlemen of great physique
who can hold water for one week
for ladies who one-quarter cup
of tea can fill completely up
for folks in urinalysis
for Viennese and Greek and Swiss
for little kids just learning this
for everyone it's pretty great
to urinate

of course for men it's much more grand
women sit or squat
we stand
and hold the fellow in our hand
and proudly watch the mighty arc
adjust the range and make our mark
on stones or posts for rival men
to smell and not come back again

women are so circumspect
but men can piss to great effect

with terrible hydraulic force
can make a stream or change its course
can put out fires or cigarettes
and sometimes
laying down our bets
late at night outside the
bars
we like to aim up at the stars.

Lamour

When I was seventeen I fell in love with Barbara Ann.
We sat together in the lunchroom. I held her hand.
Once I kissed her and she said, "That wasn't bad."
Ours was not a great romance but it was all I had.
I was lonely. I was the weirdest kid in town,
Six foot three, a crewcut, a hundred and three pounds,
High-water pants and a goofy face—if only she could see
That down inside this cartoon boy was someone lovely: me.

One night I was standing by the candy store when she drove
   by
In a pink Cadillac with this rich handsome guy
On their way to the Prom—I couldn't bear to live!
How could she be so cruel to one so sensitive?
That night I made a vow that someday I'd become
Rich and handsome, too, like him (the lousy bum!),
Well educated, suave of speech, a guy of style and grace,
And come straight back to Hoopersville and laugh right in her
   face.

And so I became and now I am and so the other day
I flew down in my Lear jet to visit Barbara A.
Got her address from her mom and drove out in my Porsche
And found her at her mobile home, hanging out her worsche.
She turned and saw me and she almost dropped her drawers—
"Is that really you, then! And is that sportscar yours?"

"It sure is!" I said and looked in those clear blue eyes
And suddenly I loved her more than I had realized.
"I love you," I said. "Come, live with me. Marry me, my
   dear."

She turned and yelled, "Hey kids, wash up! let's go! your
    stepdad's here!"
There were seven filthy children with grimy feet and hands,
And crusts of dirt around their mouths and big loads in their
    pants,
Slimy lips and greasy hair and clothes of such bad taste,
I put my arms around them all and cried, "The Lord be praste!"

We hauled them to the laundromat and got them washed and
    shined
And were married the next morning, so I guess that love is
    blind.
I think we're pretty happy, and one thing I know for sure
Is that we love each other, O viva sweet lamour.
Lamour, lamour.
Oh yes we love each other and viva sweet lamour.

In Memory of
Our Cat, Ralph

When we got home, it was almost dark.
Our neighbor waited on the walk.
"I'm sorry, I have bad news," he said.
"Your cat, the gray-black one, is dead.
I found him by the garage an hour ago."
"Thank you," I said, "for letting us know."

We dug a hole in the flower bed,
The lilac bushes overhead,
Where this cat loved to lie in spring
And roll in the dirt and eat the green
Delicious first spring buds,
And laid him down and covered him up,
Wrapped in a piece of tablecloth,
Our good old cat laid in the earth.

We quickly turned and went inside
The empty house and sat and cried
Softly in the dark some tears
For that familiar voice, that fur,
That soft weight missing from our laps,
That we had loved too well perhaps
And mourned from weakness of the heart:
A childish weakness, to regard
An animal whose life is brief
With such affection and such grief.

If this is foolish, so it be.
He was good company,
And we miss his gift

Of cat affection while he lived,
The sweet shy nature
Of that graceful creature
Who gave the pleasure of himself:
The memory of our cat, Ralph.

The Solo Sock

Of life's many troubles, I've known quite a few:
Bad plumbing and earaches and troubles with you,
But the saddest of all, when it's all said and done,
Is to look for your socks and find only one.
Here's a series of single socks stacked in a row.
Where in the world did their fellow socks go?

About missing socks, we have very few facts.
Some say cats steal them to use for backpacks,
Or desperate Norwegians willing to risk
Prison to steal socks to make lutefisk.
But the robbery theories just don't hold water:
Why would they take one and not take the odder?

Now, *some* people lose socks, and though you may scoff,
Some go to shows and have their socks knocked off.
Some use a sock to mop up spilled gin with
And some people had just one sock to begin with.
But for most missing socks, or sock migration,
Sockologists have no quick explanation.

Socks *are* independent, studies have shown,
And most feel a need for some time alone.
Some socks are bitter from contact with feet;
Some, seeking holiness, go on retreat;
Some need adventure and cannot stay put;
Some socks feel useless and just underfoot.
But whatever the reason these socks lose control,
Each sock has feelings down deep in its sole.

If you wake in the night and hear creaking and scraping,
It's the sound of a sock, bent on escaping.
The socks on the floor that you think the kids dropped?
They're socks that went halfway, got tired, and stopped.

It might help if, every day,
As you don your socks, you take time to say:
"Thank you, dear socks, for a job that is thankless.
You comfort my feet from tiptoes to ankless,
Working in concert, a cotton duet,
Keeping them snug and absorbing the sweat,
And yet you smell springlike, a regular balm,
As in Stravinsky's *Le Sacre du Printemps*,
And so I bless you with all of my heart
And pray that the two of you never shall part.
I love you, dear socks, you are socko to me,
The most perfect pair that I ever did see.
I thank you and bless you now. *Vobiscum Pax*."
Then you bend down and put on your socks.

This *may* help, but you must accept
That half of all socks are too proud to be kept,
And, as with children, their leaving is ritual.
Half of all socks need to be individual.

Mrs. Sullivan

"Function follows form,"
Said Louis Sullivan one warm
Evening in Chicago drinking beer.
His wife said, "Dear,
I'm sure that what you meant
Is that form should represent
Function. So it's function that should be followed."
Sullivan swallowed
And looked dimly far away
And said, "Okay,
Form follows function, then."
He said it again,
A three-word spark
Of modern arch-
Itectural brilliance
That would dazzle millions.
"Think I should write it down?"
He asked with a frown.
"Oh yes," she said, "and here's a pencil."
He did and soon was influential.

Guilt & Shame

A gentleman of means stood in
The exclusive Club de Joie,
Enjoying a tall glass of gin,
When suddenly he saw
A beggar lying at the door,
His face so pale and sad—
He thought he'd seen that man before.
He said, "Excuse me. Dad?"
"Oh, don't mind me," his father said.
"I'm only in your way.
I'm weak and sick, I'll soon be dead,
Perhaps later today.
I only came because I thought
That maybe you could find
A—no, I'm sorry, I forgot
You've so much on your mind.
Ah! My heart! The light grows dim!
I'll leave you now. Goodbye!"
The fine young man looked down at him
And this was his reply.

No, I won't feel guilty, Dad,
For I am not to blame,
And I won't let you put on me
A load of grief and shame.
Life is full of sunshine,
Love is a clear blue sky,
Tomorrow is a brand-new day,
God bless you and goodbye.

That evening he was standing
Underneath a bright marquee,
There to attend the gala ball
Dressed so handsomely,
Chatting with Mr. and Mrs. Saks
At the discotheque,
When suddenly a pile of rags
Reached out and touched his leg.
"Hello," she said. "It's me. Your mom.
Sorry to get in your way.
I guess you had forgotten me
And Dad, but that's okay.
I'm only your poor old relative,
There's no reason you should care,
But do you think that you might have
A couple bucks to spare?
I nursed you as a loving mother
And held you on my knee,
And now you've thrown us in the gutter,
Your poor old dad and me.
I am your flesh, I gave birth
To you—oh, the pain that night!
And now you're treating me like dirt,
Your mom. But that's all right.
I forgive. I understand.
You enjoy yourself, my child."
He took her gently by the hand
And spoke to her and smiled.

    No, I refuse to feel guilty
    For I am not to blame
    And I won't let you put on me
    A load of grief and shame.

For life is full of sunshine
And love is a clear blue sky,
Tomorrow is a brand-new day,
God bless you and goodbye.

He arrived at quarter to three
At his mansion on the hill
And sat in his library
And sipped his port, until
He heard, upstairs, a child cough
And cry: *Dad, I want you.*
He found her with her blanket off,
So feverish from the flu,
Tears streaming down the angel face.
He tried to comfort her.
She cried, "I was looking everyplace.
I didn't know where you were.
I heard some voices, I was scared,
It was too dark to see.
I thought that you had disappeared
'Cause you were mad at me.
Whydja go, Dad? Tell me. Huh?
Tell me what I did.
Left alone without no one,
Lying sick in bed.
All alone with no one here
But my old cat. And Mom."
The father brushed away a tear,
He trembled but was calm.

No, I won't feel guilty, child,
For I am not to blame
And I won't let you put on me
A load of grief and shame.

Life is full of sunshine,
Love is full of light,
Tomorrow is a brand-new day,
God bless you and good night.

He sat downstairs a little while
And thought about his kin:
His dad, his mother, and his child.
Just then the cat walked in.
She sat and stared into his face
With cool relentless eyes;
He felt the judgment in her gaze
So righteous and so wise.
She looked at him till he fell down
In anguish at her feet
And wept and threw his arms around
That cat, his shame complete.

I am guilty and ashamed
For everything I've done!
Sins that I've forgotten, now
I feel them, every one.
Life is full of sorrow,
Love is all in vain,
Tomorrow and tomorrow
Only bring us grief and pain.

He did not see the cat's expression.
She smiled to hear his sad confession.
She knew that, using this technique,
She would get tuna all next week.

Obedience

There was a boy whose name was Jim
And although life was good to him
And gave him home and food and love,
He thought that it was not enough,
That it was time for him to do
Those things that he'd been told not to.

"I am ten and must be free
To enjoy what's been denied to me,
And I shall do it all," he said.
"I'll spread some black dirt on my bread,
And spill food on my Sunday clothes
And I shall put beans up my nose."

Everything that to this kid
His mom said, "Don't," he went and did.
He gulped his sandwich, and dragged his feet,
Threw bags of garbage in the street,
Leaned out windows, ran down halls,
And wrote exciting words on walls.

Until at last, at half past two,
He could not think of more to do.
Anger, gluttony, and pride—
He'd drunk and smoked and cursed and lied,
Stuck out his tongue, dropped his britches,
And shoved old ladies into ditches
And other things good folk condemn—
He'd done it all by 3:00 P.M.,
And satisfied his appetite:
Now what was left to do that night?

From this, dear children, you should sense
The value of obedience.
When I say, "Don't," I mean, "Postpone
Some wickedness for when you're grown,
For naughty flings and wild rampages
Are much more fun at later ages."

Now brush your teeth and go to bed.
And after all your prayers are said,
Lie in the dark as quiet as mice
And whisper one word that isn't nice.
Don't say ten, a whole big group,
Just say one, like "panda poop."

Oh, what a thrill from one bad word!
Say it a second time and third.
"Poop" is a vulgar word, and vicious.
How bad of you! And how delicious!
One is enough. The rest will keep.
Now shut your eyes and go to sleep.

Upon Becoming a Doctor

Allons! This piece of poetry
Is written by a Doctor of Lit,
A degree that my friend Peter Stitt
Persuaded his college to give to me:
Gettysburg College in Pa.,
A Lutheran school in the famous town.
I drove there for Commencement Day,
Following the route of Lee
Seeking the flank of Gen. Meade,
And parked, and found a room, and peed,
Donned the honorary gown
And followed the professors down
Through the deep perspiring crowd
Who peered at me with faces bowed,
Wondering how long I'd gas,
And past the graduating class
Up to the platform where, aloof,
Imperial beneath a roof,
Our magnificent parade
Sat down and surveyed
The situation:
Youth in the sun and age in the shade,
Which has been true since creation.
Age will rule while youth must seek;
Youth must listen to age speak;
And now it was my turn.

                    I stood
And adjusted my doctoral hood,
Nodded to the classic

Brow of President Charles Glassick
And, to the right, the patient rows
Of academic buffaloes,
And with a swirl of gown and sleeve
Advanced dignified
To the podium to receive
The crowd's applause though it had died.
A long pause for the removal
From my pocket of my dark dense notes—
Down front, a storm of clearing throats—
I glanced to the sky for His approval
And took a good deep breath, and then,
Behind me where the degrees were piled,
Behind our row of distinguished men,
Came the voice of a little child,
So shrill and yet so pure:
You're no Doctor of Literature,
Never were and never will be.
Your writing goes from bad to worse.
You don't deserve a doctor degree,
You ain't even literature's nurse.
I turned and saw my old pal Pete
Leap like a champion from his seat,
Snatch that tot and slap its wrist
And make it hop
And wash its mouth with soap
And send it home to the busted shack
Down beside the railroad track,
Where it lived in squalor with its pop,
A noted deconstructionist.
Which taught the child one thing, I hope,
And that is: merit only goes so far.
People who do their best to be

The best find out they are what they are
And have to fall back upon loyalty.
I'm too old to search for truth or
Be a follower of Luther,
But I'm glad to sit beneath their tree
(Thanks to my friend Pete) a P
h. (for honorary) D.

Mother's Poem

Some mornings I get up at five.
With four to mother, one to wive,
I find the hours from light to dark
Are not enough to matriarch
With goals for matriarchy high
Among the apples of my eye.

This little girl with golden braid
Expects her toast a certain shade;
Her scrambled eggs must meet the test
Of excellence and gently rest
Upon the toast and not beside.
The little boy wants his eggs fried
Yet not be greasy on his lips,
Accompanied by bacon strips
Fried till they resemble bark.
The older boy takes his toast dark
And if his golden eggs should not
Be poached and served up steaming hot,
Two slightly liquid yellow bumps
Of yolk in solid white, he slumps
Down in his chair and has a mood.
The oldest girl eats rabbit food,
Berries, nuts, sunflower seeds,
Leaves and stems, and as she feeds,
She is displeased. It's all my fault.
I bought her seeds containing salt.
And worse—some juice containing sugar.
She glares as if I were a crook or,

Worse, a mother short on sense
And guilty of child negligence.

Negligence in the name of love
Is just what we should have more of.
Don't mother birds after some weeks
Of looking at those upturned beaks
Deliberately the food delay,
Hoping to hear their goslings say,
"What are these feathered floppy things
Attached to us? You think they're wings?"

This helpful trusty friendly *Frau*
Is starting her neglect right now.
The clothes you counted on to leap
Up while you were fast asleep
And wash themselves for you to wear
Have let you down. They just sat there.
The bicycle you thought would pick
Itself up when the rain got thick,
The homework you forgot to do,
Assuming I would tell you to—
My child, you have been betrayed.
The world you thought was neatly made,
Its corners tucked in like a sheet,
Is uncomposed and incomplete.
For years I carried on a hoax.
I made you think that scrambled yolks
Or poached or boiled, fried or shirred,
Are how they come out of the bird.
I made you think that big dustballs
Tiptoe softly down the halls
Out to the trash, that your wool skirt
(The one with emblems of dessert)

Took a cab down to the cleaner,
In answer to a court subpoena.

No matter what you have been told,
The rainbow holds no pot of gold,
Babies aren't found under rocks
Or in Sears Roebuck catalogues,
Those coins weren't put there by an elf—
The Tooth Fairy is me myself,
The Easter bunny's make-believe,
Cows don't talk on Christmas Eve,
The moon is not made of green cheese,
And eggs don't come the way you please,
Served by hens on silver trays,
And neither does much else these days.

The Finn Who Would
Not Take a Sauna

In northeast Minnesota, what they call the Iron Range,
Where a woman is a woman and some things never change,
Where winter lasts nine months a year, there is no spring or
  fall,
Where it gets so cold the mercury cannot be seen at all
And you and I, we normal folk, would shiver, shake, and
  chatter,
And if we used an outhouse, we would grow an extra bladder;
But even when it's coldest, when our feet would have no
  feeling,
Those Iron Rangers get dressed up and go out snowmobiling
Out across the frozen land and make a couple stops
At Gino's Lounge and Rudy's Bar for whiskey, beer, and
  schnapps—
And then they go into a shack that's filled with boiling rocks
Hot enough to sterilize an Iron Ranger's socks
And sit there till they steam out every sin and every foible
And then jump into a frozen lake and claim that it's enjoible—
But there was one, a shy young man, and although he was
  Finnish,
The joys of winter had, for him, long started to diminish.
He was a Finn, the only Finn, who would not take a sauna.
"It isn't that I can't," he said. "I simply do not wanna.
To jump into a frozen lake is not my fondest wish.
For just because I am a Finn don't mean that I'm a fish."
His friends said, "Come on, Toivo! Let's go out to Sunfish
  Lake!

A Finn who don't take saunas? Why, there must be some
mistake."
But Toivo said, "There's no mistake. I know that I would
freeze
In water colder than myself (98.6°)."
And so he stayed close by a stove for nine months of the year
Because he was so sensitive to change of temperature.

One night he went to Eveleth to attend the Miners' Ball.
(If you have not danced in Eveleth, you've never danced at
all.)
He met a Finnish beauty there who turned his head around.
She was broad of beam and when she danced she shook the
frozen ground.
She took that shy young man in hand and swept him off his
feet
And bounced him up and down until he learned the polka beat.
She was fair as she was tall, as tall as she was wide,
And when the dance was over, he asked her to be his bride.
She looked him over carefully. She said, "You're kinda thin.
But you must have some courage if it's true you are a Finn.
I ain't particular bout men. I am no prima donna.
But I would never marry one who would not take a sauna."

They got into her pickup, and down the road they drove,
And fifteen minutes later they were stoking up the stove.
She had a flask of whiskey. They took a couple toots
And went into the shack and got into their birthday suits.
She steamed him and she boiled him until his skin turned red;
She poured it on until his brains were bubbling in his head.
To improve his circulation and to soften up his hide,
She took a couple birch boughs and beat him till he cried,

"Oh, couldn't you just love me now? Oh, don't you think
   you can?"
She said, "It's time to step outside and show you are a man."

Straightway (because he loved her so, he thought his heart
   would break)
He jumped right up and out the door and ran down to the
   lake,
And though he paused a moment when he saw the lake was
   frozen
And tried to think just which snowbank his love had put his
   clothes in—
When he thought of Tina, Lord—that man did not think twice
But just picked up his size-12 feet and loped across the ice—
And coming to the hole that they had cut there with an ax—
Putting common sense aside, ignoring all the facts—
He leaped! Oh, what a leap! And as he dove beneath the
   surface,
It thrilled him to his very soul!—and also made him nurface!
And it wasn't just the tingling he felt in every limb—
He cried: "My love! I'm finished! I forgot! I cannot swim!"

She fished him out and stood him up and gave him an embrace
To warm a Viking's heart and make the blood rush to his face.
"I love you, darling dear!" she cried. "I love you with all my
   might!"
And she drove him to Biwabik and married him that night
And took him down the road to Carl's Tourist Cabins
And spent a sleepless night and in the morning, as it happens,
Though it was only April, it was absolutely spring,
Birds, flowers, people put away their parkas and everything.
They bought a couple acres around Hibbing, up near Chisholm,
And began a life of gardening and love and Lutheranism.

And they live happily to this day, although they sometimes
    quarrel.
And there, I guess, the story ends, except for this, the moral
Marriage, friends, is a lifelong feast, love is no light lunch.
You cannot dabble round the edge, but each must take the
    plunch.
And though marriage, like that frozen lake, may sometimes
    make us colder,
It has its pleasures, too, as you may find out when you're
    older.

5

STORIES

MEETING FAMOUS PEOPLE

W HEN BIG TIM BOWERS just happened to turn to his left and see the little guy with the battered guitar case emerge limping from Gate 4A at the Omaha International Airport on July 12, 1985, he held out his big arms to greet his best friend, which, although they had never met in person, Sweet Brian surely was. *It was Sweet Brian himself! There! In Concourse C!* His *White Boy* album was what got Tim through the divorce from Deloyne after three loving months of marriage, when she notified him that he was hopeless and the next day upped and split for Cheyenne with a bald bread-truck driver (unbelievable), after which Tim lost his security job and apartment and would've lost his mind except for Sweet Brian, so of course he yelled, "Hey, you're my man! I got to shake your hand! Hiiiiya! Sweet Brian! Hey!"

Sweet Brian made a sharp right, climbed over a railing and a row of plastic chairs, and walked fast toward Baggage Claim, which didn't surprise Tim one bit. After all, the guy who wrote "Tie Me Loose" and "That Old Highway Suits Me Pretty Well, I Guess" and "Lovers Make Good Loners" is no Sammy Davis, Jr., and Tim respected him for the uncompromising integrity and privacy and sincerity of his art, which had been crucial to Tim when his own sense of self was chewed up by Deloyne, all of which Tim now needed to say to Sweet Brian. He galloped down the concourse after the fleeing singer-songwriter, who heard his 262-pound fan and panicked and went through a door marked "NO ADMITTANCE" and clattered down two flights of steel stairs, Tim's big boots whanging and whomping on the stairs above, convincing him that death was near, and burst through a pair of swinging doors marked "WEAR EARPLUGS" and headed across the tarmac, a man once nominated for a Grammy (for "Existential Cowboy") and once described as the Dylan of the late seventies, panting and limping around some construction barriers along the terminal wall toward a red door twenty yards away. "Incredible," Tim was thinking. "I come to the airport to hang around and maybe get an idea for a song—not to meet anybody or anything, just to think about something to write about, maybe about not having anybody to meet— and I meet *him*. Fantastic." Tim was six strides behind him when he burst through the red door. There was a second, locked door a few steps beyond, and there, in the tiny vestibule, Tim expressed a lifetime of appreciation. He hugged Sweet Brian from behind and said, "Hey, little buddy, I'm your biggest fan. You saved my life, man."

The star pushed Big Tim away and sneered, "You know, it's vampires like you who make me regret ever becoming a performer. You and your twenty-nine-cent fantasies. I don't know what you— You sicken me." And he slapped Tim.

At this point Tim wasn't thinking lawsuit at all. An apology would have been enough—e.g., "Sorry, pal. I'm under too darn much pressure right now. Please understand." He'd have said, "Fine, Sweet Brian. No problem. Just want you to know I love your music. That's all. Take care of yourself. Goodbye and God bless you." Instead, Sweet Brian said those terrible things and then *slapped him* and shoved him aside and went to the hotel and wrote an abusive song about him ("Your Biggest Fan") and sang it that night at the Stockyards, and that's how they wound up in U.S. District Court two years later.

Tim had lost quite a bit of weight in those two years, ever since he got a great job at NewTech, thanks to the company's excellent weight-loss program, which, in fact, Tim himself initiated (he's executive vice-president in charge of the entire Omaha and Lincoln operations, about eight thousand employees and growing daily since NewTech bought up SmetSys, ReinTal, and Northern Gas & Hot Water), and he looked blessedly happy at the courthouse, which might have had something to do with his new wife, Stephanie, a blond six-foot former *Vogue* model who accompanied him, leaning lovingly on his chest and smiling fabulously as photographers jockeyed for position. A handsome couple. Rumor said she was two months pregnant. They looked ecstatic. Young and rich and very much in love.

Inside, Tim's lawyer described Sweet Brian as a "candy-ass has-been who can't hit the notes and can't write the hits, so he hits his fans," and asked for a half million dollars in damages. The little guy sat twenty feet away from Tim, his ankles chained together. He looked bloated, sick. His cheap green sportcoat wouldn't button in front. It had orangeade stains down the lapels. The story of his downfall was in all the papers. Sweet Brian and Tania Underwood had had to interrupt their Hawaiian sex tryst to fly to Nebraska for the trial and in Concourse C Brian was nabbed by the Omaha cops for possession of narcotics with a street value of $327. Tania was furious. She slapped him around in the police station, called him a loser, and left town. It snowed three feet that night, and his lawyer was stuck in L.A., and Sweet Brian sat in the clink for six days. That was when Tim saw him in court looking morose. "Can I help?" he asked, but the sullen singer turned away in anger. That night, a rodeo rider from Saskatchewan who was doing thirty days for bestiality beat the daylights out of Brian and knocked out four front teeth. Next morning, the county dentist, Dr. Merce L. Gibbons, had to drill out the stumps without Novocain. Brian bled so much he fainted and toppled forward, and the drill went through his cheek. The dentist panicked, thinking *malpractice suit*, and he tore his white smock slightly and roughed up his thin hair so as to claim that Brian had attacked *him*, and then he clubbed the former star hard, twice, with a mallet and yelled for the cops. They took Brian to the hospital and he got an infection from the blood test and died. There was no autopsy. The lawyer was in China. Nobody came from L.A. for the body, and finally some reporters collected $310 around the newsroom and Brian was buried in Omaha under a little headstone: "Brina Johnson, 1492–1987." The two typos weren't noticed until it was too late. So what could they do? A local columnist taped a note to the stone saying, "His name is Brian. Listen to his albums sometime. Not *White Boy*, which is too pretty, too nostalgic, too *self-conscious*, but *Coming Down from Iowa* is not bad. I think it's on the Argonaut label."

Tim was in Palm Beach when someone told him Brian was dead, and although he was extremely busy in meetings all day, he wondered, "Could this have been avoided if I had approached him differently, maybe been more low-key?"

"He was a big hero to me back then," he told Stephanie as they strolled along the beach toward The Palmery, where they were meeting some Florida associates for drinks and dinner. "I really wish we could have been friends."

*   *   *

Even today, after he settled out of court with the singer's estate for a rumored $196,000, Tim feels bad about the incident. He is not alone. Tens of thousands of people have approached very famous men and women intending to brighten the lonely lives of the great with a few simple words of admiration, only to be rejected and abused for their thoughtfulness. To the stars, of course, such encounters are mere momentary irritations in their fast-paced sensational lives and are quickly forgotten, but for the sensitive fans personal rejection by an idol becomes a permanent scar. It could easily be avoided if, when approaching the celebrated, those who practically worship them would just use a little common sense:

1. Never grab or paw the famous. They will instantly recoil and you will never ever win their respect. Stand at least thirty-two inches away. If your words of admiration move him or her to pat your shoulder, then of course you can pat back, but don't initiate contact and don't hang on. Be cool.

2. Don't gush, don't babble, don't grovel or fawn. Never snivel. Be tall. Bootlicking builds a wall you'll never break through. A simple pleasantry is enough—e.g., "Like your work!" If you need to say more than that (*I think you're the most wonderful lyric poet in America today*), try to modify your praise slightly (*but your critical essays really suck*). Or cough hard, about five times. That relieves the famous person of having to fawn back. The most wearisome aspect of fame is the obligation to look stunned by each compliment as if it were the first ever heard. That's why an odd remark (*Your last book gave me the sensation of being a horned toad lying on a hot highway*) may secretly please the famous person far more than a cliché (*I adore you and my family adores you and everyone I know in the entire world thinks you are a genius and a saint and with your permission I will fall down on the sidewalk and writhe around and foam for a while*). Be cool. Famous people *much* prefer a chummy insult to lavish nonsense: a little dig about the exorbitant price of tickets to the star's show, perhaps, or the cheesiness of the posters (*You design those yourself?*). Or a remark about the celebrity's pet (if any), like "How much did you pay for that dog?" Personal dirt (*Do you have to shave twice a day? Do you use regular soap or what? What was it like when you found that out about her going out with him?*) can wait for later. For now, limit yourself to the dog. As it gazes up in mealymouthed brown-nosed, lickspittle devotion, glance down and say, "Be cool."

3. Autographs are fine, photos are fine, but be cool. Don't truckle (*Oh, please please please—I'll do anything—anything at all*), don't pander (*This is the high point of my life*), and never cringe or kowtow (*I know that this is just about the tackiest thing a person can do and*

it makes me sick with shame but . . .), and never, never lie (*My mother, who is eighty-seven, is dying in Connecticut and it would mean the world to her if . . .*). Hand the famous person the paper and simply say, "I need you to sign this." Hand the camera to one of his hangers-on and say, "Take a picture of us."

4. When you are cool like this and don't fawn and don't grab and just go about your business as a fan and get that autograph and the photo and are businesslike about it, probably you are going to make such a big impression on the famous person that he or she will make a grab for *you* in that offhand way these people have (*Care to join Sammy and me for dinner, Roy?* or *Somebody find this guy a backstage pass, wouldja?*). Remember, these people are surrounded by glittering insincerity and false friendship and utter degradation of all personal values to such a degree that three cool words from you (*Like your work!*) will knock them for a loop. Suddenly the star recalls the easy camaraderie of a Southern small-town childhood and the old verities of love and loyalty in the circle of family, church, and community. Desperately he reaches out for contact with you (*Please. You remind me of a friend I once had. Many years ago and far away from here. Please*), wants your phone number, tries to schedule lunch with you on Thursday (*Anywhere, anytime. Early lunch, late lunch. You name it. I can send a car to pick you up. Thursday or Friday or Saturday or any day next week. Or Sunday if you'd rather. Or it doesn't have to be lunch. It could be breakfast or dinner. Or a late supper. Brunch*), tries to draw you into conversation (*You got a book you want published? Songs? Anyone in your family interested in performing? Got a favorite charity you need anyone to do a benefit for? Need a credit or job reference?*). Don't be fooled. Just smile and nod and say, "Nice to meet you," and walk away. He'll follow you (*What's your name? Please. I need you*). Walk faster. You don't want to get involved with these people. Thirty seconds can be interesting, but beyond two minutes you start to get entangled. They're going to want you to come to the Coast with them

that night and involve you in such weird sadness as you can't believe. *(Please come with us. I mean it. There's something real about you that's been missing from my life for too long. Please. Just come and talk to me for three minutes.)* Sorry. *(Please.)* No. *(Then let me come with you.)* No. *(Tell me why not.)* I'm sorry. I wish that it was possible, but it isn't, not at this time. I hope we can meet again very soon. Bye.

THE LOVER OF INVENTION

THE FIRST PERSON TO INVENT the wheel was a man named Charley Baekr, left-handed, five-foot-eight, mid-forties, a farmer (we think) and hunter who knew how to grind rocks smooth and who lived in what is now Montana if his burial site ten miles west of Billings is any indication. His remains were uncovered there last spring. "Baekr" is probably a misspelling of "Baker"; mistakes were common before man had a written language. Charley lived approximately three aeons, or two hundred sixteen eras ago, a darned long time. When dug up, he was nothing but dry bones.

His tribe was the Amminutians, a peaceable subgroup of the Western Mesa people who, like most stone-agers, were predominantly rural, religious, slow to change, preferring to squat on their rocks around a smoking fire and gnaw on semicooked caribou and watch for a change of weather, but Baekr was an exception. Two summers before he died, he produced a perfect cube carved from granite, four feet by four feet by four feet, which the Amminutians probably used for a jumping-off place. Jumping down off things was an important religious ritual for them, and his stone undoubtedly saved the lives of many virgins since it would have taken the place of a high cliff, the typical religious point of departure for persons with no sexual experience.

The perfection of the cube convinced the tribe of forty or fifty men and women that it was holy all right but some Amminutians were suspicious of Charley. His former girlfriend Verde was now hooked up with a high priest (or *spensif*) whose sacred duty it was to stand on the cliff (*presper*) and guide the faithful to the edge. When Charley's cube took its place, her new guy, Cid, ordered his disciples to tie a rock to Charley Baekr's left ankle to teach him humility (*dompa*). Perhaps the rolling of that rock inspired him to invent the wheel, we don't know. Some facts aren't completely verified but they represent a pretty accurate picture of what must have happened. At any rate, he did his work in a canyon under the sacred cliff and, early on a Tuesday morning when the dew was heavy and the air was sweet with new grass, he brought out the first man-made wheel for people to see. It was made from black quartz, ten and a half inches across, a couple inches thick, a *small* wheel. He placed it on a flat rock by the fire.

"You jump off that, you'll never get anywhere spiritually," said Verde, ruffling his long black matted hair and smiling down at him. He said, "It's not a jumping-off place, it's a roller. Look." He rolled it in the dirt. The track is visible today, you can see where the wheel wobbled. It was warm, they had eaten small birds and drunk berry juice, and he kept shifting positions where he sat. His ankle must have hurt terribly.

"It's the dumbest thing I ever saw," said Cid.

"It wasn't my own idea," said Charley, lying. "I got it from a guy I met. But it could be useful. See how easy it is to roll it. Then push this other rock through the dirt. Two rocks the same size but one is easy and the other is a bitch. Compare them and make up your own mind."

Cid did. "You're right," he said, "but so what?"

"I'm only thinking out loud now," said Charley, "but it seems to me you could put some type of load on her."

"Recidulous," said Cid. "Don't make me left."

"Look, Charley," said his former love, "you put a load on this rock, it slides off when the rock turns, you have to put the load back up, it takes more time, it's lucidous."

Charley looked up toward the sun. Around him sat his kinsmen and nearby was his perfect cube, which Cid had carved steps into and adorned with a dozen crude likenesses of bears, crows, fish, and spiders. All around them stood six hundred fifty sheep. Of that we're dead certain. Some stuff never completely goes away.

"Would you please cut this rock from off my leg so I can go show this roller to other peoples?" the inventor asked, looking at Verde.

Tears welled up in her azure eyes. "You'd go leave us? your own people? The ones who brored you and knuckled you, the ones who gave you your sven, your brodske, the people who gave you your *dialect*? We're your *people*, Charley! Nobody else in the wiemer would even understand you!"

He hunkered down, squinted, picked up a pinch of dry dust, and spat. *Ptt.* "I guess that what I'm trying to say is that I'd like to have the chance to see for myself."

"Okay," Cid said, untying the rock. "Go. But remember one thing: there is no paint."

"What?" asked Charley.

Verde touched his cheek. "Don't go. Don't."

"I meant what I said," said Cid, "and don't come back and ask me to repeat it."

*　　*　　*

The inventor of the wheel left the Amminutians and headed northeast, believing in his heart that Verde would follow him—look at those whorls, those are places where he stopped, turned around, waited, paced in circles, hoping—but after a few days he stopped and scooped out a shallow trench and lay down in it. He was forty-five, which was much older millions of years ago than it is today. A man his age really needed wheels but he had only one, a small quartz disc that he perhaps still hoped would be a hit or maybe he had quit caring. He was utterly lost. The Amminutian tongue has no word for "go away," no way to express "move," "vamoose," "cut loose," "break free," "take off," "ship out," or "make tracks." The entire linguistic family of bye-bye indicators is missing in Amminese. So we have to assume this was a pretty new cultural experience for him, much like levitation would be for us.

He lay in the trench and looked up at the constellation they called Becker, which we see as the Big Dipper but which Amminutians saw as a god holding a club in one hand, a fistful of dirt in the other, and jagged shards for teeth.

We don't know if he stayed in the trench until he died or if he got up now and then and walked around. We think he got out occasionally, but "out" was frightening to a man of his background, and soon the trench got deeper and more comfortable. Five feet down, he saw less of the god overhead. Some little pebbles bothered him in the small of his back and shoulder blades but he cleaned them out and lay and slept and slept. Dirt blew on him and against him and he probably thought, "It's only a little dust, I can shake it off." Instead he faded down and out. That's him, there. The crystal wheel is held by the left hand, flat, the perfect curve pressed against the hipbone, as if he were going to throw the discus but lay down to rest. He died of everything at once.

*   *   *

Baekr died before he could pass on his discovery, and the wheel as we know it was a team effort, not a shot in the dark by a guy with a dream but the work of King Hagged the Just, the hairy naked blood-encrusted one-eyed psychotic who led his bestial Walukas in one massacre of innocents after another, ridding the land of any humankind less wretched and horrible than themselves. One day, seeing his filthy hordes try to shove jagged boulders across uneven terrain to the killing ground to press the gentle Promosians to death with, the squat-shaped gap-toothed shit-headed leader stood up fearsomely in his stone sled pulled by three hundred Waluka women and screamed "DO—THIS—BETTER!"

The Promosians volunteered to do research. While the Walukas lurked around the perimeter, fouling the landscape, glowering, feeding on lizards and bats, the quiet and mannerly Promosians sat in the shade of the promissary trees calmly discussing geometry, considering one theory after another, deliberating in their patient and endlessly precise and cooperative and self-deprecating style the problem of moving weight across ground with less friction—"Darn, it's going to be something *so* simple, I just know it!" cried a young fellow, and sure enough it was: a CIRCLE—of *course*—the Promosians chortled for joy, shook hands all around, embraced—of *course*, the *Wheel*, what else could it be? why didn't we think of it sooner? they asked. "I was *sort of* thinking wheel," said the young guy, "but then I thought, Naw, too easy. It just goes to show, I guess." So the Walukas knocked off ten two-ton wheels, rolled them swiftly to the ancient blood-soaked killing ground, and pressed the Promosians, who died knowing they had made a great gift to civilization. King Hagged the Just went on to slay thousands and tens of thousands, happily, easily, with no pain or inconvenience to himself, and died in his sleep, drunk on excellent red wine, with eleven naked maidens pasted to him, murmuring his name.

*   *   *

How do we know all this? Well, we're not certain *how* we know but we do know. We're 100 percent certain of the results, if mystified by the process. But what is truly mysterious is the guy whose bones these are, Charley Baekr—his cracked skull, tibia, femur, radius and ulna, mandible, sternum, carpals and tarsals, and humerus, and next to the humerus, the pubic bone.

Frankly, it's pretty obvious that he missed that woman *a lot*, which explains why he stopped, on that desolate plain. He must've felt certain she'd leave Cid and follow him, that she didn't *really* see him as the religious doubter who introduced the low jump but as the inventor of the wheel and a guy she could fall in love with, so he dug in and waited for her. The ancient dilemma: he knew that once he developed the wheel and things started rolling, he'd become a somebody like Cid except bigger, and she could love him for *that*; but meanwhile, without her, he couldn't go around the block, couldn't even develop a cold. He lay in the dirt, waiting, his wheel at his side, hearing every little creak or whisper, dreaming of her, waking up believing she was close by. From trench (A) he walked out in all directions (B, C, D, E, like the spokes of a wheel) to watch for her and (F) made one last great circumference of hope before retiring to the hub to lie down and die.

* * *

It was rotten luck to invent the wheel in a rocky hilly place, among people with no concept of movement. If the land had been flatter, if the people had said, "Hey, go for it"—but no, it had to be in that rugged valley that held them like a cage, nobody daring to be movers, only jumpers, and when Charley did break out he only went 6.2 miles before he stopped.

And yet—to lie in the dark and wait for a woman to arrive—isn't that exactly how so many of our finest hours have been spent? isn't that when the poems got written, ideas thought up, jokes formulated, great art imagined? See right here how as he lay in the trench he tried to widen it to accommodate what was not yet, but which would be, the bountiful Verde, her generous body settling alongst his, saying, "Oh Charley, oh my darling lovely one," and while he lay in wait and wonderful expectation, he saw our world in his head. He invented us. He saw every use and adaptation of the wheel, from the cart to the wagon to the barrow, the windlass and mill, the coil and the ball, screw and gearwheel, drill, hinge, pulley, globe and dome, ball sports, turntable, dial, chainlink, compass, roller skate, eggbeater, lawn sprinkler, revolver, rotary press, paint roller, ballpoint pen, lazy Susan, spin dryer, roulette, Caterpillar, flywheel, floppy disc. While he lay in fragrant anticipation of her womanly waist and hips and thighs, he envisioned us in one brilliant moment like a flash of lightning over a ruined amusement park in November, its Ferris wheel and carousel and Tilt-a-whirl lit up, *wham!*

He heard steps in loose gravel and desperately wanted them to be hers, the wind in the underbrush to be her saying, "Oh sweet love, I looked so long—let me come into your bed."

If she came, the wheel didn't matter, and if she never came, it didn't matter either. Her face, her hair, her hands, her shoulders and back, her waist and belly, her legs and feet, her face, her hair, her hands, shoulders, back, and so forth. In her hand a crown of white spring flowers. Naked she bent forward and placed it in his hands and so forth. The rest nobody knows, but perhaps it was not so different then from now. Dying, he met her at last. A last faint sigh of disbelief, and then she touched him.

LONELY BOY

I MET HER AT THE BEACH a year ago June 17. I was sitting on the diving dock thinking about going home and making myself a pizza when she climbed up the ladder, putting her hand on my knee briefly. "Excuse me," she said, and dove in. I jumped up and dove after her. I had never dived headfirst before—had always held my nose and shut my eyes and jumped—but I went after her and followed her down to the murky bottom, where I bumped into her and panicked a little and grabbed on and we came up together. "That was the first time I ever did that!" I said. She said, "Aren't you that friend of Sandra Singleton's—the one who was with her cousin that time we all went to the drive-in? The one who spilled the Coke?" "Yes!" I said. (I didn't care—if that's who she thought I was, then I didn't mind being that guy; I figured I could straighten it out later, when we got to know each other better.) "You said you were going to *call* me!" she said. She put her two cool hands around my neck. I said, "Well, consider this a call."

She was at the beach with her friend Janelle, who stayed under the umbrella because the sun gave her a headache. She was fish-belly white and looked like she had a terrific headache going at the moment. She said, "It's no fun here, Rhonda, why don't we go to my house for lunch?," looking at Rhonda, not looking at me.

I said, "I'll buy us dinner," and went and got five burgers, three fries, and three shakes. Janelle said, "No, *thanks*," so I and Rhonda ate it. "By the way, I forgot your name," she said. I bit off half a burger and chewed it slowly, thinking fast. I didn't think she'd be impressed with the name Wiscnek so I gave her a name I made up when I was little, Ryan Tremaine, a name I used when I played detective. She said, "That's such a beautiful name." "Well, I'm a nice guy," I said.

She said to Janelle, "Don't you think he ought to get contacts? He'd look so much better without glasses." Janelle looked at me like contacts wouldn't make any difference at all. She said, "I'm going home. Coming, Rhon?" Rhonda said she'd come later.

We went back in the water. I said, "I don't think Janelle likes me." She said, "Don't be silly, Janelle is my best friend. We've been friends since we were six." We dove off the dock until it was almost dark, then sat on the blanket and talked. "I'm cold," she said, so I put my arm around her. We lay down and she sort of put her arm around me. I told her I loved her. She said I was sweet. We lay there in the dark, talking and getting close to each other, and then after a while she suddenly said, "No, let's not."

I said, "Why not? I love you."

"It's not that. I believe in waiting."

I thought to myself, "I have been waiting a long time already," but I said, "That's okay. I respect that," and we folded up the blanket and umbrella, and she kissed me. We talked about marriage. Sort of generally, not specifically in terms of each other, but I got the idea she liked me. Then she said goodbye.

"You're not going out toward Fennimore Parkway, are you?" I asked, taking a wild guess. "Sure," she said, "hop in."

She drove a blue 1982 Mustang convertible, a graduation present from her folks. She headed south on Lake Avenue past the Lake-Hi Drive-in Theater and East High, where I had graduated in 1976, turned right on 44th, and down the Strip past the used-car lots and over the hill past the cemetery two miles and then onto Fennimore. I had been in that part of town only a couple of times in my life. It had curving streets lined with beautiful elms and white houses as big as schools. I picked out one and said, "Here." She stopped and I got out. "What's your number?" I said. She told me.

I wonder if she would have told me if she had known I am an assistant herdsman at the zoo and live in a studio apartment. I wonder. Anyway, getting her phone number was worth the long bus ride back to Lake, where I transferred to the 16th Street bus that took me back to the beach, where I got in my car and drove home.

I thought about calling her to make sure she got home all right, but didn't because it was almost eleven o'clock, so I put a frozen macaroni dinner in the oven and watched the late movie and passed out on the couch and eventually woke up to smell smoke and see the girl in the movie alone on a deserted road being chased by bikers; then, after she ran into the woods and tripped and fell, there was a commercial, and I grabbed the phone and dialed her number. The phone rang about twenty times, then a man answered. "Hello, has Rhonda gotten home yet?" I asked. "Do you know what time it is?" he said. "She's asleep. Who the hell is this?"

"Sorry. Didn't mean to bother you. Good night." I disguised my voice so he wouldn't be mad if I met him later.

I woke up at 9:00 A.M. thinking about her, though I was late for work, and wanted to call her up and wish her a pleasant good morning and ask if she felt the same longing I felt, but raced to the zoo, where I found three angry messages on my desk with "IMMEDIATELY" underlined on each one. I was in charge of three high-school kids who worked there that summer, and so I needed a desk to sit behind when I told them what to do, but my job was not a desk job—my crew and I picked up trash and chased animals. The zoo was built with the idea that animals would be seen in their natural habitat and not stuck in little cages, a good idea, but the taxpayers got angry if they went and just saw a lot of habitat—they expected to see animals and they bitched if the moose, for example, were back in the underbrush—so our job was going into the bushes and kicking the animals' butts out of there and getting them into the open, especially the peacocks, flamingos, wolves, deer, beaver, moose, bears, and tigers. The bears and tigers we heaved corncobs at or flushed out with water hoses so they wouldn't lie around in caves or behind rocks as they tended to do. It wasn't a great job but it was what I was paid to do.

I called her at lunchtime (she was gone to play tennis) and again at five o'clock (she was eating dinner and couldn't come to the phone) and finally I reached her at 6:30. "Come on over!" she said. I knew by the address she gave that it was going to be hard to find, but I dressed up in my only good casual clothes and headed her way and in no time I was completely lost not too far from where I was sure she lived. I went around and around on little lanes and drives called Fernhill and Wooddale and Fernwood and Hilldale, where half the driveways are unmarked or say "Keep Out" and you go in to ask for directions and a minority woman in a white dress has no idea what you're talking about and of course there aren't any pay phones for miles, and it got dark and I was getting fed up—I broke out of the maze finally and hit an actual street with stores on it, and called her from a gas station. She said it was too late to come over, because Janelle was there and they were supposed to go to a play. I noticed that she didn't invite me but I didn't comment on it. I did convince her to meet me at Bingo's (minus Janelle) three days later, the soonest she could work it into her schedule.

She never looked more beautiful—to me, at any rate. She was tan and glowing and wore a white dress that really set off her features, including her long neck and perfect collarbones, the perfect picture of the sort of girl I had always wanted to know. I wanted her to love me so bad, I had spent two nights studying up on the college she had said she was going to so that, if it came up again, I could say I had gone there myself. I knew names of courses, streets, buildings, dorms, deans, a ton of material, but the subject didn't come up. Instead she asked if I sailed. She wanted her dad to buy her a sailboat.

"Oh, sure," I said, as if, to me, sailing was like crossing the street.

"I used to sail," I said, implying that I had gone on to pursue deeper interests, but wasn't sure what they should be—things she'd be interested in, of course, but, on the other hand, not things she already knew a great deal about—philosophy maybe. I decided on Nileism, the theory that nothing matters, nothing matters at all except for this little moment we have together in this dark world. But we mostly talked about her and her summer. I kissed her goodnight and she promised to see me soon. I held her, a little too long, maybe, and then she got in her car and drove away.

It was very hard, trying to be the person she thought I was, the guy who was with Sandra Singleton's cousin that night and spilled a Coke. I needed to know more about him. So that night I called up a Singleton residence in Rhonda's part of town and asked for Sandra. A girl came to the phone who was yelling at someone named Barb to keep an eye on the scallops. "Sandra, you probably don't remember me, but I'm Paul Bryant and I met you last summer, I think at the 7-Hi Drive-in, and the reason I called is I'm trying to locate that guy who was with your cousin that night—remember? The guy who spilled the Coke?"

"Gene."

"Right. How could I get ahold of him? He wanted me to call him about a car, and I couldn't remember his name."

"Parker."

"Parker! Right! Where would I find him?"

She said he went out west and she didn't know where exactly or when he might come back. "Does he owe you money?" she said. "If he does, you might as well forget it. What a fruitfly!"

"How do you mean that?" I said. She said that he was a pain in the rear and she had only been nice to him because of her cousin. I said I thought that Rhonda sort of liked him. "Ha!" she said. "Fat chance! Rhonda just likes to make Sam jealous!" Then she had to go and eat those scallops, although there was more I wanted to know. Who was Sam? for example.

I figured that, if Rhonda didn't know Gene was gone, I could go on being him for a while longer, but I should get another story ready in case of emergency ("What guy at the drive-in? A friend of Sandra who? Spilled what Coke? I don't know what you're talking about! I'm Ryan Tremaine, we met at the beach, remember?") and I had better start developing Ryan as someone she would like to know more than the guy she was mistaking me for.

I didn't have much time to work on Ryan that week, due to problems at the zoo, where a big-shot doctor who donated two Chinese peacocks brought his friends to see them and naturally they were lounging around in the back forty and had to be fetched. I wasn't around, having gone to see to the moose, so my boss had to do it and one of the peacocks attacked him. You always want to have a stick when you herd peacocks, but he was trying to play St. Francis in front of the donor, and he got scratched up. He was fried about it. He put me to work shoveling out the camel yard. Meanwhile, the moose were giving me fits. We have four, who live on a two-acre tract with manmade marsh, and when they choose to be invisible, they go into the tall grass at the back of the marsh, where they hunker down and sit all day. I don't know why people want to look at a moose, but they do, so we put up a temporary fence to keep them up front, and then Peggy developed a scalp infection and looked hideous, so we put her *behind* the fence, and then Jack tried to climb over to her and scrambled around and punctured himself, so then the fence had to come down and the tall grass had to be cut. It was hell with the moose all week, not to mention the camels. I was going to switch Ryan from Nileism into some branch of theology, maybe Methodism, which I knew something about but not nearly enough, but I didn't have time to go to the library.

That Friday she said she'd go see *The Beach of the Living Dead* with me at the Lake-Hi, and I actually found her house with the help of very specific directions that she was surprised I needed. "It's not that far from yours," she said. I couldn't remember where mine had been. Her house was a brick mansion like a foreign embassy, with a circular drive and a flagpole (American flag) and about ten acres of lawn. The man who answered the door looked at me like I had a hideous scalp infection.

"I'm sorry," I said.

"For what?"

"I don't know. I think maybe I'm a few minutes early."

He was her dad. I followed him into a dark room with dark wood walls and he sat in a leather chair and I sat in the middle of a leather couch. I should have picked the end, where I could have set my arm on the armrest. Instead I put my hands on the cushion. I was so sweaty, when I pulled them away it sounded like Velcro ripping. "So," he said, "what are you up to this summer?"

I almost gagged, my summer activities being one part of the Ryan Tremaine story I hadn't decided on. I had worked out the part about my family—my father and mother had died in 1978 in a plane crash in Bolivia, and I was just starting to get back on my feet emotionally after a pretty terrible period in my life—but what was I doing? I considered saying that I was studying wildlife management but it seemed too close for comfort, so I chose the ministry on the spot.

"What church?" he said. I said Congregational. I was going to go for Methodist, but Congregational seemed the better choice, given the layout. He grunted. "Each to his own, I suppose, but to me it's a lot of mumbo-jumbo. A lot of people pretending to be holier than everybody else."

I assured him that I did not feel holier than him, that in fact my call to the ministry was based on an awareness of my own shortcomings—"It's a big job, the ministry, the responsibility can be almost frightening sometimes"—upon which Rhonda strolled in, decked out in cutoffs and a rather bold jersey, cut as low as it could be and still be considered clothing. "Hi, Ryan," she said, bending down to give me a peck on the neck. Ordinarily, I would have been thrilled, but the terrible lies had made me awfully tired. I was pretty quiet all the way to *The Beach of the Living Dead*. She asked me what was wrong. I said, "I'm thinking about us, that's all."

She leaned her head on my shoulder, my arm around her, as zombies struggled out of their sandy graves on the tropical island, first their gruesome hands poking out and then the heads with bulging blank milky eyeballs and purplish rotting flesh hanging off, and they marched their stiff-legged zombie march, arms outstretched, toward the young couples necking on blankets under the Southern moon, and somehow this put Rhonda in a romantic mood. She kissed me a long wonderful kiss.

I said, "I wish we knew each other better." She said she thought she knew me better than I might think. "I doubt it," I said. "There's a lot you don't know, that probably you wouldn't want to know." She said, "You talk like you shot your parents or something."

Well, she was right, in a way. Betty and Bob Wiscnek were probably watching TV at that moment, sitting on the plastic-covered sofa about two miles from us, but I was all ready to have them go down in a flaming airliner over Bolivia if the situation called for it. On the other hand, Ryan was a finer person, who was more worthy of her love, which, if I won her over, could someday turn me into the finer person I had to pretend to be in order to win her. This is complicated.

I felt so bad, I had to tell her one true thing about myself. I said, "One thing you don't know is that actually I work at the zoo." She said, "Yeah? Well, that's not so bad."

A moment later, she said, "I don't go to zoos. They're so depressing." I said, "Oh, I don't know."

She said, "What gives us the right to lock up animals in little cages so we can go stare at them? How would you feel if you were in a cage?"

I said animals are treated real well in zoos. She disagreed with that. I said, "This sure is a dumb thing to argue about." She said, "You were the one who brought it up."

We talked about zoo animals a little more, then the hero and his girlfriend escaped from the island, having killed a couple dozen zombies by knocking their heads off, and then I told Rhonda how much I loved her. I said, "I really need to know that you care about me." She wanted to go home right away, and I thought we should go to Bingo's. She wasn't hungry. I knew that if I took her home I'd never see her again, and I got a little desperate, and I drove to Bingo's despite her saying, "Turn around right now, or else I'm going to jump out." So I drove around the block twice and then drove her home. It was a long drive. After a while she said that maybe I'd enjoy spending a few years in prison if I thought zoos were so wonderful. I said, "There's more than one way of looking at something. You don't necessarily have a monopoly on the truth, you know." Maybe not, she said, but she knew what she thought. I had told her, by way of explaining that our zoo didn't have cages, that part of my job was making animals come out of the underbrush, which was a mistake. She thought that was inhuman. She said, "You act like you're proud of it." I said it was my job. She said, "Some people will do anything." I pulled up in front of her house, she got out of the car, and I knew we'd never meet again.

It was a dumb way for a romance to break up that could have been so wonderful. I am still kicking myself for it. I can see now all the mistakes I made. I think there was a moment there where she would have fallen in love and married me, and if she had, I believe that things would have worked out as she got to know me better, and we would be very happy right now. Instead I feel terrible. To come so close— I keep wanting to call her and explain. The phone is on the dresser. I imagine she's sitting beside a swimming pool, by a phone. All I need to do is think of the right words to say.

WHAT DID WE DO WRONG?

T HE FIRST WOMAN TO REACH the big leagues said she wanted to be treated like any other rookie, but she didn't have to worry about that. The Sparrows nicknamed her Chesty and then Big Numbers the first week of spring training, and loaded her bed at the Ramada with butterscotch pudding. Only the writers made a big thing about her being the First Woman. The Sparrows treated her like dirt.

Annie Szemanski arrived in camp fresh from the Federales League of Bolivia, the fourth second baseman on the Sparrows roster, and when Drayton stepped in a hole and broke his ankle Hemmie put her in the lineup, hoping she would break hers. "This was the front office's bright idea," he told the writers. "Off the record, I think it stinks." But when she got in she looked so good that by the third week of March she was a foregone conclusion. Even Hemmie had to admit it. A .346 average tells no lies. He disliked her purely because she was a woman—there was nothing personal about it. Because she was a woman, she was given the manager's dressing room, and Hemmie had to dress with the team. He was sixty-one, a heavyweight, and he had a possum tattooed on his belly alongside the name "Georgene," so he was shy about taking his shirt off in front of people. He hated her for making it necessary. Other than that, he thought she was a tremendous addition to the team.

Asked how she felt being the first woman to make a major-league team, she said, "Like a pig in mud," or words to that effect, and then turned and released a squirt of tobacco juice from the wad of rum-soaked plug in her right cheek. She chewed a rare brand of plug called Stuff It, which she learned to chew when she was playing Nicaraguan summer ball. She told the writers, "They were so mean to me down there you couldn't write it in your newspaper. I took a gun everywhere I went, even to bed. *Especially* to bed. Guys were after me like you can't believe. That's when I discovered that life is essentially without meaning. That's when I started chewing tobacco—because, no matter how bad anybody treats you, it's not as bad as this. This is the worst chew in the world. After this, everything else is peaches and cream." The writers elected Gentleman Jim, the Sparrows' PR guy, to bite off a chunk and tell them how it tasted, and as he sat and chewed it tears ran down his old sunburned cheeks and he couldn't talk for a while. Then he whispered, "You've been chewing this for two years? I had no idea it was so hard to be a woman."

When thirty-two thousand fans came to Cold Spring Stadium on April 4 for Opening Day and saw the scrappy little freckle-faced woman with tousled black hair who they'd been reading about for almost two months, they were dizzy with devotion. They chanted her name and waved Annie flags and Annie caps ($8.95 and $4.95) and held up hand-painted bedsheets ("EVERY DAY IS LADIES' DAY," "A WOMAN'S PLACE—AT SECOND BASE," "ERA & RBI," "THE GAME AIN'T OVER TILL THE BIG LADY BATS"), but when they saw No. 18 trot out to second with a load of chew as big as if she had mumps it was a surprise. Then, bottom of the second, when she leaned over in the on-deck circle and dropped a stream of brown juice in the sod, the stadium experienced a moment of thoughtful silence.

One man in Section 31 said, "Hey, what's the beef? She can chew if she wants to. This is 1987. Grow up."

"I guess you're right," his next-seat neighbor said. "My first reaction was nausea, but I think you're right."

"Absolutely. She's a woman, but, more than that, she's a *person*."

Other folks said, "I'm with you on that. A woman can carry a quarter-pound of chew in her cheek and spit in public, same as any man—why should there be any difference?"

And yet. Nobody wanted to say this, but the plain truth was that No. 18 was not handling her chew well at all. Juice ran down her chin and dripped onto her shirt. She's bit off more than she can chew, some people thought to themselves, but they didn't want to say that.

Arnie (The Old Gardener) Brixius mentioned it ever so gently in his "Hot Box" column the next day:

> It's only this scribe's opinion, but isn't it about time baseball cleaned up its act and left the tobacco in the locker? Surely big leaguers can go two hours without nicotine. Many a fan has turned away in disgust at the sight of grown men (and now a member of the fair sex) with a faceful, spitting gobs of the stuff in full view of paying customers. Would Frank Sinatra do this onstage? Or Anne Murray? Nuff said.

End of April, Annie was batting .278, with twelve RBIs, which for the miserable Sparrows was stupendous, and at second base she was surprising a number of people, including base runners who thought she'd be a pushover on the double play. A runner heading for second quickly found out that Annie had knees like ball-peen hammers and if he tried to eliminate her from the play she might eliminate him from the rest of the week. One night, up at bat against the Orioles, she took a step toward the mound after an inside pitch and yelled some things, and when the dugouts emptied she was in the thick of it with men who had never been walloped by a woman before. The home-plate ump hauled her off a guy she was pounding the cookies out of, and a moment later he threw her out of the game for saying things to him, he said, that he had never heard in his nineteen years of umping. ("Like what, for example?" writers asked. "Just tell us one thing." But he couldn't; he was too upset.)

The next week, the United Baseball Office Workers local passed a resolution in support of Annie, as did the League of Women Voters and the Women's Softball Caucus, which stated, "Szemanski is a model for all women who are made to suffer guilt for their aggressiveness, and we declare our solidarity with her heads-up approach to the game. While we feel she is holding the bat too high and should bring her hips into her swing more, we're behind her one hundred percent."

Then, May 4, at home against Oakland—seventh inning, two outs, bases loaded—she dropped an easy pop-up and three runs came across home plate. The fans sent a few light boos her way to let her know they were paying attention, nothing serious or overtly political, just some folks grumbling, but she took a few steps toward the box seats and yelled something at them that sounded like—well, like something she shouldn't have said—and after the game she said some more things to the writers that Gentleman Jim pleaded with them not to print. One of them was Monica Lamarr, of the *Press*, who just laughed. She said, "Look. I spent two years in the Lifestyles section writing about motherhood vs. career and the biological clock. Sports is my way out of the gynecology ghetto, so don't ask me to eat this story. It's a hanging curve and I'm going for it. I'm never going to write about day care again." And she wrote it:

SZEMANSKI RAPS FANS AS "SMALL PEOPLE" AFTER DUMB ERROR GIVES GAME TO A'S

FIRST WOMAN ATTRIBUTES BOOS TO SEXUAL INADEQUACY IN STANDS

Jim made some phone calls and the story was yanked and only one truckload of papers went out with it, but word got around, and the next night, though Annie went three for four, the crowd was depressed, and even when she did great the rest of the home stand and became the first woman to hit a major-league triple, the atmosphere at the ballpark was one of moodiness and hurt. Jim went to the men's room one night and found guys standing in line there, looking thoughtful and sad. One of them said, "She's a helluva ball-player," and other guys murmured that yes, she was, and they wouldn't take anything away from her, she was great and it was wonderful that she had opened up baseball to women, and then they changed the subject to gardening, books, music, aesthetics, anything but baseball. They looked like men who had been stood up.

Gentleman Jim knocked on her door that night. She wore a blue chenille bathrobe flecked with brown tobacco-juice stains, and her black hair hung down in wet strands over her face. She spat into a Dixie cup she was carrying. "Hey! How the Fritos are you? I haven't seen your Big Mac for a while," she said, sort of. He told her she was a great person and a great ballplayer and that he loved her and wanted only the best for her, and he begged her to apologize to the fans.

"Make a gesture—*anything*. They *want* to like you. Give them a chance to like you."

She blew her nose into a towel. She said that she wasn't there to be liked, she was there to play ball.

*   *   *

It was a good road trip. The Sparrows won five out of ten, lifting their heads off the canvas, and Annie raised her average to .291 and hit the first major-league home run ever by a woman, up into the left-field screen at Fenway. Sox fans stood and cheered for fifteen minutes. They whistled, they stamped, they pleaded, the Sparrows pleaded, umpires pleaded, but she refused to come out and tip her hat until the public-address announcer said, "No. 18, please come out of the dugout and take a bow. No. 18, the applause is for you and is not intended as patronizing in any way," and then she stuck her head out for 1.5 seconds and did not tip but only touched the brim. Later, she told the writers that just because people had expectations didn't mean she had to fulfill them—she used other words to explain this, but her general drift was that she didn't care very much about living up to anyone else's image of her, and if anyone thought she should, they could go watch wrist wrestling.

The forty thousand who packed Cold Spring Stadium June 6 to see the Sparrows play the Yankees didn't come for a look at Ron Guidry. Banners hung from the second deck: "WHAT DID WE DO WRONG?" and "ANNIE COME HOME" and "WE LOVE YOU, WHY DO YOU TREAT US THIS WAY" and "IF YOU WOULD LIKE TO DISCUSS THIS IN A NONCONFRONTATIONAL, MUTUALLY RESPECTFUL WAY, MEET US AFTER THE GAME AT GATE C." It was Snapshot Day, and all the Sparrows appeared on the field for photos with the fans except you know who. Hemmie begged her to go. "You owe it to them," he said.

"Owe?" she said. "*Owe?*"

"Sorry, wrong word," he said. "What if I put it this way: it's a sort of tradition."

"*Tradition?*" she said. "I'm supposed to worry about *tradition?*"

That day, she became the first woman to hit .300. A double in the fifth inning. The scoreboard flashed the message, and the crowd gave her a nice hand. A few people stood and cheered, but the fans around them told them to sit down. "She's not that kind of person," they said. "Cool it. Back off." The fans were trying to give her plenty of space. After the game, Guidry said, "I really have to respect her. She's got that small strike zone and she protects it well, so she makes you pitch to her." She said, "Guidry? Was that his name? I didn't know. Anyway, he didn't show me much. He throws funny, don't you think? He reminded me a little bit of a southpaw I saw down in Nicaragua, except she threw inside more."

All the writers were there, kneeling around her. One of them asked if Guidry had thrown her a lot of sliders.

She gave him a long, baleful look. "Jeez, you guys are out of shape," she said. "You're wheezing and panting and sucking air, and you just took the elevator *down* from the press box. You guys want to write about sports, you ought to go into training. And then you ought to learn how to recognize a slider. Jeez, if you were writing about agriculture, would you have to ask someone if those were Holsteins?''

Tears came to the writer's eyes. "I'm trying to help," he said. "Can't you see that? We're all on your side. Don't you know how much we care about you? Sometimes I think you put up this tough exterior to hide your own insecurity.''

She laughed and brushed the wet hair back from her forehead. ''It's no exterior,'' she said as she unbuttoned her jersey. ''It's who I am.'' She peeled off her socks and stepped out of her cubicle a moment later, sweaty and stark naked. The towel hung from her hand. She walked slowly around them. ''You guys learned all you know about women thirty years ago. That wasn't me back then, that was my mother.'' The writers bent over their notepads, writing down every word she said and punctuating carefully. Gentleman Jim took off his glasses. ''My mother was a nice lady, but she couldn't hit a curveball to save her Creamettes,'' she went on. ''And now, gentlemen, if you'll excuse me, I'm going to take my insecurity and put it under a hot shower.'' They pored over their notes until she was gone, and then they piled out into the hallway and hurried back to the press elevator.

Arnie stopped at the Shortstop for a load of Martinis before he went to the office to write the ''Hot Box,'' which turned out to be about love:

> Baseball is a game but it's more than a game, baseball is people, damn it, and if you are around people you can't help but get involved in their lives and care about them and then you don't know how to talk to them or tell them how much you care and how come we know so much about pitching and we don't know squat about how to communicate? I guess that is the question.

The next afternoon, Arnie leaned against the batting cage before the game, hung over, and watched her hit line drives, fifteen straight, and each one made his head hurt. As she left the cage, he called over to her. "Later," she said. She also declined a pregame interview with Joe Garagiola, who had just told his NBC "Game of the Week" television audience, "This is a city in love with a little girl named Annie Szemanski," when he saw her in the dugout doing deep knee bends. "Annie! Annie!" he yelled over the air. "Let's see if we can't get her up here," he told the home audience. "Annie! Joe Garagiola!" She turned her back to him and went down into the dugout.

That afternoon, she became the first woman to steal two bases in one inning. She reached first on a base on balls, stole second, went to third on a sacrifice fly, and headed for home on the next pitch. The catcher came out to make the tag, she caught him with her elbow under the chin, and when the dust cleared she was grinning at the ump, the catcher was sprawled in the grass trying to inhale, and the ball was halfway to the backstop.

The TV camera zoomed in on her, head down, trotting toward the dugout steps, when suddenly she looked up. Some out-of-town fan had yelled at her from the box seats. ("A profanity which also refers to a female dog," the *News* said.) She smiled and, just before she stepped out of view beneath the dugout roof, millions observed her right hand uplifted in a familiar gesture. In bars around the country, men looked at each other and said, "Did she do what I think I saw her do? She didn't do that, did she?" In the booth, Joe Garagiola was observing that it was a clean play, that the runner has a right to the base path, but when her hand appeared on the screen he stopped. At home, it sounded as if he had been hit in the chest by a rock. The screen went blank, then went to a lite sausage commercial. When the show resumed, it was the middle of the next inning.

On Monday, for "actions detrimental to the best interests of baseball," Annie was fined a thousand dollars by the Commissioner and suspended for two games. He deeply regretted the decision, etc. "I count myself among her most ardent fans. She is good for baseball, good for the cause of equal rights, good for America." He said he would be happy to suspend the suspension if she would make a public apology, which would make him the happiest man in America.

Gentleman Jim went to the bank Monday afternoon and got the money, a thousand dollars, in a cashier's check. All afternoon, he called Annie's number over and over, waiting thirty or forty rings, then trying again. He called from a pay phone at the Stop 'N' Shop, next door to the Cityview Apartments, where she lived, and between calls he sat in his car and watched the entrance, waiting for her to come out. Other men were parked there, too, in front, and some in back—men with Sparrows bumper stickers. After midnight, about eleven of them were left. "Care to share some onion chips and clam dip?" one guy said to another guy. Pretty soon all of them were standing around the trunk of the clam-dip guy's car, where he also had a case of beer.

"Here, let me pay you something for this beer," said a guy who had brought a giant box of pretzels.

"Hey, no. Really. It's just good to have other guys to talk to tonight," said the clam-dip owner.

"She changed a lot of very basic things about the whole way that I look at myself as a man," the pretzel guy said quietly.

"I'm in public relations," said Jim. "But even I don't understand all that she has meant to people."

"How can she do this to us?" said a potato-chip man. "All the love of the fans, how can she throw it away? Why can't she just play ball?"

Annie didn't look at it that way. "Pall Mall! I'm not going to crawl just because some Tootsie Roll says crawl, and if they don't like it, then bull shit, they can go butter their Hostess Twinkies," she told the writers as she cleaned out her locker on Tuesday morning. They had never seen the inside of her locker before. It was stuffed with dirty socks, half-unwrapped gifts from admiring fans, a set of ankle weights, and a small silver-plated pistol. "No way I'm going to pay a thousand dollars, and if they expect an apology—well, they better send out for lunch, because it's going to be a long wait. Gentlemen, goodbye and hang on to your valuable coupons." And she smiled her most winning smile and sprinted up the stairs to collect her paycheck. They waited for her outside the Sparrows office, twenty-six men, and then followed her down the ramp and out of Gate C. She broke into a run and disappeared into the lunchtime crowd on West Providence Avenue, and that was the last they saw of her—the woman of their dreams, the love of their lives, carrying a red gym bag, running easily away from them.

YON

My name is Yon Yonson, I come from Wisconsin, I work in a lumber mill there. When I walk down the street, all the people I meet, they say, "Tell us what your name is." I say: My name is Yon Yonson, I come from Wisconsin, I work in a lumber mill there. When I walk down the street, all the people I meet, they say, "Tell us what your name is." I say: My name is Yon Yonson, I come from Wisconsin, I work in a lumber mill there. When I walk down the street, all the people I meet, they say, "Tell us what your name is." I say: My name is Yon Yonson, I come from Wisconsin, I work in a lumber mill there. But actually I left Wisconsin last fall and came to New York to visit my sister Yvonne and her husband, Don Swanson, in the Bronx. She wrote, "Come on out here and visit us, Bro, we got plenty of room, stay as long as you like." I sold my shack and came east with one cardboard suitcase. Lumbering can get awfully thin in those Wisconsin woods; sometimes a tree falls and you wish you weren't there to hear it. I hitched a ride out with a dummy named Carlson and his two dogs, neither of whom cared for me, and got to New York smelling like a dog, took a Yellow Cab to Yvonne's place hoping for a big lunch of pot roast and spuds and lemon-meringue pie and I find out the reason she has plenty of room is that she and Don Swanson got divorced last year, that she has an actor boyfriend named Gary Chalet, her hair is bright crimson, she wears three big brass rings on each wrist and has dropped forty pounds on a diet of

melon and bulgur wheat and is a painter of paintings that look like
they collided with the paint truck and is in college studying real estate,
and Don Swanson is a gay Lutheran bishop on Nantucket I tell you,
New York is full of amazing things, any one of which if it happened
in Wisconsin would stop your heart, but here it's only a news item.
"Tell me about yourself. How've you been?" she asks, pouring me
a root beer. I say, "Compared to you and Don, there frankly ain't
all that much to tell," and I think to myself, "There frankly *ain't*
and I am going to stay here until there *is* and then go back home
and tell *them*." We talked until 3:00 A.M. and I woke up at 6:00 and
went out for a breath of air; it was hot in her tiny place and her
aquarium hummed and kept me awake. I walked for blocks. I saw a
little lady in tight black pants walking fifteen little dogs on fifteen
leashes, saw a man arguing with another man in some language like
Greek that sounded fierce and furious but then they laughed, I bought
a Korean pear (very good), walked past a store that sold seashells
(nothing else, just shells) and another selling bouquets of grass
(hundreds of different types) and firewood for four dollars a pair,
dropped in at a lunch counter and sat next to a black man. The waitress
called me Love. She said, "What're we having, Love?" I had a cup
of coffee and two slices of rye toast. "Anything else, Love?" she asks,
so I got eggs, too. "Want half of this newspaper?" asks the black
man, so I take half and look at the want ads and go down to Grant
S. Pierce Flowers on 52nd Street, who needed a man to deliver full-
time, $300/week. "I can see you are an honest man," said the owner,
G.S.P., so I start right away, learning the ropes from the other
deliveryman, Elayne, and go home with forty dollars, and Yvonne
has just woke up and dressed and is hungry, so we go around the
corner to an Ethiopian restaurant where you eat food off a pancake
with your fingers. We ate three beef pancakes and one bulgur and
she informed me it was all over with Gary Chalet, she had met a
sculptor. It didn't surprise me a bit.

It surprised me that I didn't miss home, except a little bit on

Sunday during a Redskins-Giants game, somehow a note in Brent Musburger's voice recalled the cozy Sunday afternoons we lumbermen piled in together around Butch Butcherson's color TV. Billy and Butch and Pete and Tom. We'd crank up the kerosene heater and pop popcorn and sit in that steamy room in the frozen woods, watching the Vikes, and now Brent's voice at halftime made me think of things I never said to those guys, like "Maybe we ought to get out of here and go someplace else. Maybe life can be better." Third quarter, the game got lopsided. I fell asleep. When I awoke it was 6:00 A.M. The subway was peaceful so early, people sleeping on old No. K as she banged downtown, I even squeezed in some Zs myself.

It was my job to open up Grant S. Pierce at 7:30 and get the overnight orders off the answering machine. Previously, the addresses had gotten goofed up due to someone's dyslexia and Elayne got mad and threw the flowers in a ditch (which, if you know how far you got to drive to find one of those in this town, tells you how lost he was), so the day I started was the day they started to make a profit. The voices on the machine were guys phoning in at 3:00 and 4:00 A.M. and the only flower they could remember was the rose. We ordered six bales of roses every morning. Fluffed them up into bouquets and I ran around Manhattan laying them on the desks of tall wary women, not all of whom were bowled over by the gesture. "Take your lousy flowers back to that pitiful degenerate and stick them in his lap" was not such an unusual response. I drove the big green van around narrow streets as bumpy as dirt roads, not that you ever went so fast that you actually bumped, they were packed solid with traffic, so I learned to do what I had to do, to be nasty with the horn and to shove the next car aside and horn in and then—this is hard for a nice Wisconsin man to do—to park the van in the middle of the street in front of cars I had just horned in in front of and walk into a building and deliver flowers and not rush although as I wait for Miss Meyers in the thirty-first-floor reception room I can hear them calling to me from below, the forlorn long toots and anxious beeps of abandoned children, and I look out a window and see them bunched up behind the green van like ducks trying to scoot through a hole in the fence, but it's too small to squeeze through, I think, watching a black limo try to get around me, followed by a station wagon, an ambulance, a garbage truck. They look like toys. It's interesting to watch. A man gets out of the limo and walks twice around the van, fast, pounding on it with a tire iron. Furious, like Miss Meyers stabbing at the bouquet with a pencil. "I'm not even going to touch the *paper* around these," she says. I tell her that Mr. Tom Tucker didn't wrap the roses, I did, but she makes a face. "I loathe and despise him and anything he paid for whether he touched it or not." Her face brightens. "Do you sell thistles?" she asks. Honk honk, beep beep, *braaaagh*. "Do you sell and deliver bouquets of seaweed or big gobs of algae—would you deliver a bucket of green slime for me?" So much anger. It's hard for a Wisconsin man to deal with. Even in the sleepy jungle afternoons in the Grant S. Pierce greenhouse, hosing down rubber trees, pinching aphids, listening to Broadway stars reveal their thrilling lives on the "Midday Cavalcade with Adrian Adams Live from the Blue Room of the Hotel Hart High Above Eighth Avenue" and watching June bend over the tulips, there is anxiety. Angry phone calls from men wondering why the women didn't call to say thanks. A New York voice like a ratchet-tooth hacksaw: "Whaddaya mean she didn't accept the roses? You're telling me that my girl wouldn't take my roses? Is that what you're telling me? You're telling me that she doesn't think that I'm the best thing that ever happened to her? Is that it? That's what she told me two days ago. You're sayin' I'm deaf? Or stupid? Listen to me, you—" I never liked roses. Tulips beat roses anytime in my book. Once I took an armful of American Beauties to Vanelle Montage at the Hotel Hart prior to broadcast and wished it had been soft pink tulips, roses are so hard and cold. She was little and pink and talked in a tiny jewel-like voice. I whipped right past Adrian Adams and handed her the bouquet, sitting at a table for two with a clear crystal microphone, and him—he gave me the fish eye, but Miss Montage looked up and smiled a small perfect smile. "You have the kindest face, I wish that I knew you as a person and that it were possible to see you every afternoon, it would give me courage. God bless you," she whispered. She gave me a ticket to her show (she was in *Play Ball!* at the Henry James) and was unable to draw her small cold hand immediately from mine but let it rest a second. I felt a pulse beat as rapid as a bird's in her little finger; then her producer Raoul Cassette put his big paw on my shoulder. "Beat eet," he said in his fake French accent, "vi haff beezness to dô so . . . eef yeu vil be so kindt." His nose was two inches from mine and I could see that nothing in the man's face was real. I turned away. Something in Miss Montage's eyes said, *Help me please*; she blinked and again it said *Help me please*. I was triple-parked on Eighth and 43rd, the van sticking halfway into the intersection, I could hear screams and honks and glass breaking. I said, "Some other time, my dear. Goodbye." This is hard for a Wisconsin man to do: turn away from the desperate pleas of a fine woman enslaved by a vicious creep. But I was in love with June, darling June, my little Junebug, her arms full of tulips, looking at me over the ferns in the mist from the greenhouse mister, her beautiful eyes and nose and arms and legs and all of her wanting me and me wanting her, it's that way when you're around flowers constantly.

Did I tell you that she and I got married last Monday at City Hall and that we live in a $1.2-million place up in Connecticut, in the woods alongside a pond? It's a fine big house that reminds me a lot of Wisconsin houses, especially the fact that we plan to fill it with kids. When she and I stroll along under our beech and hickory trees after a busy day running our mail-order bulb business, YoYoCo, I can hear the voices of our children tearing around the woods (though she is only six days pregnant). It happened like this. Every day I got out of the Manhattan rat race by going over to the Hotel Oshkosh on West 48th for a bite of lunch, and there I got to be pals with an old guy with hair in his ears named Bob Bobson who ran a sausage factory in Queens and who hailed from Sheboygan. Everyone at the Oshkosh came from back home, it was known as "The Wisconsin Embassy" and outside on the marquee in red letters eighteen inches high was the motto "Arntcha Gladger a Badger!" which tended to keep out the uptown crowd and lure in Wisconsinites. Every day at noon the lobby filled up with men in immense plaid pants and vast yellow shirts and sportcoats in many patterns, sportcoats you could leave on a park bench and know that nobody would steal them. It doesn't take many of those gents to fill up a lobby, and they filled it with happiness and song. Their hearty voices whanged out one number after another as they patiently stood in line for a seat in the Rumpus Room and a good lunch of ham hocks and sauerkraut, songs such as "Hail Hail the Gang's All Here" and "Let Me Call You Sweetheart" and "I've Been Workin' on the Railroad" and "Let the Rest of the World Go By." Bob sat and sang along in a tuneful bass voice and his little brother Rick who worked for him writing bus advertisements'd lean over my way and say, "Listen to those wahoos, they couldn't sing their way out of a paper bag." He was only a size 46. He ate chicken wings and tuna salad, had a perm and a mustache, and wore blue shirts and gray slacks. He had been a jazz columnist in Duluth-Superior and knew the words to songs like "Stormy Weather." His plan was to crank out sausage ads until he saved a wad and then move to Vermont and write essays. When he heard I had a ticket to see Vanelle Montage (*Play Ball!* was S.R.O. into the 1990s), resentment filled his tiny red eyes and he refused to dine with me again, which was a nice deal. I would've given him the ticket except his friendship was too high a price to pay. I gave it to Bob. Big tears welled up in his eyes, his hand shook, and he set down his forkful of knockwurst. He said, "Mister, nobody ever gave me something for nothing in this town since coffee was a nickel." He swallowed. He said, "Son, I'm going to let you in on a very nice secret."

It was the Midtown-LaGuardia tunnel, the fabulous underground route to the sky that millions have dreamt about as they sat locked in place on FDR Drive watching their plane sail away to Honolulu, the tunnel begun in 1946 and shut down two years later when the Manhattan end popped up in the wrong spot. Bob leaned forward and said softly, "Take the alley behind that old building with the lady lit up on top and go down the ramp to the door marked 'RAMP' and honk twice. When it opens, go down to level 4 and through the door marked 'DANG R' and there it is, son, in two minutes you're over to Queens and take the exit marked x and you're at the United terminal."

I found it. "DANG R" opened to a dirt track through a black stone tube, a couple big puddles a quarter-mile in and a stretch of plank road but I shot through at 55 with my headlights on high beam and two minutes later was at LaGuardia, pondering the business possi- bilities. Starting the next week, I made eighteen runs daily and all of my best Grant S. Pierce customers were glad to climb in the back of my truck and be delivered to the airport so suddenly, and I started to sell more orchids and rare flowers, many of which were presented to me, their chauffeur and pal, and then I bought a used bus. With the bus, it was three tight turns driving down to level 4 but I never was one to get upset about a few scratches on a motor vehicle, it is meant to be used, not saved. I painted the windows for secrecy, carried eighteen full loads a day, screeched around those tight turns, saved my money, courted June, and quit Grant S. Pierce. They wept on my last day at work and the old man thrust immense sums of money at me, begging me to reconsider, fifties and hundreds, fistful, his big green eyes dissolved in pools of tears. June quit too. We have five hundred grand in the bank, and headed for Connecticut and bought this ten-acre spread for $6,296 in back taxes that an old customer of mine put me onto, where we aim to be happy and raise our children, like they sing about at the Oshkosh. We put down the cash, strolled around our pasture and woods, our creek, our gentle hills, our virgin pond, and drove back that afternoon to New York to sell the bus and the tunnel was blocked.

The entrance at the airport was gone, filled up, paved over. There was no trap door where the entrance had been, just asphalt. I jumped up and down on it but the pavement didn't budge. She looked pretty well shut up for the time being. So if you're heading to the airport, you ought to allow extra time.

Meanwhile I'm okay, so is June, and the baby is due in July. Yvonne has a new boyfriend, the third after the sculptor, a urologist named Cid, and is in the Bahamas with him, he loves to scuba dive. I sail, which is so relaxing for a lumberjack, though once in a while I do dearly love to bring down a tree. She and I mainly keep in touch through answering machines, mine says: "This is Yon Yonson, I've gone to Wisconsin to visit my aunts in Racine. I'll come back—when I do, I'll get back to you. Tell me what is your name."

THE ART OF SELF-DEFENSE

E D HAD READ SOMEWHERE that it's foolish to hit someone in the face because you can easily break your fingers and spend weeks unable to handle a fork, meanwhile the guy you hit suffers a small red mark on his cheek and sues you for the price of your house. Ed is forty-three, an age when bones are brittle, and yet the wisdom of having avoided injury didn't make him feel any better after the soft-ball game the Rocks lost 18–4 on Sunday afternoon to a bunch of jerks from Coleman's Irish Lounge, and especially the play in the last inning, when one jerk ran over Megan Michael at third base.

Ed played left field, he saw it all: Megan didn't play often because she was scared of the ball, but she liked to play, so, ten runs behind, they stuck her at third and the jerk came up to bat looking grim and manly and got aboard with a bloop grounder down the third-base line that she missed completely and when it then leaked through Ed's legs the jerk took off like a runaway truck. He rounded second as Ed heaved the ball toward third—she *never* could have caught it—but instead of sliding, the jerk barreled in, his knees pumping, knocked her head over heels, *stepped* on her, and chugged home as all his fellow jerks jumped up and down and ran out to pound him on the back.

It was *deliberate*. He meant to cream her, it was *obvious*, but all the Rocks could muster was a few limp words of protest. Bill was the pitcher, he could've run at them fast, but he only stepped off the mound and said, "You're ahead by ten runs, for Pete's sake." The jerk grinned and said, "Eleven!" Ed walked in from left field, saying, "Hey! What's the big idea? Cut it out!" and by the time he got to third and the little pile of Megan in her green sweatshirt, the jerk's colleagues were gathered around, asking her if she was okay. She was crying but said "Yeah," thinking a real ballplayer would say that, and the jerk said, "Sorry if I hurt you but you were standing on the bag. The runner's got a right to the basepath." And then he reached down and she took his hand and he hoisted her up, and right then and there the moment passed, the correct psychological moment for hurling yourself at the jerk in blind rage and ripping his flabby arm from its socket and beating him over the head with it and throwing him down to the ground and spitting him to death. The Rocks' chance for self-respect passed in the same moment.

He was an earnest little jerk with a mustache and no chin, watery eyes behind his horn rims, and his name was embroidered on his pocket: Nixon. He brushed some dirt off Megan's shirt. "Don't touch her," Ed thought to himself, but didn't say it. Bill said, "You're sure you're okay? Maybe you better sit down," so she did. The Rocks murmured a few more things, like "That was kind of rough, wasn't it?" and "You didn't have to do that, you know." The jerk only shrugged and said, "Hey, you want me to go back to third? Fine." "Hey, Nixon," somebody said, "you had every right, man, you got it fair and square." When the game ended, the jerk actually approached the Rocks' bench—*and the Rocks shook hands with him! Including Ed!* All except lovely Megan, who was now weeping from the pain and couldn't lift her arm. "Hey, hope you feel better," called the jerk. Ed helped her to his car. The Irish Loungers were leaning around a white van, laughing, spraying beer at each other, and they all waved as Ed drove out, and yelled "Good game!" Ed didn't get really angry until after he took Megan to St. Joseph's, where the X-ray showed a broken collarbone, after he drove her to a drugstore to pick up pain pills and then dropped her at her apartment, and after she said, "Thanks for waiting around. It was really nice of you. I could've taken a cab or something. But, thanks."

Driving home to St. Anthony Park, he imagined himself racing in from left field after the collision and decking the jerk with a flying tackle. Bashing his face in. Hard hammer blows to the jerk's gut, sharp jabs to the chinless face (Left! Right! Left! *Uppercutuppercutuppercut!*)—then, as all the other jerks came lumbering drunkenly toward him, disposing of them one-two-three with lightning karate kicks, whirling, dodging their big windmill swings, kicking kneecaps ("Arrrgghhhh!"), pounding heads together, flipping the flabby hombres up high and down flat on their fat backs ("Oooofff!"), and when they wobbled back up on their flat feet and pulled out paring knives, he dispatched them with quick little jujitsu brick-breaker thrusts to the throat, *wap wap wap wap*, and they went down like pigs at Hormel: Wham! Bam! Pow! Wham! Krrack!

He coasted around Madison School and up Dowell Street. The yellow backhoe sat up on his grass, the deep trench lay along the curb. He parked in front of Spander's and jumped the trench to his yard. Two months of sewer work and still no pipe in sight. In the cool house nothing stirred except a breeze through the white curtains; the white kitchen smelled faintly of lemon. The flowers in the back garden perched on the hill in ranks, an audience, divided by rows of stones. Leonie was at her mother's, because Ethel was having her lymph nodes removed on Monday morning, or was it a gland? Mel was sick, too. Then Ed remembered the faint little peep of protest that came out of his mouth in left field, the timid ladylike petulance, the stamping of his tiny foot, when mayhem was what the situation called for, assault with a baseball bat. *Coward.* Why had he walked toward third base so slowly if not to make sure he'd get there too late?

He could recall other occasions when he had backed away from trouble. And it wasn't nonviolence, it was failures of nerve. He hadn't turned the other cheek, he had merely averted his eyes and walked away from fights. People could see this weakness in him. People were walking on him, and he would have to put a stop to it. The answer was so simple, it floated into the kitchen into plain view, like the glass of beer on the table in front of him. *Hit someone.* He'd have to go out and pop somebody to cure his cowardice. Maybe it wasn't exactly cowardice but more like an eye-hand coordination problem, that he couldn't pull the trigger on his fist. Some brain cells were flabby up in the anger circuit. Anger mounting in the brain, creating conditions likely to bring on a stroke. If he did nothing, soon his hands would shake, he'd become an old man who berates children. One good shot at a jerk would flush out the system and restore him to health.

He threw the beer down the sink and went for a walk. Down the alley behind the fine old colonial houses, past the school and the tennis courts and a little way into the park, and he stopped in a grove of poplars. How to stand to get off a good punch? Like a pitcher on the mound. Body relaxed, eyes narrowed to slivery dark slits. Step off the rubber with left foot, bring right arm forward, fist clenched. Pow! He set the next Sunday as the deadline for the punch. No. Wednesday. A real punch. No shoving, no "Oh yeah?"s and "Look out"s and nonsense like that, a straight-on assault on somebody who deserved it.

That night Leonie called. Her mother was in a panic about the operation. Ed could hear weeping in the background. Leonie was worn out. "How's your dad?" he asked. "Useless," she said. Monday morning, he had two chances. The bus driver told him in a brusque tone of voice to step to the rear, and briefly Ed considered letting him have it, but then the guy said it to the next person, too. Ed got off downtown, crossed the street, and a vicious punk in a beat-up tan station wagon swerved right into the crosswalk, honked, gave him the finger, zoomed away. Ed yelled "Hey! You!" and ran a couple steps after the car as if he might chase it to the next stoplight, rip the door open, haul the kid out, and beat the buttons off him, but the next intersection was a long way off and the light there was green. The kid sailed on. Ed went to work. "Today's the day," he said. "Your time is coming." Several times that day he said, "Be ready. It'll come. Don't let it pass." He heard his boss talking to secretaries in his fruity, pompous voice, and Ed strained to pick up some blatant sexist remark that might warrant a good pop in the snoot but heard none. Later, the clown strolled into his office wearing brilliant red-plaid pants and a lurid green bozo jacket. "How's it going, old boy?" he asked. Ed let it pass.

En route home, a marquee he never noticed before, two blocks from work: "Live Continuous Sex ON STAGE See Hear Smell Touch And Much More SPECIAL SURPRISE ACTS & Things You Thought Were Illegal GROUPS WELCOME." He tried the door. Chained. What kind of jerk would run a slimy business like this, hanging out garbage for children to see and disturbing their delicate sense of the *beauty* of things—maybe he could return in the evening, jump onstage, and cream the emcee, a pimply little creep in lizard pants. Wipe the smirk off his face, put a little life into his blank eyes. Get arrested, be interviewed by TV: "Why did I do it? Because I have the capability of outrage at outrageous things, that's why!"

There was some good slugging on TV that night. James Garner pasted a guy in a men's toilet and tied his ankles with his belt and hung him upside down from a stanchion. Two welterweights went the distance at the Sands, standing toe to toe and banging the sweat off each other. Even Michael Landon connected on "Little House on the Prairie," an evil teamster who kidnapped Laura from the dry-goods store. Dan Rather didn't, but he looked like he could go a couple rounds. Leonie called at 10:00. The operation was a success. Six hours. "I wish I could come home," she said, on the verge of tears. Ed wanted to tell her: Your husband could be in jail tomorrow, or the hospital, maybe a cold marble slab, you may be talking to your Ed for the last time. Later, he gave himself a good pep talk in bed. "Your whole life is dedicated to stepping out of people's way! You're so good at it, you don't even know that you're doing it! You've got to get out there and hit! Smash 'em! Knock 'em down! Otherwise, something worse is going to happen. You turn into a shadow. A pale polite presence, a slight coolness that moves from room to room." He lay in the dark and it seemed to him that hitting somebody was a deeply moral undertaking: horrible deeds had come of men exactly like him being afraid to duke it out who were slowly crazed by cowardice until some psychopathic official policy let them ease the strain by commanding insane acts of violence at a safe distance: tons of bombs dumped on remote villages by order of pleasant men who, if someone had shoved them on the street, would've been aghast; Indian tribes wiped out by guys afraid of Indians, who despised themselves for it and avenged this fear through brutal and dishonest documents. Paperwork! Paper that worked vicious cruelty a thousand miles away while the authors went home, kissed their wives, and bounced their babies.

Tuesday, instead of his old 6A, he took the 11A bus, which would drop him at Hell's Corners, leaving a hike of eight blocks along West 4th. It was a section of downtown known for heavy street action, a no-man's-land, people he knew told him that if you had a flat tire you should sit and wait for the cops and don't get out of your car and walk. But what those folks were afraid of was exactly what he was looking for. Little bands of minority persons lounging on the hoods of cars and yelling things at whites, insults that nice people didn't know about and couldn't always recognize. Even cabdrivers stayed away from there. He carried his Swiss army knife in his suitcoat pocket and put his medical-insurance card in his shirt pocket, where an ambulance crew could find it.

The driver of 11A was a bald little man who looked locked in position, hunched down over his big wheel, his eyes straight ahead, and when Ed asked if 11A went to West 4th, the man whispered, "Please. Not now. Please. I m going through something now, I can't deal with this. Please." The bus was packed full; the passengers weren't like the old 6A crowd, who sang "Happy Birthday" for the old regulars and the driver, Fred Thompson, sometimes bringing a cake. These people looked beaten down, scared, and they stared sadly into space. One man was weeping. Ed sat next to a woman in a lime-green pants suit who kept wringing her hands and humming a mournful tune. "I need to talk to someone," she said softly after a few blocks. It was about her hair. Doctors said she was going to lose her hair. She was distraught. Ed said, "Your hair looks fine," but in fact it did look dull and lifeless. Hell's Corners was deserted. With its cheap liquor stores, porno shops, burned-out shells of buildings boarded up, vacant lots full of trash, it looked like a street Charles Bronson would walk in his campaign against crime, but the only people Ed saw were panhandlers. Old men with the shakes saw him coming and stepped into his path and made their pitch. "I played with Bix Beiderbecke." "I am a World War II veteran. I was wounded in North Africa." "I'm Skeeter from the Little Rascals movies. You remember. Spanky's friend." Ed had seen the Rascals on TV and the man actually did resemble Skeeter. Ed pressed a ten-dollar bill into his hand.

Word of this gift traveled on ahead, evidently. Perhaps, as Ed continued along West 4th, Skeeter waved his arms in a signal known to all panhandlers. Ed saw people on the next block turn and look, and men stepped out of doorways, rose up from the weeds, emerged from the back seats of hulks of cars to greet him. An old woman ran across the street. "I'm dying of cancer," she said. On the block beyond this one, ragged people stood in clumps. "I haven't eaten in three days." "My kids are sick." "I'm out of work. I was a teacher. I used to live in Golden Valley." The man's front teeth were brown, rotten. "I was on the radio. I was Singin' Slim of the Bunkhouse Buddies. I have emphysema." A man sitting against a trash barrel waved weakly and Ed leaned down. "Remember me?" the man whispered in a horrible pained voice. Remember? You said you'd come and take me back to Fargo."

Eight blocks, and it cost him everything in his billfold, about eighty-seven dollars. Nobody challenged him. Everyone looked like they had been banged around enough already. The fight was out of him; he knew it; he didn't try to argue with himself. That night on the "Six O'Clock Eyewitness News," Todd Withrow led off with three harrowing stories: foster children killed in Texas when a bus skidded off the road in the rain en route to a picnic; a weak, dying child held up to the camera as her parents pleaded for a liver donor; a screaming mother held back by firemen as smoke and flames billowed up from the tiny house— Todd's voice broke, and when Melanie came on with the weather, tears ran down her tan cheeks. "Sometimes the weather doesn't seem very important," she whispered.

It was a week later, the Tuesday after his Wednesday deadline, when, unbelievably, he hit a man. In the men's room at a restaurant. Dinner with Leonie, home at last, Ethel and Mel having left for a week with Judy, and he ordered snails to impress her. He'd never eaten snails before. They were probably okay but he thought too much about them during the meal and retired to a cubicle for a break. Its gray steel walls were scratched with dozens of ancient messages. One said: "You Too?" Someone came in the room and sat in the next cubicle. The man blew his nose and cleared his throat. "Can I come in there with you?" he whispered.

"Beg your pardon?"

"I need to be with someone right now," the man said. "I feel— God, I can't tell you—I've got a wife and three kids. I love them an awful lot. Oh, Jesus—" He started to cry. "Nobody knows what this is like. Do you have any idea? No, you don't. My God." "I'm leaving now," said Ed.

"Please, try to understand this. Just for one minute. Look at this." A hairy hand passed a snapshot under the partition. Ed saw that he had a wife and three kids all right. The wife looked tired and kind and the children, in their teens, well dressed, at a confirmation perhaps. Two tall girls wore white shoes. "You're looking at one hell of a family, mister," the man said. "So you tell me—" Ed handed the picture back. "You must love them very much to feel so guilty about being attracted to other men," he said. The man pounded on the steel wall and screamed, "What am I doing talking to *you* about it? You faggot!" He jumped up and yanked the door to Ed's cubicle off the hook. He was a big bald guy in a suit. Ed shoved him and the man stepped back. He swatted a rolled-up newspaper at Ed and the edge of a page scratched his left eye. A razorlike pain, tears flooding his eyes, without a single thought his right hand hauled off and slugged the man hard just above his ear. He staggered and Ed reached out to grab him, but when Ed tried to open his fist, the pain made him settle right down to his knees like a balloon descending, he knelt on the wet floor, bent over, holding the fist with his left hand. "You didn't hurt me! Just grazed me!" the man said, his speech slurred. Ed's hand was numb, getting fat. The man sat down on the sink. He said, "Gotcha pretty good, didn' I."

Leonie paid the bill. She was amused. "Boxing? In the bathroom? Oh my." She drove him to St. Joseph's and sat with him on the bench in the hall outside Emergency. His hand was swollen up as big as a breadloaf. "The world is full of jerks," he said, "and ever so often you have to deal with one so the word gets around to the others and they settle down for a while." He wasn't so sure about this, actually, but the deed was done. That part of his life was over for good and now something else could happen. He hoped the man was all right. He hoped the doctor would prescribe something strong, with codeine in it. He wished he were home in the dark.

END OF AN ERA

WHEN LARRY ROSE DIED suddenly while cleaning out his garage one sunny day, his death came as a big shock to some people around Market Falls, Vermont, who knew him fairly well and who visited the house that evening to comfort Sarah, Larry's friend, and bring her food, including homemade rye bread, home-smoked whitefish, garbanzo salad, and a meatless lasagna—one of Larry's favorites, though he wasn't a vegetarian (he *had* been one for a while but then he quit). They spread the dishes on a table he had made from an immense wooden spool, which stood on his new sundeck between the little yellow house and the garage, and they sat around it and talked in low voices about the man they had known, who, a few hours before, had pitched forward and fallen on the concrete floor he was sweeping. They also noticed that his table was tippy.

They agreed that death must have come as a big shock to Larry, too, since he was only forty-three and looked not so bad—if, that is, he had been aware of himself dying, which Sarah's sister Star hoped that he had been. She felt that a moment of awareness, a clear split second, would enable a dying man, even while falling forward, to make his peace with the world. Star, whose real name was Starflower, said, "The brain has these almost incomprehensible powers when it is focused and I think that in one incredible flash it could give up this life and reach for the next one, and I feel Larry would have wanted that as a matter of dignity, like knowing your address or something." Some others hoped he had gone instantly, without knowing, because he was so committed to life.

"When I go, I want to go *bang*," said Stan, Larry's best friend, or so he told Sarah—she didn't know Stan; she and Larry had only been together a few weeks. She was wrapped in a white chenille robe, a gift from Larry, and though her eyes were red, she looked serene and lovely. Larry's children, Angelina and Andrew, were with his ex-wife, Jessica, in Boston, and Sarah was meaning to call them with the sad news the next morning. "I think it's better to hear about something like this in the morning, when you have a stronger sense of life," she said. "Of course, I'm a morning person."

His friends didn't stay long, because Sarah was beat and also it was sort of depressing around there. *To die while cleaning out your garage*, Stan thought—to die in a heap of rusty tools, bike parts, stuff to be recycled, some sad little plastic toys, some rotten pumpkins from last fall, and four or five of your unfinished projects, including a busted rocker and the workbench you started to build three years before. It was also depressing to sit on Larry's sundeck, which, frankly, was an eyesore, built of three-quarter-inch plywood that sagged under their weight. *Why couldn't he have learned about joists*, Stan wondered.

Still, everyone planned to give him a good sendoff, of course. Star and Sarah sat down the next morning to call up all the numbers Larry had written on the wall by the telephone in the kitchen and invite those people to his funeral. "I'm sorry to be the one to have to tell you this," Star said to one of the people who answered. The man on the other end was quiet after she gave him the bad news. Then he said, "Larry . . . Larry. Larry? Was he the little guy in the red cowboy boots who slept in the Chevy?"

After he divorced Jessica in 1972, Larry moved around quite a bit for about a decade, doing a variety of things, including joining the Sky Family, a communal operation in the mountains, where people came and went freely. Now, a few years later, not many of the Skys remembered exactly who Larry was, perhaps because there had been an emphasis on seeking new identities at the time. The Family believed in renaming yourself every day as a way of recognizing the new possibilities of life, and this ritual sometimes occupied most of a morning: meditating under a tree or in a car or up in a tree, seeking to know one's true name for that day, trying to free oneself from preconceptions such as Larry or Janice or Stanley, and to find the one word that most perfectly expressed your aspirations, such as Radiance or Bear or Venus, and then going around and introducing yourself to the others, some of whom wanted to know why: *Why* did you decide to be California? Or Peaches. Or Brillo.

So the name of Larry Rose didn't ring a universal bell. "No," said Sarah to a woman who thought Larry was a guy she remembered from a trip to Mexico, "he wasn't like that at all. You must be thinking of someone else. Larry is a very *nice* person, very gentle, very caring. I mean he *was*—he's dead now, of course." She hadn't been in the Sky Family—that was long before her time; she was only a kid then— so she looked through Larry's stuff for an old picture so she could describe him to his old friends, and while rummaging through a cardboard box of his papers she found his will, typed on three pages of yellow paper, single-spaced.

The will made it clear that Larry had thought a lot about his death. He wanted no funeral but, rather, a "Celebration of Life," and as for his remains, he asked to be cremated and his ashes be divided up and put in manila envelopes and mailed to people he admired, such as writers, actors, teachers, healers, religious people, and rock stars— hundreds of them—as gifts. Those people also were to be invited to the Celebration of Life (and given a chance to perform or speak "if they want to, it's entirely up to them, and nobody should bad-mouth them if they don't, maybe they just want to sit and rest or be part of the crowd"), and so were Larry's extended family of Sky people across America, everyone in Market Falls, and motorists on Highway 7. Friends of his were to stop cars on Celebration Day and hand out printed invitations that began, "Dear Traveler, Can you take just a moment to join us in a celebration of another human being?" Friends also were supposed to organize the Celebration, which would be "a free-form coming-together (nonsorrowing) of Survivors to share music, games, food, history, personhood—to exchange tokens, totems, lifelore, etc." It was to take place in the country, in a grove of trees by a river. There was more about the friends' duties (sharing memories of Larry and pledging themselves to carry on his life in their own lives and nurturing each other and being happy), but her mind had wandered off toward some practical questions. *Who did she know who owned property in the country who would want to host a bunch of campers for a few days, some of them drunk, most of them with large dogs?*

*   *   *

About twenty people attended the funeral service at the Rothman Chapel two days later. It was sad, and some of them cried, but then the Methodist minister pronounced the deceased's name Lawrence *Rosé*, like the wine, and that cracked everyone up, and then Stan stood up to give a personal tribute. Though Larry's best friend, he was a stand-in for Sarah's first choice, Star, who had decided that morning to go to Montreal instead, with a former ballplayer named Roy. "There is so much a person could say about Larry it is hard to know where to begin," Stan said. "It's hard to tell just one story and leave out all the hundreds of others. He was a good man, but, then, you know that already, otherwise you wouldn't be here. I wish we had time for each one of you to share your personal memories of Larry, I know it'd be great. But perhaps we should just have a moment of silence and each of us remember him in our own way."

Sarah remembered the morning he went out to clean the garage. He'd had a cup of coffee and a bran muffin, smoked another Pall Mall, and said, "I'm getting tired of all this junk of mine. I keep saving all this *stuff* and I don't know why." Those were the last words she heard him say. It wasn't an ignoble way to die, she thought—trying to get your life out from under the debris. Had he lived longer, he might have thrown away his stupid will. She felt a little guilty about not having the Celebration but not as guilty as she had expected to feel. The service was over in twenty minutes, and after a few hugs and handshakes on the sidewalk everyone went away. She took Angelina and Andrew to lunch, and then Jessica picked them up at the house. She honked; she didn't come in. Sarah gave the kids some of his rings and a couple of old hats. The next day, the garbageman came and emptied the garage of everything. Sarah put the house up for sale. A lawyer told her she was entitled to part of Larry's estate, he thought, though the will was reticent on the subject of material things. The real-estate woman advised her to get rid of the sundeck, so the garbageman came and got that, too. It was surprisingly easy to remove. Underneath was a patch of bare dirt, and a few weeks later the place was thick with green grass and weeds.

GLASNOST

During four days of speeches, delegates broke one taboo after another, adding new zest to Gorbachev's policy of *glasnost*, or openness. One delegate attacked Politburo members. Another touched off debate over whether the party should relinquish its monopoly over Soviet politics. Two others feuded publicly. By the time the meeting ended, the sense of openness had built up so strongly that Gorbachev declared *glasnost* a hero of the gathering.

—Washington *Post*, July 3, 1988

SOME GENIUS FROM MINSK with yogurt in the corners of the mouth making a stinky speech against the Politburo *gospodin* and you call this *glasnost*, my friend? *Ha!* And the "debate" about monopoly schmopoli—*tovarishch*, in my city, Kiev, we stuff that stuff in chickens but you call it *glasnost*? In Moscow, the intelligentsia belch and it's called a debate. And then two sturgeon snappers in baggy blue suits and white polyestiya shirts and shlumpy ties with tractors stand up and trade three wimpnik insults and this is *glasnost*?

Give me a break.

Stop with your stories of Moscow and the great historic "*open*" party conference. Moscow is a parking lot. Bad food, bad whiskey, no ice. Beds full of bedboogi. City full of Amyerikans shlepping cameras looking for samizdat, refuseniks, raskolniks, what a laugh. Ha! This is me, Leonid, being open with you, sharing. Stop wasting the time. COME TO KIEV. In Kiev it is completely open city, the Center of Openness, Kiev the Honest it is known to all peoples, it is THE GATEWAY TO *GLASNOST*.

Don't take the word of me for it. Come on to Kiev and see this for yourself all right out in the open. Babushkas, borsch, shashlik, the real Russia. I drive you myself in my big car (free), we to go to GUM (open til ten) and buy pair of Levi dzhinsi, listen to Amyerikan dzhass on the dzhyukbaks down at Boris Nikolayevich's BaBaKyu

348

Russé (yes!). Here the light bulbs are dim to permit the special openness and they sell vodka cheap (a hundred kopecks, you get a snootful), chase it with a *glasnost* of beer, have a big plate *zakuski*, get crazy, and open yourself up if you wish or just watch me. *Nichevo*. It doesn't matter.

* * *

October is when to come to Kiev, the month of the Congress of Peoples, a hundred thousand people will be there, lot of action, big fun, no shyit, it makes Moscow look sick. Moscow is Plastyinki Mir. Kiev is Openville. It is good morning, U.S.S.R. Wide open. Total *glasnost*. Guys in hotels dropping water balloons, guys in little hats with tassels riding around on big motorcycles. Vroom, vroom. Big fatniks and little shmoozers making whoopee in the Hotel Lenin lobbiya, singing "Volga Boatman," getting shnockered—

You don't care for that? *Nyet?* Guess what. Neither do I. No! Cossacks is what those guys are, fools, crooks. Pigs. We'll round them up and throw them in a dump truck and—*poof*—they're all gone faraway bye-bye.

* * *

We got something much more open: surfing. Big waves in October on the Crimea, we'll get a board and two wet suits from the Surfburo and find the beach, what do you say, Sonya? Surfing opens a person up. You don't care for it?

I don't either. There's a difference between openness and emptiness. I admire you very much for that you choose right. You're an okaynik, you're so honest. Your purity appeals to me.

What should we to do? I am open. Whatever you want, baby.

Shall we ride the hydrofoil?

Do you play chess? volyibol? tenyisneya? Or should we sit in the cafeteriya and enjoy big glasses of hot tea with all the sugar and talk and talk and talk.

* * *

What do you wish to talk about, my little *pirogi?* My beauty.
Speak.

* * *

You request to know the truth about me?

Me, Leonid? Hey, baby.

That question is exactly the question I hoped you would ask. You
want me to be open, I *want* to be open. I am sick of lies. Time for
complete openness, my *blini,* my little *muzhitshka.* I am not like
other men, they *lie* because they have no eyes to see beauty but I
look upon you, my darling, my *stupendous dumpling,* and you inspire
me to tell the truth from my heart— O Tanya your eyes are the blue
of Lake Baikal, your hair is the brown of a new-plowed field in the
Caucasus, your lips are the red of you know what, and your breasts,
my gosh, your breasts . . .

Your breasts.

How can a man once given the opportunity to look upon your
beautiful young breasts ever tell a lie again?

Your body has the power to make a man good.

Let me see your breasts.

Be open with me as I will be open with you.

* * *

Now I reveal the truth in a few simple clumsy words, this is no speech
memorized by me to tell to every girl who rides in my cab. Nyet. I
was one-hundred-percent open *years* before Gorbachev. He is an old
man, I am thirty-seven, a different generation. Women are my best
friends. Always have I stood on the side of women in their struggle
against lies and cruelty and the closed doors of prejudice. Openness
is my middle name. *Leonid Glasnostyevich.* It is true. I changed my

name to say who I really am. I am a man but I am a true feministiya!
I am a liberatchik!

*   *   *

I have chocolate, nylon stockings, and *cigaryeti*. Also a twentiya-
carat gold bracelyet and a bikinyi. For you. I take you anywhere. I
am free. We go to Gastronom and buy all the best. Caviar, sausage
and crackers, cheese of all kinds. You say. Anything you want.

I say this so you know I am yours completely and openly. I am
a warm person and sensitive, who is crazy about you. Touch me. See
how warm I am, don't take my word for it, see for yourself.

I give you my body.

*   *   *

Don't speak right now, *devushka*. *Glasnost* is beautiful and extremely
delicate. A careless word can shatter it forever.

*   *   *

Here in Kiev, tonight, a man and a woman are not to be ashamed to
take *glasnost* further and more beautiful than ever it has been before.

*   *   *

Take off your *platye*, Natasha. Your *bluzka*, your *kombinatsiya*. My
beautiful one. You trust me. Your puyas, your liyifchik, your *trusiki*.
Liebchen, darling. You *are* openness, dear delicious Galina, you make
it real, daring me to know you as you are. Now have I told you
everything that can be said.

Kiss me, you fool. Love me!

AFTER A FALL

WHEN YOU HAPPEN TO STEP off an edge you didn't see and lurch forward into space waving your arms, it's the end of the world for a second or two, and after you do land, even if you know you're okay and no bones are broken, it may take a few seconds to decide whether this is funny or not. Your body is still worked up about the fall—especially the nervous system and the adrenaline-producing areas. In fact, I am *still* a little shaky from a spill that occurred two hours ago, when I put on a jacket, walked out the front door of this house and for no reason whatever took a plunge down five steps and landed on the sidewalk flat on my back with my legs in the air. I am in fairly good shape, not prone to blackouts or sudden dizziness, and so a sudden inexplicable fall comes as a big surprise to me.

A woman who was jogging down the street—a short, muscular young woman in a gray sweatshirt and sweatpants—stopped and asked if I was okay. "Yeah! Fine!" I said and got right up. "I just fell, I guess," I said. "Thanks," I said. She smiled and trotted away.

Her smile has followed me into the house, and I see it now as a smirk, which is what it was. She was too polite to bend over and hoot and shriek and guffaw and cackle and cough and whoop and wheeze and slap her thighs and stomp on the ground, but it was all there in the smile: a young woman who through rigorous physical training and feminist thinking has gradually taken charge of her own life and rid her attic of self-hatred and mindless competitiveness and other artifacts of male-dominated culture is rewarded with the sight of a middle-aged man in a brown suit with a striped tie falling down some steps as if someone had kicked him in the pants.

I'm sorry if I don't consider this humorous. I would like to. I wish she had come over and helped me up. We might have got to talking about the fall and how each of us viewed it from a different perspective: that she perceived it as symbolic political theater, whereas I saw it as something that was actually happening to me at the time. I might have understood that the sight of a tall man in a suit folding up and waving his arms and falling helplessly and landing flat on his back was the punch line of a joke she had been carrying around with her for a long time.

I might have seen it her way, but she ran down the street, and now I can only see my side of the fall. I feel cheapened by the whole experience. I understand now why my son was so angry with me a few months ago when he tripped on a shoelace and fell in the neighbor's yard—a yard where the neighbor's sheepdog had lived for years—and I laughed at him.

"It's not funny!" he yelled.

"Oh, don't be so sensitive," I said.

Don't be so sensitive! What a dumb thing to say! Who has the right to tell someone else how to feel? It is the right of the person who falls on the dog droppings to decide for himself or herself how he or she will feel. It's not up to a jury. The fallen person determines whether it's funny or not.

*   *   *

My son and I are both tall fellows, and I suppose tall people are the funniest to see fall, because we try so hard not to. We work hard for our dignity, trying to keep that beanpole straight, keep those daddy longlegs coordinated, keep those big boats from tangling with each other. From a chair through a crowded room to the buffet dinner and back to the chair with a loaded plate is a long route for a tall fellow—

a route we have to study for tricky corners and edges, low doorways, light fixtures, rug wrinkles, and other low-lying obstacles that we, being tall, don't see at a glance. A tall fellow has got his hands full on a maneuver like that. He is pulling strings attached to all his joints, knowing that, if he lets himself go or makes a mistake, it's a long way down.

Short, compact persons can trip and recover their balance quickly, maybe even turn that stumble into a casual Twyla Tharp–type dance move or a Buster Keaton fall, but when tall fellows stumble they go down like cut timber. We're not like Walter Payton, who bounces right up from the turf when he's tackled. We're more like the tall trees in the National Basketball Association. When they fall, usually there's ligament damage or torn cartilage; the stretcher crew runs onto the floor, and the crowd applauds sympathetically as the debris is stacked and carried away. "The knee feels good," the tree says six months later. "I am lifting weights with it, and I am now almost able to bend over," but he knows that his pro tree career is done gone, that he has begun a new career as a guy who hurts a lot.

All this can happen in one quick fall, and so a tall fellow is cautious when he threads his way through the party to reload his plate with spareribs. One misstep and down he goes, to the vast amusement of all present, who don't realize that he has wrenched something in his back and will be in a body cast for months and not be so good a friend again. Only a tall fellow knows how major his fall might be.

*   *   *

Five years ago, I got on a bus with The Powdermilk Biscuit Band and rode around for two weeks doing shows every night. They played music; I told jokes and sang a song. One night, in the cafeteria of a junior college in Rochester, Minnesota, we happened to draw a big crowd, and the stage—four big plywood sheets on three-foot steel legs—was moved back twenty feet to make room for more chairs. The show was late starting, the room was stuffy, the crowd was impatient, and when finally the lights dimmed and the spotlight shone on the plywood, I broke from the back door and made a run for the stage, to make a dramatic entrance and give these fine people the show they were waiting for.

What I could not see in the dark was the ceiling and a low concrete overhang that the stage had been moved partly under, and then the spotlight caught me straight in the eyes and I couldn't see anything. I leaped up onto the stage, and in mid-leap my head hit concrete and my right leg caught the plywood at mid-shin. I toppled forward, stuck out my hands, and landed on my hands and knees. The crowd drew a long breath. I got right up—I had been doing shows long enough to know not to lie onstage and cry in front of a paying audience— and, seeing the microphone about ten feet ahead, strode up to it and held out my arms and said, "Hello, everybody! I'm happy to be here!"

Then they laughed—a big thunderstorm of a laugh and a big round of applause for what they now saw had been a wonderful trick. But it wasn't funny! My neck hurt! I hurt all over! On the other hand, to see a tall man in a white suit jump directly into a ceiling and then fall down—how often does a person get to see that? Men dive off high towers through fiery hoops into tiny tanks, men rev up motorcycles and leap long rows of trucks and buses, but I am the only man in show business who takes a good run and jumps Straight Up into Solid Concrete Using Only His Bare Head. Amazing!

Let's see that once more in slow motion:

Me in the hallway saying, "Now?" Stage manager saying, "Not yet, not yet," then, "Okay, *now*." He opens door, I take two steps, see bright circle of light onstage, take five long running strides. In mid-run, the circle moves, man is blinded by the light, looks for edge of stage, then leaps—pushing off with left foot, right leg extended. Head hits concrete, stopping upward motion. Forward momentum carries body onto stage but right leg fails to clear plywood. Body falls, lands on hands and knees, stands up—like a dropped puppet

picked up by puppeteer—walks forward, speaks. *Laughter & applause.*
Looking at this footage one more time, you can see how hard this
poor guy hit. The head jerks, the eyes squeeze shut, the hands fly
up like birds, the body shudders.

Look now as the tall fellow who has had a load of concrete dropped
on his head starts singing. It's a song he has sung for years and knows
by heart, so it doesn't matter that he is senseless; these lyrics are
stored not in his head but at the lower end of the spinal cord. "Hello,
hello, it's time for the show! We're all dressed up and rarin' to go!"
But his eyes are glazed, and it's clear that something is terribly wrong.
Stop the show! This man is hurt! Is there a doctor in the house? This
fellow may have broken his neck! Friends, this entertainer who always
gave you everything he had has now given you too much. His life
is now shattered, owing to one last effort to jump headfirst into a
ceiling for your pleasure and amazement.

     —You've now seen in slow motion the play that led to the
injury that so tragically ended your career. Tell us in your
own words, if you can, what goes through your mind as you
see yourself jump into the ceiling.

     —Howard, I've tried to put all that behind me. I have no
hard feelings toward the guy who moved the stage or the
audience that laughed—they were only doing their job. Right
now my job is to regain my sense of humor and go back to
work. I feel like I'm making real good progress. Howard, I
consider myself to be one lucky guy.

Oh, it is a sad story, except for the fact that it isn't. My ceiling
jump got the show off to a great start. The band played three fast
tunes, and I jumped carefully back onstage and did a monologue that
the audience, which now *knew* I was funny, laughed at a lot. Even
I, who had a headache, thought it was funny. I really did feel lucky.
So do I still—a tall man who fell now sitting down to write his

memoirs. The body is so delicate, the skeleton so skinny; we are stick men penciled in lightly, with a wooden-stick cage to protect the heart and lungs and a cap of bone over the brain. I wonder that I have survived so many plunges, so many quick drops down the short arc that leads to the ground.

The Haymow Header of 1949: Was playing in Uncle Jim's haymow and fell through a hole, landing in the bull's feed trough, barely missing the stanchion, and was carried into the house, where Grandma put brown paper on my head. *The Milk Jar Mishap of 1951:* Tripped on the cellar steps while carrying two gallon glass jars full of milk from the grocery, dropped the jars (which broke), and then landed on them but didn't cut myself. Went to my room and cried. My dad said, "That's all right, it doesn't matter." But it did matter. I had ruined us—my poor family! A week's worth of milk gone bust, and it was my fault. *Miscellaneous Bike Bowls, 1954–* : Biking no-handed. Going over the bike jump. Going down a steep hill and hitting loose gravel. Practicing bike skids. Swerving to avoid a dog. *The Freshman Composition Class Collapse of 1960:* After staying up all night to write an essay on a personal experience, rose in Mr. Cody's class to read it, blacked out, and fell on top of people sitting in front of me. Got up and went home. *Miscellaneous Sports Spills:* Basketball collision that dislocated left elbow in 1961. Skating, skiing, tobogganing. Two memorable outfield collisions, after one of which a spectator said she could hear our heads hit 250 feet away.

Falls of Fatherhood: Walking across the room, thinking long-range thoughts. Suddenly there's an infant at my feet, whom I am just about to step on! And instantly I lift the foot and dive forward, sometimes catching myself short of a fall and sometimes doing a half-gainer into the furniture. (I also fall for cats.) *The Great Ladder Leap of 1971:* Climbing up to install a second-story storm window, felt the extension ladder slip to one side, dropped the window and jumped, landing in a flower bed, barely missing my two-year-old boy standing nearby. *Dreams of Falls:* Too numerous, too common, to mention. Always drawn toward the edge by some powerful force, tumble through space, then wake up and go get a glass of water.

*   *   *

The first time I ever went naked in mixed company was at the house of a girl whose father had a bad back and had built himself a sauna in the corner of the basement. Donna and I were friends in college. Both of us had grown up in fundamentalist Christian homes, and we liked to compare notes on that. We both felt constricted by our upbringings and were intent on liberating ourselves and becoming more open and natural. So it seemed natural and inevitable one night to wind up at her house with some of her friends there and her parents gone and to take off our clothes and have a sauna.

We were nineteen years old and were very cool ("Take off my clothes? Well, sure. Heck, I've taken them off *dozens* of times") and were careful to keep cool and be nonchalant and not look at anybody below the neck. We got into the sauna as if getting on the bus. *People do this,* I thought to myself. *There is nothing unusual about it! Nothing! We all have bodies! There is no reason to get excited! This is a normal part of life!*

We filed into the little wooden room, all six of us, avoiding unnecessary body contact, and Donna poured a bucket of water on the hot rocks to make steam. It was very quiet. "There's a shower there on the wall if you want to take a shower," she said in a strange, nervous voice.

"Hey! How about a shower!" a guy said in a cool-guy voice, and he turned on the water full blast. The shower head leaped from the wall. It was a hand-held type—a nozzle at the end of a hose—and it jumped out at us like a snake and thrashed around exploding ice-cold water. He fell back, someone screamed, I slipped and fell, Donna fell on top of me, we leaped apart, and meanwhile the nozzle danced and flew from the force of the blast of water. Donna ran out of the sauna and slipped and fell on the laundry-room floor, and another girl yelled, "Goddamn you, Tom!" Donna scrambled to her feet. "God! Oh, God!" she cried. Tom yelled, "I'm sorry!" Another guy laughed a loud, wicked laugh, and I tiptoed out as fast as I could move, grabbed my clothes, and got dressed. Donna grabbed her clothes. "Are you all right?" I said, not looking at her or anything. "No!" she said. Somebody laughed a warm, appreciative laugh from inside the sauna. "Don't laugh!" she yelled. "It isn't funny! It isn't the least bit funny!"

"I'm *not* laughing," I said, though it wasn't me she was angry at. I *still* am not laughing. I think it's a very serious matter, twenty years later. Your first venture as a naked person, you want it to go right and be a good experience, and then some joker has to go pull a fast one.

All I can say is, it's over now, Donna. Don't let it warp your life. We were young. We meant well. We wanted to be natural and free. It didn't mean we were awful. God didn't turn on the cold water to punish us for taking off our clothes—Tom did, and he didn't mean it, either. It was twenty years ago. Let's try to forget it. Write me a letter and let me know how you're doing. I would like to hear that you're doing well, as I am, and that our night of carnal surprise did you no lasting harm. Life is so wonderful, Donna. I remember once, after I lost track of you, I ran on the dock of a summer camp where I worked as a counselor—ran and slipped on the wet boards and did a backward half-somersault in the air and, instead of hitting the dock and suffering permanent injury, I landed clean in the water headfirst and got water up my nose and came up sneezing and choking, but *I was all right*, and is that so surprising? It was luck, I suppose, but, then, two-thirds of the earth's surface is water, so our chances are not so bad, and when you add in the amount of soft ground, bushes, and cushions in the world and the amazingly quick reactions of the body to protect itself, I think the odds of comedy are better than even. God writes a lot of comedy, Donna; the trouble is, He's stuck with so many bad actors who don't know how to play the scenes. When I dropped the window off that falling ladder back in 1971, I didn't know that my son had come around the corner of the house and was standing at the foot of the ladder watching me. The window hit the ground and burst, the ladder hit the ground and bounced, and his father landed face first in the chrysanthemums; all three missed him by a few feet. Quite a spectacle for a little boy to see up close, and he laughed out loud and clapped his hands. I moved my arms to make sure they weren't broken into little pieces, and I clapped, too. Hurray for God! So many fiction writers nowadays would have sent the window down on that boy's head as if it were on a pulley and the rope were around his neck, but God let three heavy objects fall at his feet and not so much as scratch him. He laughed to see me and I laughed to see him. He was all right and I wasn't so bad myself.

I haven't seen you since that night, Donna. I've told the sauna story to dozens of people over the years, and they all thought it was funny, but I still don't know what you think. Are you all right?

MY LIFE IN PRISON

E VER SINCE THE DAY I FIRST WALKED out onstage and blinked and cleared my throat, people have written some terrible things about me that aren't true, but it doesn't matter. I've done a lot of terrible things in secret that nobody wrote about, so it all evens out.

My sister used to say terrible untrue things about me to my parents, but it didn't matter, because they didn't believe in innocence anyway. When they caught us pounding on each other, they just grabbed the nearest one and sent him up to his room, and if I said, "She hit me first!" (the truth) it made no difference: I still got punished to make up for the times they probably had made a mistake in my favor.

Their punishment backfired in my case. I loved to be sent up to my room. My books were there, my tablets, my plastic soldiers, it was good up there. If they wanted to punish me, they should have sent me out to play with other children. Solitary confinement was my idea of fun. It was a chance to sit down and talk to myself, and that's what naturally led me into radio, which led to so much more, including those terrible untrue things.

This is the sort of thing I mean, which happens often: A reporter calls up and says how much he's always liked my work, could he take me to lunch, so he does, something expensive like walleye sushi, and he asks me ten questions about life and love and laughter, and then he turns on his tiny tape recorder and asks, "What's the worst thing your folks ever did to you?" I tell him that sometimes they punished me for nothing, and he writes his story, "RICH WRITER BITTER TOWARD MOM, 74."

I understand, he's only doing his job, there's nothing personal about the piece. Journalism is a moral art, it draws pictures in bold strokes. The newspaper columnist back in St. Paul who combed the town for children whom I had disappointed is a deeply moral writer:

TIMMY LIES IN PAIN WHILE "HERO" LAPS UP N.Y. GLITZ AND GLAMOUR

A very sick little boy lies on a broken bed in a dank basement apartment on the South Side waiting for hours for the mailman. A few minutes after one o'clock, when he hears the rustle of mail in the fetid hallway, he climbs painfully from the soiled sheets and limps to the door and stops with his little hand on the cold knob and says an Our Father.

But so far it hasn't been answered.

Every day Timmy whispers Garrison Keillor's name and looks for an envelope containing the autographed photo he requested from the former "Prairie Home Companion" host way back in March 1987. Doctors say that such a signed photo could give Timmy the spark of hope he needs in order to live. His Aunt Brenda, Timmy's custodian since his parents and sister died at the hands of a furloughed maniac on Christmas Eve, says, "If only Garrison knew how much it means to us, surely as a Christian he would spare thirty seconds to autograph a picture."

But would he?

Keillor, who sleeps all day and spends his nights cavorting with the glitterati in the niteries of Sodom, is said to be quite satisfied with his new famous friends and his new life of luxury and excess.

Last Tuesday night, while Timmy was running a 110° fever and moaning, "Please, please, an autograph," over and over in an inaudible voice, Keillor was stuffing his face with expensive crab salad in the company of fancy-pants friends at the Stork Club, two of them known homosexuals.

With so many Americans unemployed, you might think that the bard of Lake Wobegon would at least choose a domestic wine.

Well, guess again.

A 1984 Pouilly-Fuissé.

Thirty-five bucks.

Meanwhile a little boy lies waiting.

Hoping. Believing.

A lot of folks could probably use $35 to put food on the table, but never mind. I can understand a big shot wanting to indulge himself, and that's his right. Still, couldn't he take ten seconds to put his John Hancock on a napkin and maybe save a kid's life?

I understand very well the idealism behind a column like that, and should I complain that the columnist has left out a few facts that might have favored me? Should Moses in his description of the Midianites have mentioned that sometimes they sang songs and were fun to be with? No, certainly not. Nevertheless, I have canceled my subscription to that paper, and I've gone from bookstore to bookstore, collecting copies of *Geek: An Unauthorized Biography of You Know Who (The Big Jerk)* and reshelving them in Religion, behind C. H. Mackintosh's *Commentary on Ephesians*. My sense of guilt is as powerful as a locomotive. I don't appreciate a book that's packed full of people grumbling at me.

"He was awful darn hard to work with," recalls Chuck Frick, who parked cars behind the World Theater. "He'd come in here before the show and hardly speak to us, maybe say,

'Hi, how ya doin'—what kinda recognition is that for guys who bust their butts parking cars so he can have an audience? Once I gave him a tape of my songs and didn't hear back about it for *three weeks*, and then he didn't offer any constructive criticism or anything, just said, 'Sorry, it isn't quite right for us'—what kind of thing is that to say? I worked on those songs for six years and he dismisses them with six words. Those were good songs. He treated them like they were *nothing* to him. He didn't even invite me out to lunch. He was a crummy tipper, too. And his car was messy. Burger wrappers on the back-seat floor. Once I saw him get in the car with a woman who worked on the show. They were talking real quiet, and you can't tell me there wasn't some hokey-pokey going on there. But people are afraid to talk, otherwise there'd be a lot more that'd come out that you wouldn't believe.''

I read that book and suddenly realized why PR people send out gallons of Johnny Walker at Christmas and serve prime-rib sandwiches in hospitality suites in hotels. Journalists are hungry people. The PR guy, courtly, English, walks up to the sleaziest writer in the room and lays an arm across his dandruffy shoulders and murmurs, ''You know who you remind me of? Edward R. Murrow. I mean it. You've got that same intensity, that kind of grace, like what Yeats wrote about—how does that line go? 'Nor law nor duty bade me fight / Nor public men nor cheering crowds / A lonely impulse of delight / drove to this tumult in the clouds.' Can I get you a Scotch?''

The reporter, a man with watery eyes and forty pounds of old cheeseburgers around his waist, blushes and stares down at his Hush Puppies, and for the next twenty years you will have no problem with him at all. He will go chase the university president (''TAX MONEY LAVISHED ON EXECUTIVE SUITE WHILE THE DYING LIE IN DIM ALCOVES AT U HOSPITAL'') or snipe at the archbishop (''PRELATE FAILS TO ATTEND CRIPPLES' DINNER FOR THIRD YEAR IN ROW'') or haul off and slug the mayor ("POLITICIAN DENIES PERSISTENT RUMORS OF PET MOLESTING"), and he will not go writing your unauthorized biography full of everybody who has a grudge against you. He'll write:

> Everyone in this town knows Garrison Keillor as a wonderful entertainer and devoted father, but I wonder how many of us are aware of those dozens of little unsung deeds he does for the poor and unfortunate every week.

A PR guy would sing some of those deeds in a nice low voice so that a columnist could hear them. I don't have a PR guy, but once I did hire someone named Milo to attend rehearsals and yell "All *right!*" every time I sang a song. I was sensitive about my voice and needed affirmation in order to do my best. He sat among the band and in that awkward silence after a song, when the musicians reach for a smoke, Milo yelled, "All *right!* Far out! *Whoooo!* You sang that one, all right!" Milo is quoted in *Geek* as saying that I was selfish.

I was selfish, and I'm sorry about it, but the one thing a PR guy can't do is the one thing you really need, which is to resolve your guilt, compared with which bad publicity is a picnic. A rotten story by a jerk who snapped the picture when your face was blank and your finger was in your ear is a mild heartache compared with the violence a man can do to himself, given the right start in life.

One deed my parents never sent me to my room for was hitting my cousin on the head with a pair of stilts one summer day behind our garage, back in Brooklyn Park, Minnesota. (I don't want to use his real name so I'll just call him Abel.) The stilts were mine. Abel had them, and I grabbed them away, and when he grabbed at me I whacked him with the stilts across the side of his skinny head. He had good presence of mind for a ten-year-old. When he looked around and saw no adult to appeal to, he turned and said to me in a clear small voice, "You know what's going to happen to you someday? You're going to go to prison for the rest of your life."

The quiet way he said it made me believe him instantly, absolutely. I offered him the stilts and he accepted them, but that didn't change anything. It would be prison for me: no trial, no judge or jury; a policeman would simply pick me up and drive me to the state prison and take me to the children's cellblock. The steel doors would clang shut and the big key turn, the officer's footsteps fade away back down the long concrete hall *tap tap tap tap tap* toward the light, and not far away a maniacal laugh and the squeaking of mice and water dripping in the dank sewers below. Prison.

When you're a little kid, your heart is open and tender and a harsh word can go straight in and become part of your life. I've been living under his sentence for almost forty years now, going along from year to year, waiting, knowing that all the good things I've done won't matter one bit when the cops come and take me away. Once, I was helping Grandma and she said, "I never saw anyone who could grease a cake pan half as good as you can." Her kind compliment made me feel talented and useful, and I still feel talented, even competent sometimes, but that doesn't change fate. Probably I'll be making a useful contribution to society right up to the day I go to prison, and then I'll make good license plates.

Will the police arrest a performer, a man who stands onstage in his tuxedo singing and saying funny things, a microphone in hand, a smile on his face, delighting the big audience? Will Sergeant D'Agostino march out from the wings and into the spotlight and grab that man's wrists as he sings "O you, it's you I adore, I give my life to you" to the beautiful audience and slap the cuffs on him and advise him of his right to remain silent? Maybe if the audience is big, and if the biggest ones sit in the first row, and if it's a *good* audience, with a lot of liberals, some nuns and community organizers, some extremely good people like vegetarian Danish Catholic theologians who are fasting for the salvation of South America and sit smiling weakly in their wheelchairs enjoying the show as they weave simple cotton garments for the poor on tiny handlooms, then the police may decide to wait until the show is over, but they'll come eventually, and then I'll be on "Eyewitness News" that night, cringing, holding a newspaper over my face, a forty-six-year-old humorist being hauled away to the precinct station for something like Failure to Declare Value of Illegal Drugs on 1979 Income Tax Return. If I'd been caught in 1979 I'd have done twelve months in the county workhouse, but each year the penalty doubles and now I'm going to the pen for 512 years. There's no trial, because under this particular set of circumstances, after six years you forfeit your right to one. So ruled the Supreme Court in a 1985 case exactly the same as mine.

"You could deny everything and make them prove it," says a lawyer who is in the holding tank with me, charged with a minor securities infraction, "but I'm afraid guilt is written all over your face." He's right. Sweat pops from every pore, my eyes dart back and forth furtively, and I cannot stop biting my lips and humming. I jump at the slightest sound. My heart pounds. My knees buckle as they lead me into the tiny green interrogation room.

"Care for a cup of coffee?" Lieutenant Matthews asks. I drink the bitter black municipal coffee and wait, but there is no interrogation. He and his partner, Sergeant Sloan, know everything. I know they know everything and they know I know they know, so we're cool and relaxed. "The van should be here in twenty minutes," Sloan says, offering me a Pall Mall. I light it. I quit smoking four years ago, but now that I'm bound for the Big House all bets are off. It tastes good. The van arrives. The guards are four guys I went to high school with, who used to call me Foxfart. They're glad to see me. "Hey, Fox, we've been reading about you for years, man," they say. "You really made us proud, the way you were going along so great there for a while, but then you went to Denmark and you got sloppy. You must've figured you were in the clear. Too bad you came back so soon. The statute of limitations would've come into effect in three more days. *Three days.* Now you're going to spend the rest of your life in prison. Five hundred years. That's a tough break, huh? Oh

well. You're tough. You'll be okay. See ya, Fox." And Carl pops me
in the shoulder the same way he always did in English when I got
an A and he got a D.

They drive me to LaGuardia and put me on board a Northwest
flight to Minneapolis. All fugitives are sent to prison in Minnesota
on Northwest, which preboards us on a conveyor belt that carries us
into a special section to the rear, behind Smoking, where flight at-
tendants prod us with sharp sticks to make us squeeze in tight. We
sit on the steel floor of the aircraft. There are two hundred of us, all
fugitives and their families, plus fifty head of sheep and quite a few
goats and some crates of chickens. The others carry big shopping bags
full of clothes, and after takeoff, when the captain turns off the "NO
COOKING" sign, they light fires and cook up some pork fat and suc-
cotash in old bean cans. Children sob in the corners and old women
rock back and forth moaning and praying for the good earth to return
to the bottoms of their feet. We men sit hunkered around the fire,
smoking, not talking. We're all going to spend the rest of our lives
in prison and we know it and what is there to say about a thing like
that? The plane bucks and the fires flicker. Night comes on. We sit
and chew and spit. The plane shakes as the flaps are lowered. Through
the tiny window appear the lights of Minneapolis, a big city where
I attended Sunday school regularly for many many years and worked
hard and tried to be a good citizen, but it's too late to think about
that now, or about the neat book reports that received gold stars, the
maps of the states correctly labeled by me and carefully colored using
forty-eight different crayons, the bowline hitch I tied that was shown
to other Scouts as a model of how that knot looks when it is perfect,
the certificate from the American Legion Auxiliary for the prize-
winning essay "America the Beautiful"—they are immaterial evidence now that I am a crook.

The press waits at the gate, a blaze of lights, a thicket of micro-
phones, and my cousin Abel—they are interviewing him. He says
that he feels no bitterness at all, only relief. My sister is there, her

children in tow, her husband, Buck, smiling. He always thought I thought I was better than him, so this is a sweet moment and he has brought his Super-8 movie camera. "We'll always love you," my sister says. "We'll do everything we can." One thing she did years ago was bang me on the head with a cast-iron skillet as I stood washing dishes at the kitchen sink. I could see the Milky Way shining between the bright-blue veins in my eyeballs. She yelled, "It was an accident— it slipped when I was putting it away!" and my mother accepted that story even though we kept the skillets in a low cupboard by the oven and if she had really been putting it away she'd have banged me in the ankle. But it doesn't matter.

In the airport terminal some Lutheran women are allowed behind the ropes to feed us peanut-butter sandwiches and green nectar while the cameras roll, and then we get into buses for the long ride to Stillwater Prison, through the streets of St. Paul past the Cathedral and the Civil War monument and the State Capitol and out east to the slammer, or "facility," as they call it. The walls of my cell are beige tile with green trim, similar to my old high school, and it smells of the same disinfectant. The bed is not unlike what we had at YMCA camp, where I hid in the woods to avoid swim class. The army blankets are like old friends, my dad having bought all our bedding from surplus stores. The food is the same as what I ate for years, fish sticks and string beans and Jell-O, and every day we get the St. Paul paper, whose world view mirrors that of Mr. Magendanz, our basketball coach who taught world history. His view was: Us or Them, Which One Are You? The voices in prison are the same. Every morning the guard, Rich, who was in Sunday school with me, stops at my door and says, "So how's everything this morning then?" "Oh, about the same then," I say. "They treatin' you okay then?" They're treating me fair and square. It's not home but it's not so bad. Pretty soon it's like I never left.

WE ARE STILL MARRIED

O NE DAY LAST AUGUST, after the vet said that Biddy had only months to live, Willa and I took her for a cruise around Lake Larson on our pontoon boat. She was listless and depressed from the medication, and we thought the ride might cheer her up, but she sat with her head in Willa's lap, her eyes closed, and when a flock of geese flew down and landed alongside the boat she paid no attention. I felt desolate to see her that way, and angry at other boats zipping around without a care in the world, and so when we got home and I found a message on the answering machine that said, "Hi, this is Blair Hague at *People* magazine, and I'd like to come to Minnesota and do a piece about your poor dog," I was relieved to know that someone cared.

Willa and I discussed it that night, and although she felt that the illness of a pet is a private matter, eventually I convinced her that we should agree to the story as a tribute to Biddy and also because, as Blair said on the tape, our experience might help others who were going through the same thing.

Blair arrived on Thursday with Jan, a photographer, and he explained that they wanted to live with us, so they could do a better job. "You get more nuance that way," he said. He had lived with a number of people in order to write about them, including Joe Cocker, Jean Shepherd, Merv Griffin, and the Pointer Sisters, he said. I could see his point, so they moved in, and Jan set up a darkroom in the laundry, which was fine with us—one thing we realized, with Biddy dying, was that we didn't have many pictures of her—and Blair got to work gathering background. Willa and I opened up our scrapbooks to him and Willa even let him read her diary. I wondered about that, but she said, "Honesty is the only policy. There's a lot about Biddy in there."

We lived in a two-bedroom condominium overlooking Lake Larson, and although Blair and Jan were extremely pleasant and helped with the dishes and made their beds and kept the stereo turned down after ten o'clock, I started to feel crowded after a few days. I'd be shaving and Blair would stick his head in the bathroom door and ask, "How much do you earn a year, Earl? Do you consider yourself a religious person? Do you normally wear boxer shorts? Is that your real hair?" After work, when I like to sit down with a beer and watch television, he sat next to me. How would I describe myself? Had I ever wanted to be something other than a bus driver? How much beer did I consume per day, on the average? Was it always Bub's Beer? What were my favorite books? What was on my mind? What did I think of the future? What sorts of people made me angry?

I wanted to say, "People who ask too many questions," but I held my tongue. I did mention to Willa that I thought Blair was pushy. "The article is about Biddy, not us," I said. She thought Blair was doing an excellent job. She said, "I feel like he is helping me to understand a lot of things about us that I never thought about before."

Soon after they arrived, we noticed that Biddy was getting better. Her appetite improved, and she got so she liked to go for walks again. I told Willa I thought we should tell Blair that there was no story. She said, "There's a lot more story here than you know, Earl. Biddy is just the tip of the iceberg."

Two weeks passed, then three, and Blair wasn't running out of questions to ask. He kept coming back to the subject of our marriage.

"Do you feel you have an excellent, good, average, or poor marriage? Do you regret not having had children? How many times per week do you have sexual relations? On the average—just a ballpark figure. Do you think Willa is happy?"

I said, "You ought to ask her."

"I have," he said.

Right up to the day they left, I had no idea he was going to write the story he did. Once, he said, "As so often happens, the story changes as a reporter works on it. You start out to do one thing and you wind up doing something entirely different." I thought he was referring to Biddy's improvement.

The story was entitled "Earl: My Life with a Louse, by Willa Goodrich as told to Blair Hague, photographs by Jan Osceola," and the day it came out Willa took Biddy and moved to her mother's. I wasn't home so I didn't know she left. I was driving a charter to New Orleans. Some passengers picked up *People* in Des Moines, and as I drove south I could hear them whispering about me. In southern Missouri, a man came to the front and crouched down in the aisle beside me. "I thought you had a right to know this," he said, and he read me some parts. I couldn't believe the stuff Willa said about me! My personal grooming, my food preferences, my favorite TV shows, our arguments. And her referring to me as "stubborn and unreasonable"—why would she say that? In print!

In New Orleans, I discovered that the man had skipped some of the worst parts. Willa said she had often wanted to leave me. She said that I was uncaring and cold, that Biddy's illness didn't mean "beans" to me, and that I had talked about getting another dog soon. She said that I had "Victorian ideas about women and sex." She said I was often personally repulsive. To back her up, *People* printed three pictures with the story: me in my shorts, bending over to adjust the TV picture; me with my mouth open, full of baked potato; and me asleep on the La-Z-Boy recliner, in my shorts, with my mouth open.

I tried to reach Willa at her mother's, but she was in New York, and I saw her the next morning on "America, How Are You?" Essentially, she told Monica Montaine the same stuff, plus she said that I was "compulsive." She said, "He walks around humming the same tune over and over, usually 'Moon River.' He taps his fingers continuously, and he taps his foot in his sleep. His breath is very bad. He compulsively rips the labels off beer bottles. And at dinner he always eats all his meat first, then the potato, then the vegetable." Monica Montaine got a big kick out of that. "Sounds like he's missing the Up button," she said.

Two days later, someone from "Today" called and wanted me to get on a plane to New York and join Willa on the show for a dialogue. He said, "I think the country would like to hear your side, Earl." I told him I had no desire to engage in a public debate with my wife over matters I considered personal. Willa did the show herself, then a number of other daytime shows, and though I made a point of not watching, my friends were starting to ask questions. "Is it true about the almost total lack of any attempt at communication?" a mechanic at work wanted to know. "And you wearing socks in bed—any truth to that?" He said the story had given him a lot to think about.

In October, Willa testified before a House subcommittee, revealing new details about our marriage under oath. Several congressmen expressed shock at what she said about my lack of affection, my "utter insensitivity" to her needs. "What was he *doing* all this time while you were suffering?" one asked. She said, "He watched football on television. He played seven different types of solitaire. He carved a new stock for his shotgun. He acted like I didn't exist." That was the quote they used on "ABC World News Tonight."

I was lonely as winter approached. I'm not a man who can live by himself. Some men are cut out for the single life, but not me. So I told my boss I was available for all the charters I could get. I spent November and December mostly on the road, going to Orlando six times, Disneyland four, making two runs to San Francisco. Meanwhile, I read in *People* that Willa had sold her story to Universal Pictures and was in California ironing out some wrinkles in the deal. The next week, she got a call from the Pope, who expressed hope that efforts would be made to reach a reconciliation. "I'm ready any time Earl is," she told the Holy Father. She told him that although she was not a Catholic she respected the Church's view on marriage. "It's a two-way street, though," she said.

Finally, we met in New York, where I had driven a four-day "New Year's Eve on the Great White Way" tour and was laying low at the Jaylor Hotel, and where she had rented a great apartment on the Upper West Side and was on her way to a cocktail party. We met at her place. It was in a new building on Broadway, with a beautiful view from the twenty-fifth floor. Biddy was living with her, of course. Biddy looked wonderful, though she was a little hostile toward me. So were Willa's three friends, who worked in publishing. "What do you do?" one man asked, though I was sure he knew. The other man mentioned something about socks. The woman didn't talk to me at all. She kept telling Willa, "We've got to get going—the invitation said five o'clock." Willa kissed me goodbye. "Let's be friends," she said. "Call me sometime."

I did call her, four or five times, and we talked, mostly about her projects—she was writing a book, she was being considered as a substitute host. We didn't talk about our marriage until one day in April, when she mentioned that Biddy was sick again, and she said she missed me. Biddy died a week later, and Willa brought the body back to Minnesota for interment. She came to the condo for dinner one night and wound up staying.

My friends can't believe I took her back after all those things she said about me, but I can't see where it's any of their business. I told her there was no need for her to apologize, so she hasn't. She did scrap the movie project and the book, though. The substitute-host deal fell through when the regular host decided he wasn't so tired after all. Except for our two dogs, Betty and Burt, we're almost where we were last summer. The ice has melted on Lake Larson, the lilacs and chokecherries are in bloom, soon the goslings will hatch and their mothers will lead them down to water, and everything will be as if none of this ever happened.

"Maybe You Can, Too," "The Current Crisis in Remorse," "Who We Were and What We Meant by It," "We Are Still Married," "End of the Trail," "The People vs. Jim," "What Did We Do Wrong?," "End of an Era," "Hollywood in the Fifties," "Your Book Saved My Life, Mister," "Three New Twins Join Club in Spring," "Meeting Famous People," and "How the Savings and Loans Were Saved" first appeared as signed contributions in *The New Yorker*. "After a Fall" was originally published in *The New Yorker* and later in the Penguin edition of Mr. Keillor's *Happy to Be Here*.

In addition, twenty-one essays, observations, and reflections appeared as "Notes and Comment" and "Talk of the Town" pieces in *The New Yorker*. "Country Golf" appeared as "A Reporter At Large" piece in *The New Yorker*.

Other selections in this book first appeared, some under different titles or in slightly different form, in *The Atlantic*, *The Gettysburg Review*, *Harper's*, *Life*, *Minnesota Monthly*, *The New York Times*, *Newsweek*, *Sports Illustrated*, and *TWA Ambassador*.

Grateful acknowledgment is made for permission to reprint the following copyrighted works:

"How to Write a Letter" (originally entitled "How to Write a Personal Letter"). Reprinted by permission of International Paper.

Excerpts from "Gentle on My Mind," by John Hartford. Copyright © 1967, 1968 by Ensign Music Corporation.

Excerpt from *The Washington Post* article, July 3, 1988. © The Washington Post, 1988.

Excerpt from "An Irish Airman Foresees His Death," from *The Poems of W. B. Yeats: A New Edition*, by W. B. Yeats, edited by Richard J. Finneran. Copyright 1919 by Macmillan Publishing Company, renewed 1947 by Bertha Georgie Yeats. Reprinted with permission of Macmillan Publishing Company and A. P. Watt Ltd. on behalf of Michael B. Yeats and Macmillan London Ltd.